Where the Rain is Born

Where the Rain is Born

Writings About Kerala

Edited by Anita Nair

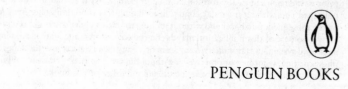

PENGUIN BOOKS

PENGUIN BOOKS
Published by the Penguin Group
Penguin Books India Pvt Ltd, 11 Community Centre, Panchsheel Park, New Delhi
110 017, India
Penguin Group (USA) Inc., 375 Hudson Street, New York, New York 10014, USA
Penguin Group (Canada), 90 Eglinton Avenue East, Suite 700, Toronto, Ontario,
M4P 2Y3, Canada (a division of Pearson Penguin Canada Inc.)
Penguin Books Ltd, 80 Strand, London WC2R 0RL, England
Penguin Ireland, 25 St Stephen's Green, Dublin 2, Ireland (a division of Penguin
Books Ltd)
Penguin Group (Australia), 250 Camberwell Road, Camberwell, Victoria 3124,
Australia (a division of Pearson Australia Group Pty Ltd)
Penguin Group (NZ), cnr Airborne and Rosedale Roads, Albany, Auckland 1310,
New Zealand (a division of Pearson New Zealand Ltd)
Penguin Group (South Africa) (Pty) Ltd, 24 Sturdee Avenue, Rosebank, Johannesburg
2196, South Africa

Penguin Books Ltd, Registered Offices: 80 Strand, London WC2R 0RL, England

First published by Penguin Books India 2002

This anthology copyright © Penguin Books India 2002
Introduction © Anita Nair 2002
The copyright for individual pieces vests with the authors or their estates

Page 316 is an extension of the copyright page. While every effort has been made to
trace copyright holders and obtain permission, this has not been possible in all
cases; any omissions brought to our attention will be remedied in future editions.

Typeset in Venetian by Mantra Virtual Services, New Delhi
Printed at Pauls Press, New Delhi

Contents

Introduction: Making Do

Anita Nair

This much is certain: it is impossible to get two people in Kerala to agree upon anything. Give them a subject—nuclear weapons, the American Presidential elections, earthquakes, Maxim Gorky, or the family next door and they will argue about it with as much acumen and aplomb as any star attorney in a TV soap would. And yet, bring up the principle of make do and everyone will hasten to agree that it is the only way to survive Kerala. Make do is the deity everyone worships. Make do is the reason why the average Malayali goes through life convinced that he is the liveliest, shrewdest and most intelligent of all Indians. This despite the high rate of lunatics and suicides. Make do is just about the only thing a Malayali does with little rancour or debate.

Each time I go home to a little village called Mundakotukurussi in Kerala, this business of make do confronts me with a sly giggle, starting with the jeep that jumps and leaps, screeches and roars in turns as it crunches up miles between the railway station and my ancestral home. If there was a road once, it exists in the memories of the residents of the village as a few mounds of gravel patched with tar. Right now, they have learnt to make do with a well-trodden path wide enough for a jeep to negotiate and navigate through.

How omnipresent the principle of make do really is I discovered on my last trip home. When I reach my parents' house, it is to discover that the power is off. The level in the water tank is low. Around the house are clusters of giant plastic drums and traditional bronze vessels. This being the month of October, when the power fails, the rains have been known to oblige. I take a deep breath and look around me. Nowhere else in the world have I seen so many hues of green. The velvety green of the moss on the wall. The deep green of the hibiscus bush. The dappled green of the jackfruit. The jade green of the paddy...Leaves. Parakeet's wings. Tree frogs. The opaque green of silence. In the evening, darkness will run amok on this canvas of green and it will be time to visit the temple where make do reigns supreme. Muthasikavu or the grandma's grove is a little shrine edging the village. My grandfather re-built the broken down temple. Since none of the idol-makers could comprehend what it was he wanted hewn out of stone or fashioned in metal, he set up a sandalwood pedestal and made do. In the Muthasikavu, there is no deity. Only a lamp that glows from within the sanctum sanctorum. You make do with what your imagination can conjure up and that is the face of divinity. In this village that has neither a guardian deity nor a regular place of worship, they have learnt to make do with this family shrine. And so when they require divine intervention, they make their request to the old lady of the grove. The drummers begin to tune their instruments in preparation for the Velluchapad. The oracle is a tall lean man with gaunt cheekbones and eyes that burn. His hair is wet and straggly after the ritual bath and hangs to his shoulders. He walks into the temple with giant strides and breaks into a guttural scream every few minutes. The drumbeats drown all thought and the Velluchapad begins to dance. As abruptly as the dance began, it ends and the Velluchapad begins to run, circling the temple. His body trembles and he flicks his wet hair with a toss of his hand as if to signal that now he is possessed by the force of the temple. Sometimes the divine power refuses to let go of the Velluchapad and then he begins to slash his head till blood drips down his nose. Slowly his body loosens and the clenched-in look on his face dissipates. Being a Velluchapad, I decide, takes a lot of making do. It can't be easy being a repository of divinity; pitching yourself into a state of nervous energy, cutting your head open to appease a savage god; all to keep a family fed and clothed. There is enormous prestige attached to the position but these days, Velluchapads have few rituals to officiate at and hence have to make do with alternate sources of income. This one is an electrician's assistant by day.

I trudge the narrow path back home. The power goes off. It comes back in a minute and then goes off again. On and off, on and off. Three times is a signal to indicate that the power won't be switched on till next morning. Little lanterns shaped like glass eggs light up rooms. In more affluent homes, the emergency light comes on. There are no harsh surprises, none of the not-knowing-what-to-do. Palm leaf fans and mosquito nets; transistor radios that will bring the world into the homes even if the TV can't; candles in saucers and generators. With these the village will make do till morning or whatever time the power chooses to return.

I sit in the veranda and watch the rainfall. A frog leaps joyous with wetness. A baby scorpion scuttles out; flooded out of its dry home, it seeks refuge in a crack in the floor. In the morning, coconut clusters that would have sagged from the assault and battery of the storm will be propped up and tied. Rotten plantain trees will be uprooted and new ones planted. The land will be repaired. Nature that kills will also heal. And perhaps it is based on this seminal knowledge that the principle of make do thrives. Kerala when offered to the world is a package wrought of colour, traditions, dainty foods, coconut lined lagoons and marvellous beaches, where green and light, 100% literacy and ayurveda, boats and elephants, all find their place. God's own country, the brochures tell you. If you've been there, you've been to paradise, they cajole.

What of the total lack of industry, high unemployment, a competitive and conspicuous consumerism, bureaucracy, corruption, or the stifling conservative attitudes, the average Malayali asks. Does the world really know what Kerala is all about? Only if you have lived here will you understand, I am told again and again. As I collated material for this anthology, it is this I sought. Writers who have a congenital craving to want to read between lines and see beyond what is on display. To probe beyond the surface and tap into the seams of everyday. To shrug aside recycled nostalgia and to see Kerala for what it truly is. Voices that haven't succumbed to the sheer beauty of Kerala and who have been able to decipher, if not appreciate, the conundrum that Kerala is. A repertoire of voices that either in English or in Malayalam, in essays, fiction and poetry, have made definite forays into understanding Kerala.

The corridor

Balachandran Chullikkad

On the cold floor of the
corridor
poems like headless bodies
smeared in blood and phlegm
lie scattered.
Ants come in hordes
and drag them away
to store as food
for dreamless winters.

Once in a while
The tired steps of a
Death-song
Climb up the stairs
When darkness and sorrow
Fill the corridor.

Inside a room
the bleeding heart of a
gramophone
groans with pain,
a love-lorn Saigal
on wings wet with liquor
wafts along the corridor
like a delirium-dazed dream.
From the bath shower
the sad sound of a violin
overflows like a blue river
carrying the abandoned body
of summer.

A drunk shadow
comes walking
along the corridor
with faltering steps,
knocks at every door and
calls,
his own door has shut behind
him, shut for ever
as eyelids in death.

—Translated from the Malayalam by N. Kunju

R. Prasanna Venkatesh/Wilderfile

Chasing the monsoon

Alexander Frater

2 JUNE

The wind woke me before dawn. It came from the south-west with a curious singing note, steady and melodic. A deeper accompaniment was discernible in the background which, at first, I took to be breaking seas. Thinking they were breaking outside my window I went to investigate but found only the wild thrashing of coconut palms.

I returned to bed but couldn't sleep. The monsoon seemed to be on its way and my journey in its company could commence. The fact that it had finally made its move was one worry less, but new doubts began to assail me over the travel arrangements. An eccentric monsoon, starting and stopping at whim, perhaps making unscheduled diversions, would make life very complicated. And what was happening about the Cherrapunji permission? I made a mental note to call Delhi but then, remembering I would have to use the Indian telephone system, immediately cancelled it. That problem could be faced nearer the time.

Dawn revealed a deep cumulus overcast and flayed, streaming coconut fronds. The crows had been blown away (even now they were probably hurtling backwards, wildly cawing, over Goa) and replaced by flights of brown sea eagles. These had taken up station fifty feet above the brow of the cliff beyond my window, ranged along it like sentinels, perfect flying machines hanging almost motionless as they waited for fish in the boiling sea below.

Half a mile out men waited for fish in fleets of flimsy, high-prowed canoes which, later today, Julius Joseph would order ashore; spinning like compass needles they kept vanishing beneath the huge

This extract is taken from *Chasing the Monsoon*, published by Penguin Books India.

swell and reappearing, dizzyingly, far from where they started.
Periodically a sunbeam touched the dark sea and ignited it in a wild,
irradiating flash.

The bay below my hotel had become a white tidal race, the waves
surging up the beach and over the road. A foolhardy cyclist venturing
on to the road with a milk pail was knocked flat. Hoisting the bike
shoulder-high he staggered on, pail in the crook of an arm, surf surging
about his ankles. The coast, running north for many miles, lay semi-
obscured under an opaque ribbon of spray which, touched by those
sunbeams, briefly glittered with a rainbow luminescence.

'Monsoon coming!' said the waiter at breakfast.

'When?'

'I think this afternoon.'

I nodded, unsettled by the behaviour of my watch, a 25-year-old
Swiss Omega which, ever since I had owned it, lost precisely 4½
minutes a day. Nothing could apparently be done about this; a droll
Zurich expert to whom I once showed it said the 4½-minute lapse
lay so deep in the mechanism it was more a matter of metaphysics
than watchmaking, accessible to God perhaps, but not to him. This
morning, though, routinely checking it against my undeviating
electronic alarm clock as I strapped it on, I noted with astonishment
that it was running eight minutes *fast*. Such a bewildering development,
I decided, must have been caused by charged particles or a strange
force field moving up in the van of the burst.

Still preoccupied I walked to the village through salvoes of flying
vegetation, bought a paper and took shelter in a coffee shop. 'Monsoon
Due in 48 Hours' proclaimed a front page headline. The story, filed
in New Delhi and dated the previous day, said:

> Though there have been some pre-monsoon showers in
> certain parts of southern India in the last few days, south-
> west monsoon is likely to break out in its normal run along
> the Kerala coast in the next 48 hours.
>
> Giving the information on the basis of satellite imagery of
> monsoon conditions, Dr N. Sen Roy, Additional Director of
> the Meteorological Department, said once the monsoon
> breaks out of Kerala it would spread to the neighbouring

Karnataka, Andhra Pradesh, Tamil Nadu and other States in the next week.

UNI adds from Trivandrum: Conditions are becoming 'favourable' for the onset of the south-west monsoon over Kerala and Lakshadweep during the next three days, meteorological sources said here today. It said that isolated heavy rain was likely to occur over Kerala during the next 48 hours.

If it arrived here today—or tomorrow—when might it be expected in Cochin, my next stop on its route? Julius Joseph must now be one of the most sought-after men in South India but, even so, I would soon need a word with him. A voice said, 'Well, well, sod this for a game of soldiers!' and my bespectacled friend from the bus parked himself on the bench opposite, grinning.

I was pleased to see him. 'What are you late for this time?' I asked.

'Nothing. I am taking day off. All it will do is make me one day later for all things for which I am hopelessly late already.' He laughed and placed a dog-eared school exercise book on the table. 'Today I am sitting here writing.'

'Writing what?'

'A short story, sir. That is my trade.'

I said I had once written short stories too and we talked happily of the problems of finding good beginnings, credible endings and themes that lent themselves to the subtle brush strokes of miniaturists like ourselves. He told me he admired the work of Maupassant, Chekhov, John Cheever, William Trevor and Rabindranath Tagore.

The Trivandrum bus would be leaving in a few minutes. I finished my coffee and asked what story he would be working on today.

'It is based on a true incident,' he said. 'About local farming village with bad water shortage. A dozen girls went into the paddy fields with a priest, took off their clothes and danced naked. The girls are doing this quite willingly, you understand—it is traditional dance to bring rain. But nudity is illegal in India so police are coming along and arresting them.'

'And did they bring rain?'

He smiled and tapped his nose. 'Read the story! I am giving it twist in tail!'

Aboard the bus I opened the paper again. Water shortages remained very much in the news. The Andhra Pradesh government had begun transporting water in special trains, with celebrations attendant upon the departure of the first, *aarti* being offered and coconuts broken as the fifty-tanker 'rake' set off. And here, by way of a contrast, was a report about the Delhi authorities going under water to look for shipwrecks near Lakshadweep. 'Archaeologist S.R. Rao said that the search for treasure-carrying vessels would be taken up only after the monsoon.'

The mood at the Meteorological Centre was like that in a theatre before the curtain went up on an important first night. People moved with quickened tread and an urgent sense of purpose. Mr Rajagopalan, the Director, came pacing by with furrowed brow and hands clasped behind his back, the leading man mentally rehearsing his lines. He didn't remember me, and looked startled when I interrupted his reverie. 'We are talking hours and minutes now!' he declaimed. 'Hours and minutes!'

Julius Joseph stood outside his office, speaking to an attentive young assistant. The lines of worry had vanished from his face; he suddenly looked as relaxed as someone back from a long holiday. 'Tell them to be here at four o'clock for an official announcement,' he said.

'Yes, sir!' said the young man, rushing off.

'That's for the local media,' said Mr Joseph, smiling. 'To put them out of their misery.'

'So today's the day,' I said.

'Undoubtedly—though, as is customary, we will not formally announce it until tomorrow. We think it will arrive between 3 and 3.30. This morning the wind was gusting at 40 knots from the south-west—the classic prelude to the burst.'

'When will it get to Cochin?'

'Tomorrow.'

'Maybe I should get up there tonight.'

'Through a great barrage of rain and wind? No one would take you. My advice is to wait and watch its arrival here. And the best place for that will be out at Kovalam beach. It should be quite a spectacle.'

His secretary, wearing a burst-day sari of rain-cloud-coloured silk, called to him. Delhi was on the line! Mr Joseph sighed and hurried away.

I set off for the florist's shop in Mahatma Gandhi Road, noting that an electric mood had come over the city. People stood in groups on street corners, talking animatedly and looking at the sky. The traffic moved faster and more eccentrically than usual, and the thin wheeping sound of police whistles filled the air. Then, on impulse, I asked the trishaw driver to take me to a hospital. 'A traditional hospital,' I added. 'South Indian.'

He nodded, unsurprised. 'We go to Ayurvedic Teaching,' he said.

The matter of the watch still puzzled me. Now, following that and almost as weird, the stiffness in my neck and hands had been replaced by a faint tingling sensation. It was pleasant, even exhilarating, providing the kind of lift you might get from tiny cardiac implants dispensing cold gin. These two factors had to be connected. Perhaps they pointed to a course of treatment, even a cure.

The hospital stood in a tree-filled garden, a large, airy building suffused with the heady smells of a spice bazaar. A friendly woman in a white coat sat at the reception desk. She listened to my tale of whiplashed necks, stiff hands and fast watches without ceasing to smile, though I noted a little tension appearing behind the eyes. I was asked to take a seat. One of the doctors would see me shortly. The corridors were full of stunningly pretty trainee nurses and lounging male patients wearing nothing but breechclouts, their heavily oiled skins gleaming like varnished mahogany. The heavily oiled women, presumably, had remained in the seclusion of their wards.

Several battered Ayurvedic medical journals lay on a nearby table. I leafed through them, learning that victims of cholera or acute gastroenteritis were given intravenous drips of coconut milk. Powdered seeds of bastard teak could, if eaten daily with gooseberry juice, ghee and honey, turn an old man into a youth.

A 22-year-old college student had been cured of chronic headaches by being purged with *gandharva hastadi* castor oil, then, each day before lunch, swallowing an ounce of *pippalyadi arishtam*. He took a tablespoon of *chavana prasa* and a cup of milk before bed and, on rising, had unconcentrated *ksheerabala* oil applied to the head; on twenty-one occasions the oil had also been administered nasally.

I saw how these head applications were done. A shiny, well-built young man came by in a wheelchair, pushed by one of those flashing-eye child nurses, a small leather crown set atop his shaven scalp. The receptionist said he suffered from migraines.

'The hat contains a tank which we are filling daily with oils of cider and concentrated milk extracts. The mixture is absorbed naturally and, quite soon, he will be getting better.'

The doctor who saw me was a busy, plump, middle-aged lady with beautiful skin. Though interested in the accelerating watch—'I heard of town hall clock that once chimed thirteen times during monsoon burst'—she offered little comfort.

'I am not denying there may be force fields and charged particles in the atmosphere today,' she said briskly. 'Only a physicist could tell us that. And if such things exist it is possible they may be affecting you. But I doubt they could help us make you better. Perhaps we could ease the symptoms, but our methods are very slow. Take pain, for instance. We don't treat pain, we treat only the cause. This can take many weeks. Even we Ayurvedic doctors sometimes suffer pain ourselves and would gladly kill for an aspirin! We too become impatient. But nothing must be allowed to interfere with the natural healing process. So you will need plenty of time.'

'I must go to Cochin tomorrow,' I said.

She shook her head. 'You Westerners! Always demanding instant results. Look, I am trying to tell you, we work in different areas. Factors like the time of your birth, the influence of your father and mother, are important to us. You would consult holy men as well as doctors. We use leeches for blood-letting. This is not Harley Street, or your famous National Health Service.' She glanced pointedly at her watch.

I stood. 'Is it gaining much?' I asked.

She gave a small, gurgling laugh, unexpectedly sexy but, by the time I had reached the door, was already calling for her next patient.

At the flower shop Babu, in a state of some excitement, asked if I would like to meet Kamala Das. He had called her and she was prepared to see me at 5 p.m. 'We must take flowers, but what kind would she like?'

I stared at him. 'Babu, I haven't the faintest idea what you're talking about. Anyway, I'll be out at Kovalam watching the burst.'

He looked dismayed. 'Kamala is one of India's greatest poets. In 1984 she was nominated for the Nobel Prize for Literature and she lives here, in Trivandrum. She understands better than most what the monsoon means to us. And I thought it might be interesting for you to sit and talk while the first rains are falling.'

'My word!' I said.

He smiled. 'Come back after your burst. We will go together. Meanwhile, I shall sit and ponder the matter of the bouquet.'

A line of spectators had formed behind the Kovalam beach road. They were dressed with surprising formality, many of the men wearing ties and the women fine saris which streamed and snapped in the wind. Their excitement was shared and sharply focussed, like that of a committee preparing to greet a celebrated spiritual leader, or a victorious general who would come riding up the beach on an elephant; all they lacked was welcoming garlands of marigolds. As I joined them they greeted me with smiles, a late guest arriving at their function. The sky was black, the sea white. Foaming like champagne it surged over the road to within a few feet of where we stood. Blown spume stung our faces. It was not hard to imagine why medieval Arabs thought winds came from the ocean floor, surging upwards and making the surface waters boil as they burst into the atmosphere.

We stood rocking in the blast, clinging to each other amid scenes of great merriment. A tall, pale-skinned man next to me shouted, 'Sir, where are you from?'

'England!' I yelled.

The information became a small diminishing chord as, snatched and abbreviated by the elements, it was passed on to his neighbours.

'And what brings you here?'

'This!'

'Sir, us also! We are holiday-makers! I myself am from Delhi. This lady beside me is from Bangalore and we too have come to see the show!' He laughed. 'I have seen it many times but always I come back for more!'

The Bangalore woman cried, 'Yesterday there were dragonflies in our hotel garden. They are a sign. We knew monsoon was coming soon!' She beamed at me. 'It gives me true sense of wonder!'

More holiday-makers were joining the line. The imbroglio of inky cloud swirling overhead contained nimbostratus, cumulonimbus and Lord knows what else, all riven by updraughts, downdraughts and vertical wind shear. Thunder boomed. Lightning went zapping into the sea, the leader stroke of one strike passing the ascending return stroke of the last so that the whole roaring edifice seemed supported on pillars of fire. Then, beyond the cumuliform anvils and soaring castellanus turrets, we saw a broad, ragged ban of luminous indigo heading slowly inshore. Lesser clouds suspended beneath it like flapping curtains reached right down to the sea.

'The rains!' everyone sang.

The wind struck us with a force that made our line bend and waver. Everyone shrieked and grabbed at each other. The woman on my right had a plump round face and dark eyes. Her streaming pink sari left her smooth brown tummy bare. We held hands much more tightly than was necessary and, for a fleeting moment, I understood why Indians traditionally regard the monsoon as a period of torrid sexuality.

The deluge began.

She relinquished her grip and went scampering back into the trees, chiding her clerky husband for not raising his umbrella fast enough. The umbrella, raised, almost lifted him off his feet before being blown inside out. The rain hissed on the sea and fell on us with a buzzing, swarming noise. The air was suddenly fluid and fizzing. As a child in the islands I once attempted to walk across the lip of a waterfall. I slipped midway over and the plunge to the pool below seemed to take for ever; the sensation I felt then, of being cocooned inside a roaring cataract of falling, foaming water, was very similar to the one I felt now.

Elated, I made my way slowly back to the hotel. Water sheeted off the hillside, a rippling red tide carrying the summer's dust down to the sea. I changed and persuaded a taxi driver to take me to the flower shop. He muttered and sighed and asked for many rupees. But passing through Kovalam I spotted a place offering traditional

Ayurvedic massages and, on the spur of the moment, asked the driver to wait.

The masseur, a lugubrious brahmin with small, muscular hands, bade me strip and lie on a table. For twenty minutes he rubbed me down with thick, spicy gingili oil, pausing every few minutes to walk to the window and spit into the streaming rain. The procedure was soothing and faintly soporific and, afterwards, I felt an inexplicable sense of well-being. The masseur, though, remained wary when questioned about this. All he would say was, 'There are three places on body you cannot massage—gent's penis' (he called it 'pennies'), 'lady's chests and face of both sex; face massage make muscles go slack and give wrinkles.'

Babu, wearing a tie, his hair combed for Kamala Das, awaited me with purple orchids in a basket. The axle of his car had been repaired and we set off through flooded, gurgling streets strewn with flamboyant and flame-of-the-forest blossoms knocked down by the rain. Some were carried along in the gutters, making them resplendent, more lay heaped and scattered across the pavements; beneath their shiny umbrellas the passers-by moved across this glowing, lambent surface like fire-walkers. Many shops and offices had closed, their workers awarding themselves an unofficial public holiday.

I told Babu about the massage. 'Yes, I know of that man,' he said. 'He is quite good. But did he bless the oil before he rubbed it on?'

'I've no idea,' I said.

'He is supposed to hold each application cupped in his hand for a few seconds while he offers it to the gods. With you being a foreigner, though, he probably didn't bother. If an Indian had caught him just pouring and slapping it on he would have complained.'

He handed me Volume 1 of Kamala Das's *Collected Poems* and I leafed through it in the waning light. The poems were moving and very fine, with the monsoon a recurring symbol of, it seemed to me, sadness, wistful regret and tenderness. In 'The Time of the Drought' she had written:

When every night my littlest child awakes and
Limpets to my side, I am heavy with unshed tears,

I am the grey black monsoon sky
Just before the rain . . .

And, in 'A Souvenir of Bone':

How often
Have I wished as a child to peel the night like old
Wallpaper and burn it, to hold at monsoon time
The wounded wind in my arms, to lull it back to sleep.

But when, half an hour later, I put the sadness theory to her she crisply dismissed it. 'Nonsense!' she said. 'It's the most beautiful time! It means rejuvenation, greenery, new growth. It's nothing less than the reaffirmation of life.'

We sat drinking tea in a lofty blue room piled with books. The house was rambling and comfortable, the sounds of the dripping garden audible through the open shutters. A small, bespectacled woman with a teenager's complexion, Kamala Das wore a vivid blue sari with great panache and I reflected that she must have been a great beauty.

She continued, 'The monsoon's arrival is quite magnificent. It comes towards you like an orchestra and, not surprisingly, has inspired some of our loveliest music, ragas which evoke distant thunder and falling rain. For centuries our artists have painted monsoon pictures and our poets serenaded the monsoon; I am simply in that tradition.' She smiled and said, 'What I would really like to talk about, however, is the forests—or, rather, the lack of them. Some friends will be joining us shortly. They share my concern and I hope you will listen to them. The problem is inextricably linked with the monsoon so should be relevant to your researches.' She gave me a keen, questing look. 'I gather you plan to travel up India in its company?'

'That's the idea,' I said.

'You may find it an unreliable, even treacherous, companion. These days it has become very elusive. It is often late. Deforestation is one of the reasons for this. Trees help to make rain. Forests seed the passing clouds. Before they cut them down the monsoon was always scrupulously punctual. My grandmother planned everything around it—washing the clothes, drying the grain, visiting relatives in the certain expectation that it would arrive on the appointed day. The rains were heavier then. Within minutes of the burst small rivers had formed around our houses in which we children sailed paper boats. The monsoon was part of our lives, like sleep. We watched the world being reborn around us while the rain seeped into the house's foundations, making it creak and wobble. In the last two weeks of July we picked ten sacred herbs that grew in the puddles, took them inside and blessed them.'

'It was always the morning we went back to school after the long Ramadan holiday,' said Babu. 'My parents made a terrible fuss. They were scared of chills and implored me to stay out of the rain. But how could I?'

'Parents are much more enlightened now,' said Mrs Das. 'Children are encouraged to go out into the rain to enjoy this "gift from heaven". Also on a practical note, it helps them build up a resistance to monsoon complaints.' She cocked an eye at him. 'But morning? I distinctly remember it coming during the early afternoon, at about two. We always had an early lunch and hurried through the washing-up so that we could enjoy the spectacle. And when it arrived each villager would crack a raw egg, swallow the contents, fill the empty shell with sweet oil and swallow that too. They believed it did them a power of good.' To me she said, 'One aspect you should look into is health. The monsoon cure is big business in Kerala these days.'

I told her of my attempt to find a cure that morning. I also told her about my watch.

'Your watch may have been accurate. Perhaps we have all gained eight minutes without realizing it. As for your cure, I would send you to a place near here where your physician prays before an oil lamp and shrine dedicated to Dhanwanthari, the god of medicine; occasionally mantras are chanted also, the chief reason being that the sound is beneficial to the patient. Then his four assistants place you in a large wooden tub filled with warm medicated oil. Different types may be prescribed. Women wanting shiny skin, for example, have a particular red oil with a very sweet smell. The assistants massage you for an hour. (A curious thing about the massage is that it improves the vision; half blind old men have been known to throw away their spectacles.) You get only bland food, to cool the system, and you may not go into the sun. This goes on for twenty-one days and takes years off your age. My father had it regularly because he wanted to stay young. He died at eighty-four and, apart from his white hair, he had the appearance of a forty-year-old.'

To me Babu said, 'But you must always do exactly what the doctors tell you.'

'Oh, goodness, yes,' said Mrs Das. 'Last year two rich socialite girl friends of mine flew down from Bombay for the monsoon cure. But each evening, as soon as their physician left them, they came over here to carouse. They'd sit with me, chain-smoking and drinking scotch until dawn (they were a damned nuisance, actually), then sneak back to be in their rooms when the physician returned at 9 a.m. But after twenty-one days a terrible thing happened. They began to age. They became wrinkled old hags, their youth and beauty gone for ever. When I last heard they were at home in Bombay awaiting plastic surgery.'

Mrs Das's anti-deforestation committee arrived, shaking and furling their umbrellas, half a dozen courteous young people and an intense, middle-aged man referred to as the doctor. They took tea and before commencing their meeting, put the problem into perspective for me.

They said India was once a sylvan country. When Alexander the Great invaded in 327 BC he encountered dense, close-canopied, almost impenetrable forests. But peasants were already pursuing a slash-and-burn policy and, after the Emperor Ashoka came to power, the reforms proposed in his Rock Edicts included the planting of 'useful trees' along roads and on military camping grounds. The Marathas and Gonds planted mangoes beside their marching routes.

Trees play a crucial role in the monsoon cycle. By seeding clouds they encourage the rain to fall; by trapping it they help recharge the aquifers and hold groundwater in store for the common good. Some water, rising with the cell sap, is returned to the sky by transpiration through the leaves. A well-stocked teak forest gives off the equivalent of 1,000 mm of precipitation. Great rain forests act on the atmosphere like tropical seas; they supply it with water vapour and help replenish the rains.

By and large India is a natural tree-bearing country. Though it has five million hectares of eternal snow, most of its soil groups will support something—oaks and conifers in slightly acidic higher-altitude soils, sandalwood in coarse, shallow soils, casuarina in deep coastal sands, rosewood on riverine alluvium, babul, neem and palas in alkaline soils, bamboos just about anywhere.

Many Indians, though, have never visited a forest and are perhaps unaware that ever widening man-made gaps in the canopy will allow heavy rains to wash away the herbs, grasses and leaf-mould carpeting the floor. Then the soil itself is washed away, leaving the underlying rock exposed. Silting and flooding follow. Some of India's most tragic floods have been caused by denudation of forests once so thick that tigers lived in them.

'We have reached the stage now,' said Mrs Das, 'where only four per cent of the state of Kerala lies under forest. Within a short time, due to private greed and public indifference, we could be another Ethiopia. So I go to the villages and hold sapling-planting seminars, mostly with the women. I start with a prayer—one should always do that in India—and then I say a few words about the hardness and injustice of life and we have a little cry, and then I get on to the subject of trees. And they understand. They really do.'

'A thick forest,' said the doctor, 'traps and keeps its rainfall. It seeps through the floor into the subsoil and feeds the streams during the rainless period. Forests are great natural reservoirs. But today, with so many gone, 80 per cent of the monsoon rainfall simply runs away into the sea. This means that if next year's monsoon fails, or is late, there will be intense personal suffering. Once again people must go thirsty and hungry. There will be a 40 per cent drop in our agricultural output and that affects people right down the line, from the State Treasury to the humblest peasant.'

Suddenly the lights went out, came on again and then, for several minutes, flickered weakly and erratically. Mrs Das gave a loud, contented laugh. 'That is the monsoon!' she cried. 'Just as I remember it. All is back to normal!'

Charlis and I

Shashi Tharoor

I was about eight or nine when I first came across Charlis.

A few of us children were kicking a ball around the dusty courtyard of my grandmother's house in rural Kerala, where my parents took me annually on what they called a holiday and I regarded as a cross between a penance and a pilgrimage. (Their pilgrimage, my penance.) Balettan, my oldest cousin, who was all of thirteen and had a bobbing Adam's apple to prove it, had just streaked across me and kicked the ball with more force than he realized he possessed. It soared upward like a startled bird, curved perversely away from us, and disappeared over our high brick wall into the rubbish heap at the back of the neighbour's house.

'Damn,' I said. I had grown up in Bombay, where one said things like that.

'Go and get it, *da*,' Balettan commanded one of the younger cousins. *Da* was a term of great familiarity, used especially when ordering young boys around.

A couple of the kids, stifling groans, dutifully set off toward the wall. But before they could reach it the ball came sailing back over their heads toward us, soon followed over the wall by a skinny, sallow youth with a pockmarked face and an anxious grin. He seemed vaguely familiar, someone I'd seen in the background on previous holidays but not really noticed, though I wasn't sure why.

'Charlis!' a couple of the kids called out. 'Charlis got the ball!'

Charlis sat on the wall, managing to look both unsure and pleased with himself. Bits of muck from the rubbish heap clung to his shirt and skin. 'Can I play?' he asked diffidently.

Balettan gave him a look that would have desiccated a coconut.

This extract is taken from *India: From Midnight to the Millennium*, published by Penguin Books India.

'No, you can't, Charlis,' he said shortly, kicking the ball toward me, away from the interloper who'd rescued it.

Charlis's face lost its grin, leaving only the look of anxiety across it like a shadow. He remained seated on the wall, his leg—bare and thin below the grubby *mundu* he tied around his waist—dangling nervously. The game resumed, and Charlis watched, his eyes liquid with wistfulness. He would kick the brick wall aimlessly with his foot, then catch himself doing it and stop, looking furtively at us to see whether anyone had noticed. But no one paid any attention to him, except me, and I was the curious outsider.

'Why can't he play?' I finally found the courage to ask Balettan.

'Because he can't, that's all,' replied my eldest cousin.

'But why? We can always use another player,' I protested.

'We can't use *him*,' Balettan said curtly. 'Don't you understand anything, stupid?'

That was enough to silence me, because I had learned early on that there was a great deal about the village I didn't understand. A city upbringing didn't prepare you for your parents' annual return to their roots, to the world they'd left behind and failed to equip you for. Everything, pretty much, was different in my grandmother's house: there were hurricane lamps instead of electric lights, breezes instead of ceiling fans, a cow in the barn rather than a car in the garage. Water didn't come out of taps but from a well, in buckets laboriously raised by rope pulleys; you poured it over yourself out of metal vessels, hoping the maidservant who'd heated the bathwater over a charcoal fire had not made it so hot you'd scald yourself. There were the obscure indignities of having to be accompanied to the outhouse by an adult with a gleaming stainless-steel flashlight and of needing to hold his hand while you squatted in the privy, because the chairlike commodes of the city had made you unfit to discharge your waste as an Indian should, on his haunches. But it wasn't just a question of these inconveniences; there was the sense of being in a different world. Bombay was busy, bustling, unpredictable; there were children of every imaginable appearance, colour, language, and religion in my school; it was a city of strangers jostling one another all the time. In my grandmother's village everyone I met seemed to know one another and be related. They dressed alike, did the same things day after day,

shared the same concerns, celebrated the same festivals. Their lives
were ordered, predictable; things were either done or not done,
according to rules and assumptions I'd never been taught in the city.
Some of the rules were easier than others to grasp. There were, for
instance, complicated hierarchies that everyone seemed to take for
granted. The ones I first understood were those relating to age. This
was absolute, like an unspoken commandment: everyone older had to
be respected and obeyed, even if they sent you off on trivial errands
they should really have done themselves. Then there was gender: the
women existed to serve the men, fetching and carrying and stitching
and hurrying for them, eating only after they had fed the men first.
Even my mother, who could hold her own at a Bombay party with a
cocktail in her hand, was transformed in Kerala into a dutiful drudge,
blowing into the wood fire to make the endless stacks of thin, soft,
crisp-edged *dosas* we all wolfed down. None of this had to be spelled
out, no explicit orders given; people simply seemed to adjust naturally
to an immutable pattern of expectations, where everyone knew his
place and understood what he had to do. As someone who came from
Bombay for a month's vacation every year, spoke the language badly,
hated the bathrooms, and swelled up with insect bites, I adjusted less
than most. I sensed dimly that the problem with Charlis, too, had
something to do with hierarchy, but since he was neither female nor
particularly young, I couldn't fit him into what I thought I already
knew of Kerala.

We finished the game soon enough, and everyone began heading
indoors. Charlis jumped off the wall. Instinctively, but acting with
the casual hospitability I usually saw around me, I went up to him
and said, 'My mother'll be making *dosas* for tea. Want some?'

I was puzzled by the look of near panic that flooded his face. 'No,
no, that's all right,' he said, practically backing away from me. I could
see Balettan advancing toward us. 'I've got to go,' Charlis added,
casting me a strange look as he fled.

'What's the matter with him?' I asked Balettan.

'What's the matter with *you*?' he retorted. 'What were you saying
to him?'

'I just asked him to join us for some *dosas*, that's all,' I replied.

Seeing his expression, I added lamely, 'You know, with all the other kids.'

Balettan shook his head in a combination of disgust and dismay, as if he didn't know whether to be angry or sad. 'You know what this little foreigner did?' he announced loudly as soon as we entered the house. 'He asked Charlis to come and have *dosas* with us!'

This was greeted with guffaws by some and clucks of disapproval by others. 'Poor little boy, what does he know?' said my favourite aunt, the widowed Rani-*valiamma*, gathering me to her ample bosom to offer a consolation I hadn't realized I needed. 'It's not his fault.'

'What's not my fault?' I asked, struggling free of her embrace. The Cuticura talcum powder in her cleavage tickled my nose, and the effort not to sneeze made me sound even more incoherent than usual. 'Why shouldn't I invite him? He got our ball back for us. And you invite half the village anyway if they happen to pass by.'

'Yes, but which half?' chortled Kunjunni-*mama*, a local layabout and distant relative who was a constant presence at our dining table and considered himself a great wit. 'Which half, I say?' He laughed heartily at his own question, his eyes rolling, a honking sound emerging from the back of his nose.

I couldn't see why anyone else found this funny, but I was soon sent off to wash my hands. I sat down to my *dosas* feeling as frustrated as a vegetarian at a kebab-shop.

'Who *is* Charlis, anyway?' I asked as my mother served me the mild chutney she made specially since I couldn't handle the fiery spiced version everyone else ate.

'I don't know, dear, just a boy from the village,' she responded. 'Now finish your *dosas*, the adults have to eat.'

'Charlis is the Prince of Wales, didn't you know?' honked Kunjunni-*mama*, enjoying himself hugely. 'I thought you went to a convent school, Neel.'

'First of all, only girls go to convent schools,' I responded hotly. 'And anyway the Prince of Wales is called Charles, not Charlis.' I shot him a look of pure hatred, but he was completely unfazed. He soaked it in as a paddy field would a rainstorm, and honked some more.

'Charlis, Charles, what's the difference to an illiterate Untouchable with airs above his station? Anyway, that's how it sounded in Malayalam, and that's how he wrote it. Charlis. So you see how the Prince of Wales was born in Vanganassery.' He exploded into self-satisfied mirth, his honks suggesting he was inhaling his own pencil-line mustache. I hadn't understood what he meant, but I vowed not to seek any further clarification from him.

My mother came to my rescue. I could see that her interest was piqued. 'But why Charles?' she paused in her serving and asked Kunjunni-*mama*. 'Are they Christians?'

'Christians?' Kunjunni-*mama* honked again. 'My dear *chechi*, what do these people know of religion? Do they have any culture, any traditions? One of them, that cobbler fellow, Mandan, named his sons Mahatma Gandhi and Jawaharlal Nehru. Can you imagine? The fellow didn't even know that 'Mahatma' was a title and 'Nehru' a family surname. His brats were actually registered in school as M. Mahatma Gandhi and M. Jawaharlal Nehru. So of course when this upstart scavenger shopkeeper has to name *his* offspring, he went one better. Forget nationalism, he turned to the British royal family. So what if they had Christian names? So what if he couldn't pronounce them? You think Charlis is bad enough? He has two sisters, Elizabeth and Anne. Of course everyone in the village calls them Eli and Ana.'

This time even I joined in the laugher: I had enough Malayalam to know that *Eli* meant 'rat' and *Ana* meant 'elephant'. But a Bombayite sense of fairness asserted itself.

'It doesn't matter what his name is,' I said firmly. 'Charlis seems a nice boy. He went into the rubbish heap to get our ball. I liked him.'

'Nice boy!' Kunjunni-*mama*'s tone was dismissive, and this time there was no laughter in his honk. 'Rubbish heaps are where they belong. They're not clean. They don't wash. They have dirty habits.'

'What dirty habits?' I asked, shaking off my mother's restraining hand. 'Who's *they*?'

'Eat your food,' Kunjunni-*mama* said to me, adding, to no one in particular, 'and now this Communist government wants to put them in our schools. With our children.' He snorted. 'They'll be drinking out of our wells next.'

*

A few days later, the kids at home all decided to go to the local stream for a dip. On earlier Kerala holidays my mother had firmly denied me permission to go along, sure that if I didn't drown I'd catch a cold; but now I was older, I'd learned to swim, and I was capable of towelling myself dry, so I was allowed the choice. It seemed a fun idea, and in any case there was nothing better to do at home: I'd long since finished reading the couple of Biggles books I'd brought along. I set out with a sense of adventure.

We walked through dusty, narrow lanes, through the village, Balettan in the lead, half a dozen of the cousins following. For a while the houses we passed seemed to be those of relatives and friends; the kids waved cheerful greetings to women hanging up their washing, girls plaiting or picking lice out of each other's hair, bare-chested men in white *mundus* sitting magisterially in easy chairs, perusing the day's *Mathrubhumi*. Then the lane narrowed and the whitewashed, tile-roofed houses with verdant backyards gave way to thatched huts squeezed tightly together, their interiors shrouded in a darkness from which wizened crones emerged stooping through low-ceilinged doorways, the holes in their alarmingly stretched earlobes gaping like open mouths. The ground beneath our feet, uneven and stony, hurt to walk on, and a stale odour hung in the air, a compound of rotting vegetation and decaying flesh. Despair choked my breath like smoke. I began to wish I hadn't come along.

At last we left the village behind, and picked our way down a rocky, moss-covered slope to the stream. I didn't know what I'd expected, but it wasn't this, a meandering rivulet that flowed muddily through the fields. At the water's edge, on a large rock nearby, women were beating the dirt out of their saris; in the distance, a man squatted at a bend in the stream, picking his teeth and defecating. My cousins peeled off their shirts and ran into the water.

'Come on, Neel,' Balettan exhorted me with a peremptory wave of the hand. 'Don't be a sissy. It's not cold.'

'Just don't feel like it,' I mumbled. 'It's okay. You go ahead. I'll watch.'

They tried briefly to persuade me to change my mind, then left me to my own devices. I stood on the shore looking at them, heard their squeals of laughter, then looked away at the man who had completed his ablutions and was scooping water from the river to wash himself. Downstream from him, my cousins ducked their heads underwater. I quickly averted my gaze.

That was when I saw him. Charlis was sitting on a rocky overhang, a clean shirt over his *mundu*, a book in his hand. But his eyes weren't on it. He was looking down at the stream, where my cousins were playing.

I clambered over the rocks to him. When he spotted me he seemed to smile in recognition, then look around anxiously. But there was no one else about, and he relaxed visibly. 'Neel,' he said, smiling. 'Aren't you swimming today?'

I shook my head. 'Water's dirty,' I said.

'Not dirty,' he replied in Malayalam. 'The stream comes from a sacred river. Removes all pollution.'

I started to retort, then changed my mind. 'So why don't you swim?' I asked.

'Ah, I do,' he said. 'But not here.' His eyes avoided mine, but seemed to take in the stream, the washerwomen, my cousins. 'Not now.'

Bits of the half-understood conversation from the dining table floated awkwardly back into my mind. I changed the subject. 'It was nice of you to get our ball back for us that day,' I said.

'Ah, it was nothing.' He smiled unexpectedly, his pockmarks creasing across his face. 'My father beat me for it when I got home, though. I had ruined a clean shirt. Just after my bath.'

'But I thought you people didn't—' I found myself saying. 'I'm sorry,' I finished lamely.

'Didn't what?' he asked evenly, but without looking at me. He was clearly some years older than me, but not much bigger. I wondered whether he was scared of me, and why.

'Nothing,' I replied. 'I'm really sorry your father beat you.'

'Ah, that's all right. He does it all the time. It's for my own good.'

'What does your father do?'

Charlis became animated by my interest. 'He has a shop,' he said, a light in his eyes. 'In our part of the village. The Nair families don't come there, but he sells all sorts of nice things. Provisions and things. And on Thursdays, you know what he has? The best *halwa* in Vanganassery.'

'Really? I like *halwa*.' It was, in fact, the only Indian dessert I liked; Bombay had given me a taste for ice cream and chocolate rather than the deep-fried *laddoos* and bricklike *Mysoor-paak* that were the Kerala favourites.

'You like *halwa*?' Charlis clambered to his feet. 'Come on, I'll get you some.'

This time it was my turn to hesitate. 'No, thanks,' I said, looking at my cousins cavorting in the water. 'I don't think I should. They'll worry about me. And besides, I don't know my way about the village.'

'That's okay,' Charlis said. 'I'll take you home. Come on.' He saw the expression on my face. 'It's really good *halwa*,' he added.

That was enough for a nine-year-old. 'Wait for me,' I said, and ran down to the water's edge. 'See you at home!' I called out to the others.

Balettan was the only one who noticed me. 'Sure you can find your way back?' he asked, as my cousins splashed around him, one leaping onto his shoulders.

'I'll be okay,' I replied, and ran back up the slope as Balettan went under.

*

Charlis left me at the bend in our lane, where all I had to do was to walk through a relative's yard to reach my grandmother's house. He would not come any farther, and I knew better than to insist. I walked slowly to the house, my mind full of the astonishment with which his father had greeted my presence in his shop, the taste of his sugary, milky tea still lingering on my palate, my hands full of the orange-coloured wobbling slabs of *halwa* he had thrust upon me.

'Neel, my darling!' my mother exclaimed as I walked in. 'Where have you been? I've been so worried about you.'

'Look what I've got!' I said proudly, holding out the *halwa*. 'And there's enough for everyone.'

'Where did you get that?' Balettan asked, a white *thorthumundu*, a thin Kerala towel, in his hand, his hair still wet from his recent swim.

'Charlis gave it to me,' I said. 'I went to his father's shop. They.—'

'You did *what*?' Balettan's rage was frightening. He advanced toward me.

'I—I—'

'Went to Charlis's shop?' He loomed over me, the towel draped over his shoulder making him look even older and more threatening. 'Took food from Untouchables?' I began to shrink back from him. 'Give that to me!'

'I won't!' I snatched the *halwa* away from his hands, and as he lunged, I turned and ran, the precious sweet sticky in my grasp. But he was too fast for me; I had barely reached the yard when he caught up, seized me roughly by the shoulders, and turned me around to face him.

'We don't do this here, understand?' he breathed fiercely. 'This isn't Bombay.' He pried my hands apart. The *halwa* gleamed in my palms. 'Drop it,' he commanded.

'No,' I wanted to say, but the word would not emerge. I wanted to cry out for my mother, but she did not come out of the house.

'Drop it,' Balettan repeated, his voice a whiplash across what remained of my resistance.

Slowly I opened my hands outward in a gesture of submission. The orange slabs slid reluctantly off them. It seemed to me they took an age to fall, their gelatinous surfaces clinging to the soft skin of my palms until the last possible moment. Then they were gone, fallen, into the dust.

Balettan looked at them on the ground for a moment, then at me, and spat upon them where they lay. 'The dogs can have them,' he barked. He kicked more dust over them, then pulled me by the arm back toward the house. 'Don't you ever do this again.'

I burst into tears then, and at last the words came, tripping over themselves as I stumbled back into the house. 'I hate you! All of you! You're horrible and mean and cruel and I'll never come back here as long as I live!'

*

But of course I was back the next year; I hardly had any choice in the matter. For my parents, first-generation migrants to the big city, this was the vital visit home, to their own parents and siblings, to the friends and family they had left behind; it renewed them, it returned them to a sense of themselves, it maintained their connection to the past. I just came along because I was too young to be left behind, indeed too young to be allowed the choice.

In the year that had passed since my last visit, there had been much ferment in Kerala. Education was now universal and compulsory and free, so all sorts of children were flocking to school who had never been able to go before. There was talk of land reform, and giving title to tenant farmers; I understood nothing of this, but saw the throngs around men with microphones on the roadside, declaiming angry harangues I could not comprehend. None of this seemed, however, to have much to do with us, or to affect the unchanging rhythms of life at my grandmother's house.

My cousins were numerous and varied, the children of my mother's brothers and sisters and also of *her* cousins, who lived in the neighbouring houses; sometimes the relationship was less clear than that, but as they all ran about together and slept side by side like a camping army on mats on the floor of my grandmother's *thalam,* it was difficult to tell who was a first cousin and who an uncle's father-in-law's sister's grandson. After all, it was also *their* holiday season, and my parents' return was an occasion for everyone to congregate in the big house. On any given day, with my cousins joined by other children from the village, there could be as many as a dozen kids playing in the courtyard or going to the stream or breaking up for cards on the back porch. Sometimes I joined them, but sometimes, taking advantage of the general confusion, I would slip away unnoticed, declining to make the effort to scale the barriers of language and education and attitude that separated us, and sit alone with a book. Occasionally someone would come and look for me. Most often, that someone was my aunt Rani-*valiamma.*

As a young widow, she didn't have much of a life. Deprived of the status that a husband would have given her, she seemed to walk on the fringes of the house; it had been whispered by her late husband's family that only the bad luck her stars had brought into his life could account for his fatal heart attack at the age of thirty-six, and a whiff of stigma clung to her like a cloying perfume she could never quite wash off. Remarriage was out of the question, nor could the family allow her to make her own way in the world; so she returned to the village house she had left as a bride, and tried to lose herself in the routines of my grandmother's household. She sublimated her misfortune in random and frequent acts of kindness, of which I was a favoured beneficiary. She would bring me well-sugared lime-and-water from the kitchen without being asked, and whenever one of us brought down a green mango from the ancient tree with a lucky throw of a stone, she could be counted upon to return with it chopped up and marinated in just the right combination of salt and red chilli powder to drive my taste buds to ecstasy.

One day Rani-*valiamma* and I were upstairs, eating deviled raw mango and looking out on the kids playing soccer below, when I saw something and nearly choked. 'Isn't that Charlis?' I asked, pointing to the skinny boy who had just failed to save a goal.

'Could be,' she replied indifferently. 'Let me see—yes, that's Charlis.'

'But he's playing in our yard! I remember last year—'

'That was last year,' Rani-*valiamma* said, and I knew that change had come to the village.

But not enough of it. When the game was over, the Nair kids trooped in as usual to eat, without Charlis. When I asked innocently where he was, it was Balettan, inevitably, who replied.

'We play with him at school, and we play with him outside,' he said. 'But playing stops at the front door.'

I didn't pursue the matter. I had learned that whenever any of the Untouchable tradespeople came to the house, they were dealt with outside.

With each passing vacation, though, the changes became more and more apparent. For years my grandmother, continuing a tradition handed down over generations, had dispensed free medication (mainly aspirins and cough syrup) once a week to the poor villagers who queued for it; then a real clinic was established in the village by the government, and her amateur charity was no longer needed. Electricity came to Vanganassery: my uncle strung up a brilliant neon light above the dining table, and the hurricane lamps began to disappear, along with the tin cans of kerosene from which they were fuelled. The metal vessels in the bathroom were replaced by shiny red plastic mugs. A toilet was installed in the outhouse for my father's, and my, convenience. And one year, one day, quite naturally, Charlis stepped into the house with the other kids after a game.

No one skipped a beat; it was as if everyone had agreed to pretend there was nothing unusual. Charlis stood around casually, laughing and chatting; some of the kids sat to eat, others awaited their turn. No one invited Charlis to sit or to eat, and he made no move himself to do either. Then those who had eaten rose and washed their hands and joined the chatter, while those who had been with Charlis took their places at the table. Still Charlis stood and talked, his manner modest and respectful, until everyone but he had finished eating, and then they all strolled out again to continue their game.

'Charlis hasn't eaten,' I pointed out to the womenfolk.

'I know, child, but what can we do?' Rani-*valiamma* asked. 'He can't sit at our table or be fed on our plates. Even you know that.'

'It isn't fair,' I said, but without belligerence. What she had stated was, I knew, like a law of nature. Even the servants would not wash a plate off which an Untouchable had eaten.

'You know,' honked Kunjunni-*mama*, tucking into his third helping, 'They say that boy is doing quite well at school. Very well, in fact.'

'He stood first in class last term,' a younger cousin chimed in.

'First!' I exclaimed. 'And Balettan failed the year, didn't he?'

'Now, why would you be asking that?' chortled Kunjunni-*mama* meaningfully, slapping his thigh with his free hand.

I ignored the question and turned to my aunt. 'He's smarter than all of us, and we can't even give him something to eat?'

Rani-*valiamma* saw the expression on my face and squeezed my hand. 'Don't worry,' she whispered. 'I'll think of something.'

She did; and the next time Charlis walked in, he was served food on a plantain leaf on the floor, near the back door. I was too embarrassed to hover near him as I had intended to, but he seemed to eat willingly enough on his own.

'It's just not right!' I whispered to her as we watched him from a discreet distance.

'*He* doesn't mind,' she whispered back. 'Why should you?'

And it was true that Charlis probably ate on the floor in his own home.

When he had finished, a mug of water was given to him on the back porch, so that he could wash his hands without stepping into our bathroom. And the plantain leaf was thrown away: no plate to wash.

We returned to the game, and now it was my turn to miskick. The ball cleared the low wall at one end of the courtyard, hit the side of the well, teetered briefly on the edge, and fell in with a splash.

It had happened before. 'Go and get it, *da*,' Balettan languidly commanded one of the kids. The well was designed to be climbed into: bricks jutted out from the inside wall at regular intervals, and others had been removed to provide strategic footholds. But this was a slippery business: since the water levels in the well rose and fell, the inside surface was pretty slimy, and many of those who'd gone in to retrieve a floating object, or a bucket that had slipped its rope, had ended up taking an unplanned dip. The young cousin who had received Balettan's instruction hesitated, staring apprehensively into the depths of the well.

'Don't worry,' Charlis said quietly. 'I'll get it.' He moved toward the edge of the well.

'No!' There was nothing languid now about Balettan's tone; we could all hear the alarm in his voice. 'I'll do it myself.' And Charlis, one half-raised foot poised to climb onto the well, looked at him, his face drained of expression, comprehension slowly burning into his cheeks. Balettan ran forward, roughly pushing aside the boy who had been afraid to go, and vaulted into the well.

I looked at Rani-*valiamma*, who had been watching the game.

'Balettan's right,' she said. 'Do you think anyone would have drunk water at our house again if Charlis had gone into our well?'

*

Years passed; school holidays, and trips to Kerala, came and went. Governments fell and were replaced in Kerala, farm labourers were earning the highest daily wage in the country, and my almost toothless grandmother was sporting a chalk-white set of new dentures under her smile. Yet the house seemed much the same as before. A pair of ceiling fans had been installed, in the two rooms where family members congregated; a radio crackled with the news from Delhi; a tap made its appearance in the bathroom, though the pipe attached to it led from the same old well. These improvements, and the familiarity that came from repeated visits, made the old privations bearable. Kerala seemed less of a penance with each passing year.

Charlis was a regular member of the group now, admitted to our cardplaying sessions on the porch outside, joining us on our expeditions to the cinema in the nearest town. But fun and games seemed to hold a decreasing attraction for Charlis. He was developing a reputation as something of an intellectual. He would ask me, in painstaking textbook English, about something he had read about the great wide world outside, and listen attentively to my reply. I was, in the quaint vocabulary of the villagers, 'convent-educated,' a label they applied to anyone who emerged from the elite schools in which Christian missionaries served their foreign Lord by teaching the children of the Indian lordly. It was assumed that I knew more about practically everything than anyone in the village; but all I knew was what I had been taught from books, whereas they had learned from life. Even as I wallowed in their admiration, I couldn't help feeling their lessons were the more difficult, and the more valuable.

Balettan dropped out of school and began turning his attention to what remained of the family lands. It seemed to me that his rough edges became rougher as the calluses grew hard on his hands and feet. He had less time for us now; in his late teens he was already a full-fledged farmer, sitting sucking a straw between his teeth and watching the boys kick a ball around. If he disapproved of Charlis's growing familiarity with all of us, though, he did not show it—not even when Charlis asked me one day to go into town with him to see the latest Bombay blockbuster.

I thought Charlis might have hoped I could explain the Hindi dialogue to him, since Keralites learned Hindi only as a third language from teachers who knew it, at best, as a second. But when we got to the movie theatre, Charlis was not disappointed to discover the next two screenings were fully sold out. 'I am really wanting to talk,' he said in English, leading me to an eatery across the street.

The Star of India, as the board outside proclaimed, was a 'military hotel'; in other words, it served meat, which my grandmother did not. 'I am thinking you might be missing it,' Charlis said, ushering me to a chair. It was only when the main dish arrived that I realized that I was actually sitting and eating at the same table with Charlis for the first time.

If he was conscious of this, Charlis didn't show it. He began talking, hesitantly at first, then with growing fluency and determination, about his life and his ambitions. His face shone when he talked of his father, who beat him with a belt whenever he showed signs of neglecting his books. 'You can do better than I did,' he would say before bringing the whip down on Charlis. 'You will do better.'

And now Charlis was aiming higher than anyone in his family, in his entire community, had ever done before. He was planning to go to university.

'Listen, Charlis,' I said gently, not wanting to discourage him. 'You know it's not going to be easy. I know you're first in class and everything, but that's in the village. Don't forget you'll be competing for places with kids from the big cities. From the—convents.'

'I am knowing that,' Charlis replied simply. Then, from the front pocket of his shirt, he drew out a battered notebook filled with small, tightly packed curlicues of Malayalam lettering in blue ink, interspersed with phrases and sentences in English in the same precise hand. 'Look,' he said, jabbing at a page. 'The miserable hath no other medicine / But only hope.—Shakespeare, *Measure for Measure*, III.i.2,' I read. And a little lower down, 'Men at some time are masters of their fates; / The fault, dear Brutus, is not in our stars, / But in ourselves, that we are underlings.' Charlis had underlined these words.

'Whenever I am reading something that inspires me, I am writing it down in this book,' Charlis said proudly. 'Shakespeare is great man, isn't it?'

His Malayalam was of course much better, but in English Charlis seemed to cast off an invisible burden that had less to do with the language than with its social assumptions. In speaking it, in quoting it, Charlis seemed to be entering another world, a heady place of foreign ideas and unfamiliar expressions, a strange land in which the old rules no longer applied.

'For the Colonel's Lady an' Judy O'Grady,' he declaimed at one point, '"are sisters under their skins!"—Rudyard Kipling,' he added. 'Is that how you are pronouncing it?'

'Rudyard, Roodyard, I haven't a clue,' I confessed. 'But who cares, Charlis? He's just an old imperialist fart. What does anything he ever wrote have to do with any of us today, in independent India?'

Charlis looked surprised, then slightly averted his eyes. 'But are we not,' he asked softly, 'are we not brothers under our skins?'

'Of course,' I replied, too quickly. And it was I who couldn't meet his gaze.

The following summer, I was sitting down to my first meal of the holiday at my grandmother's dining table when Rani-*valiamma* said, 'Charlis was looking for you.'

'Really?' I was genuinely pleased, as much by Charlis's effort as by the fact that it could be mentioned so casually. 'What did he want?'

'He came to give you the news personally,' Rani-*valiamma* said. 'He's been admitted to Trivandrum University.'

'Wow!' I exclaimed. 'That's something, isn't it?'

'Untouchable quota,' honked the ever-present Kunjunni-*mama*, whose pencil-line moustache had gone from bold black to sleek silver without his ever having done a stroke of work in his life.

'Reserved seats for the Children of God. Why, Chandrasekhara Menon's son couldn't get in after all the money they spent on sending him to boarding school, and here Charlis is on his way to University.'

'The village *panchayat* council is organizing a felicitation for him tomorrow,' Rani-*valiamma* said. 'Charlis wanted you to come, Neel.'

'Of course I will,' I responded. 'We must all go.'

'All?' snorted Kunjunni-*mama*, who was incapable of any action that could be called affirmative. 'To felicitate Charlis? Speak for yourself, boy. If you want to attend an Untouchable love-in organized by the Communists who claim to represent our village, more's the pity. But don't expect to drag any members of the Nair community with you.'

'I'll come with you, Neel,' said a quiet voice by my side. It was Rani-*valiamma*, her ever-obliging manner transformed into something approaching determination.

'And me,' chirped a younger cousin, emboldened. 'May I go too, Amma?' asked another. And by the next evening I had assembled a sizable delegation from our extended family to attend the celebration for Charlis.

Kunjunni-*mama* and Balettan sat at the table, nursing their cups of tea, and watched us all troop out. Balettan was silent, his manner distant rather than disapproving. As I passed them, I heard the familiar honk: 'Felicitation, my foot.'

The speeches had begun when we arrived, and our entry sparked something of a commotion in the meeting hall, as Charlis's relatives and the throng of well-wishers from his community made way for us, whispers of excitement and consternation rippling like a current through the room. I thought I saw a look of sheer delight shine like a sunburst on Charlis's face, but that may merely have been a reaction to hearing the *panchayat* president say, 'The presence of all of you here today proves that Charlis's achievement is one of which the *entire* village is proud.' We applauded that, knowing our arrival had given some meaning to that trite declaration.

After the speeches, and the garlanding, and Charlis's modest reply, the meeting broke up. I wanted to congratulate Charlis myself, but he was surrounded by his own people, all proud and happy and laughing. We made our way toward the door, and then I heard his voice.

'Neel! Wait!' he called out. I turned, to see him pulling himself away from the crush and advancing toward me with a packet in his hands. 'You mustn't leave without this.'

He stretched out the packet toward me, beaming. I opened it and peered in. Orange slabs of *halwa* quivered inside.

'It's the last bag,' Charlis said, the smile never fading from his face. 'My father sold the shop to pay for me to go to University. We're all moving to Trivandrum.' I looked at him, finding no words. He pushed the *halwa* at me. 'I wanted you to have it.'

I took the bag from him without a word. We finished the *halwa* before we got home.

*

Years passed. Men landed on the moon, a woman became prime minister, wars were fought; in other countries, coups and revolutions brought change (or attempted to), while in India elections were won and lost and things changed (or didn't). I couldn't go down to Kerala every time my parents did; my college holidays didn't always coincide with Dad's leave from the office. When I did manage a visit, it wasn't the same as before. I would come for a few days, be indulged by Rani-*valiamma*, and move on. There was not that much to do. Rani-*valiamma* had started studying for a teacher's training diploma. My grandmother spent most of her time reading the scriptures and chewing areca, usually simultaneously. Balettan, tough and taciturn, was the man of the house; now that agriculture was his entire life, we had even less to say to each other than ever. My cousins were scattered in several directions; a new generation of kids played football in the yard. No one had news of Charlis.

I began working in an advertising agency in Bombay, circulating in a brittle, showy world that could not have had less in common with Vanganassery. When I went to the village the talk was of pesticides and irrigation, of the old rice-levy and the new, government-subsidized fertilizer, and, inevitably, of the relentless pace of land reform, which was taking away the holdings of traditional landlords and giving them to their tenants. It was clear that Balettan did not understand much of this, and that he had not paid a great deal of attention to what was happening.

'Haven't you received any notification from the authorities, Balettan?' I asked him one day, when his usual reticence seemed only to mask ineffectually the mounting level of anxiety in his eyes.

'Some papers came,' he said in a tone whose aggressiveness betrayed his deep shame at his own inadequacy. 'But do I have time to read them? I'm a busy man. Do I run a farm or push papers like a clerk?'

'Show them to Neel,' Kunjunni-*mama* suggested, and as soon as I opened the first envelope I realized Balettan, high-school dropout and traditionalist, had left it too late.

'What are these lands here, near Kollengode?'

'They're ours, of course.'

'Not anymore, Balettan. Who's T. Krishnan Nair, son of Kandath Narayananunni Nair?'

'He farms them for us, ever since Grandfather died. I farm here at Vanganassery, and Krishnan Nair takes care of Kollengode, giving us his dues after each harvest. It's the only way. I can't be at both places at the same time, can I?'

'Well, it says here he's just been registered as the owner of those lands. You were given fourteen days to show cause as to why his claim should not have been admitted. Why didn't you file an objection, Balettan?'

We were all looking at him. 'How can they say Krishnan Nair owns our land? Why, everybody knows it's our land. It's been ours ever since anyone can remember. It was ours before Grandmother was born.'

'It's not ours anymore, Balettan. The government has just taken it away.'

Balettan shifted uneasily in his chair, a haunted, uncomprehending look on his face. 'But they can't do that,' he said. 'Can they?'

'They can, Balettan,' I told him sadly. 'You know they can.'

'We've got to do something,' honked Kunjunni-*mama* with uncharacteristic urgency. 'Neel, you've got to do something.'

'Me? What can I do? I'm a Bombay-wallah. I know less about all this than any of you.'

'Perhaps,' admitted Kunjunni-*mama*. 'But you're an educated man. You can read and understand these documents. You can speak to the Collector. He's the top IAS man in the district, probably another city type like you, convent-educated. You can speak to him in English and explain what has happened. Come on, Neel. You've got to do it.'

'I don't know,' I said dubiously. The advertising life had not brought me into contact with any senior Indian Administrative Service officers. I hadn't the slightest idea what I would say to the Collector when I met him.

And then I saw the look in Balettan's eyes. He had grown up knowing instinctively the rules and rituals of village society, the cycles of the harvest, how to do the right thing and what was never done. He could, without a second thought, climb trees that would make most of us dizzy, descend into wells, stand knee-deep in the slushy water of a paddy field to sprout grain into the world. But all these were skills he was born with, rhythms that sang in his blood like the whisper of his mother's breath. He wore a *mundu* around his waist, coaxed his buffalo across the fields, and treated his labourers and his family as his ancestors had done for thousands of years. He was good at the timeless realities of village India; but India, even village India, was no longer a timeless place. 'Don't you understand anything, stupid?'

he had asked me all those years ago; and in his eyes I saw what I imagined he must have seen, at that time, in mine.

'I'll go,' I said, as Balettan averted his eyes. In relief, perhaps, or in gratitude. It didn't matter which.

*

The Collector's office in Palghat, the district capital, was already besieged by supplicants when I arrived. Two greasy clerks presided over his antechamber, their desks overflowing with papers loosely bound in crumbling files held together with string. Three phones rang intermittently, and were answered in a wide variety of tones, ranging from the uncooperative to the unctuous, depending on who was calling. People crowded round the desks, seeking attention, thrusting slips of paper forward, folding hands in entreaty, shouting to be heard. Occasionally a paper was dealt with and a khaki-uniformed peon sent for to carry it somewhere; sometimes, people were sent away, though most seemed to be waved toward the walls where dozens were already waiting, weary resignation on their faces, for their problems to be dealt with. All eyes were on the closed teak door at the corner, bearing the brass nameplate M.C. THEKKOTE, I.A.S., behind which their destinies were no doubt being determined.

'It's hopeless,' I said to Balettan, who had accompanied me. 'I told you we should have tried to get an appointment. We'll be here all day.'

'How would we have got an appointment?' Balettan asked, reasonably, since we did not yet have a phone in the village. 'No, this is the only way. You go and give them your card.'

I did not share Balettan's faith in the magical properties of this small rectangular advertisement of my status, but I battled my way to the front of one of the desks and thrust it at an indifferent clerk.

'Please take this to the Collector-*saar*,' I said, trying to look both important and imploring. 'I must see him.'

The clerk seemed unimpressed by the colourful swirls and curlicues that proclaimed my employment by AdAge, Bombay's smartest new agency. 'You and everyone else,' he said skeptically, putting the card aside. 'Collector-*saar* very busy today. You come back tomorrow, we will see.'

At this point Balettan's native wisdom asserted itself. He insinuated a five-rupee note into the clerk's palm. 'Send the card in,' he said. 'It's important.'

The clerk was instantly responsive. 'I am doing as you wish,' he said grudgingly. 'But you will still have to wait. Collector-*saar* is so so very busy today.'

'You've told us that already,' I replied. 'We'll wait.'

A peon wandered in, bearing tea for the clerks. Once the man at the desk had satisfied himself that his tea was sugared to his taste, he added my card to the pile of papers he gave the peon to take in to the Collector. 'It will take some time,' he added curtly.

It didn't. Soon after the door had closed behind the peon, the black phone on the clerk's desk jangled peremptorily. 'Yes, saar. Yes, saar,' he said, perspiring. 'No, saar. Not long. Yes, saar. At once, saar.' He had stood up to attention during this exchange, and when he replaced the receiver there was a new look of respect in his eyes. 'Collector-*saar* will be seeing you now, *saar*,' he said, with a *salaam*. 'You didn't explain who you were, *saar*.' The five-rupee note re-emerged in his hand. 'You seem to have dropped this by mistake, *saar*,' he said shamefacedly, handing it to Balettan.

'Keep it,' Balettan said, as mystified as I by the transformation in the man's attitude. But the clerk begged him to take it back, and bowed and scraped us toward the imposing doorway.

'Obviously Bombay's ad world counts for more than I thought with these government-wallahs,' I whispered to Balettan.

'He's just happy to be able to speak English with someone,' Balettan suggested.

The clerk opened the door into a high-ceilinged office. The Collector rose from behind a mahogany desk the size of a Ping-Pong table, and stretched out a hand. 'It's so good to see you again, Neel,' he said.

It was Charlis.

'Charlis!' I exclaimed, astonishment overcoming delight. 'B-but— the name—the IAS—'

'You never did know my family name, did you? After all these years.' Charlis spoke without reproach. 'And yes, I've been in the IAS for some time now.' The Administrative Service, too, I found myself thinking unworthily, offered one more of the quotas Kunjunni-*mama* liked to complain about. 'But this is the first time I've been posted so close to Vanganassery. I've barely got here, but once I've settled in, I'm planning to visit the village again soon.' He added casually, 'It's part of my district, after all. That'd make it an official visit, you see.'

He seemed to enjoy the thought, and I found myself looking at Balettan. I didn't know what I expected to find in his expression, but it certainly wasn't the combination of hope, respect, and, yes, admiration with which he now regarded the man across the desk.

Charlis seemed to catch it, too. 'But what is this? We haven't even asked Balettan to sit down.' He waved us to chairs, as tea appeared. 'Tell me, what can I do for you?'

We explained the problem, and Charlis was sympathetic but grave. The law was the law; it was also just, undoing centuries of absentee landlordism. In our case, though, thanks to Balettan's inattention (though Charlis didn't even imply that), it had been applied unfairly, leaving Balettan with less land than his former tenant. Some of this could be undone, and Charlis would help, but we would not be able to get back all the land that had been confiscated. Charlis explained all this carefully, patiently, speaking principally to Balettan rather than to me. 'Some changes are good, some are bad,' he concluded, 'but very few changes can be reversed.'

'Shakespeare or Rudyard Kipling?' I asked, only half in jest, remembering his little notebook.

'Neither,' he replied quite seriously. 'Charlis Thekkote. But you can quote me if you like.'

Charlis was as good as his word. He helped Balettan file the necessary papers to reclaim some of his land, and made sure the files were not lost in the bureaucratic maze. And the week after our visit, knowing I would not be staying in Vanganassery long, Charlis came to the village.

I will never forget the sight of Charlis seated at our dining table with the entire family bustling attentively around him: Rani-*valiamma*, on leave from the school where she was now vice-principal, serving him her soft, crisp-edged *dosas* on Grandmother's best stainless-steel *thali*; Kunjunni-*mama*, honking gregariously, pouring him more tea; and half the neighbours, standing at a respectful distance, gawking at the dignitary.

But the image that will linger longest in my memory is from even before that, from the moment of Charlis's arrival at the village. His official car cannot drive the last half-mile to our house, on the narrow paths across the paddy fields, so Charlis steps down, in his off-white safari suit and open-toed sandals, and walks to our front door, through the dust. We greet him there and begin to usher him into the house, but Balettan stops us outside. For a minute all the old fears come flooding back into my mind and Charlis's, but it is only for a minute, because Balettan is shouting out to the servant, 'Can't you see the Collector-*saar* is waiting? Hurry up!'

I catch Charlis's eye; he smiles. The servant pulls a bucketful of water out of the well to wash Charlis's feet.

Marthanda Varma

C.V. Raman Pillai

Towards the first quarter of the eighteenth century, the Native State of Travancore in South India, where today more than fifty lakhs of loyal subjects worship an enlightened ruler on the throne, was a hotbed of unrest, bordering on open rebellion. In opposition to custom and rigid rules of convention, an idea had taken root among a certain section of the people of the State, that the matriarchal system of succession that had been followed hitherto was fundamentally wrong, since it violated the basic principle of birthright, ignoring the prerogative of the male, and should therefore be changed forthwith. This new revolutionary school of thought was led by no less a person than Sri Padmanabhan Thampi, the elder son of the then ruling Maharajah, aided by his younger brother Sri Raman Thampi, and the Eight Nair Chieftains, who enjoyed vast resources in men and money, besides owning strategic positions along the frontier of the State.

Consequent upon the protracted illness of the Maharajah, the administrative head of the State could not, for the time being, concentrate his attention on vital matters affecting the State, much less suppress the activities of the anarchists, and it was openly stated in the streets, that the matriarchal dynasty would end in the historic state of Travancore with the death of the old Maharajah, who was visibly ailing, and that in its place would come a new patriarchal royal house, and perhaps a new era in the annals of the country. Although traditional loyalty, imbibed through centuries of blind worship, naturally swayed the minds of the masses, an open avowal of sympathy with the royal house would have been tantamount to an act of suicide, owing to the power wielded by the revolutionary party, and people held their tongue in fear and practical wisdom, till the

This extract is taken from *Marthanda Varma*, published by Sahitya Akademi, Delhi.

atmosphere became clear and congenial once more.

In the days of which we write, at the place called Charote, like the forgotten relic of a more distant past, when, instead of Trivandrum, Padmanabhapuram was the capital of the State of Travancore, there still stood a palace within whose mudstained, moss covered walls unknown to the absentee caretaker, now lived only legions of blind bats, bandicoots and hooded serpents. The whole compound was overgrown with weeds and wild undergrowth, and from the dirty dust-laden rooms of the dilapidated palace, emanated the stench of foulsome vapour.

One fine morning, some two years after the memorable events described in the prologue, a young Brahmin, scarcely over his 'teens was seen to be sitting in the outer verandah of the aforesaid palace. Although the simplicity of his attire and the tell-tale sacred thread proclaimed him to be a Brahmin, it was hard to say to which sect of Brahminism he belonged. For, besides a thick mop of hair and a curly beard, both of which he wore long, as if observing deeksha for some departed elder of his family, his face shone more with martial valour than with Vedic piety! piety! piety! He was decidedly fair, with a classic cast of countenance, and except for the long hawk-like nose which leant an added majesty to the face, his features were regular and of rare regal distinction. Nor did the shape of the body indicate much of the Brahmin. The long sinewy arms that reached up to the knees, the thick column of the neck that stood erect like a pillar of strength in the centre of those massive shoulders, and the arching beauty of the deep muscular chest, all belied the simple attire of the Brahmin, stamping every line and limb of his wonderful physique with the unmistakable hallmark of the high-born Kshatriya warrior.

But then, as he sat staring towards the heights of the Veli Hills in front of him, a thin film of sadness seemed to shadow the serene gravity of his face, sometimes contorting it into hard lines of uncontrollable anger. He seemed to be musing over some secret worry, tossing on the uncertain seas of life, sinking in despair, rising up the surface buoyed up by hope, and again falling back in hopeless exhaustion.

Suddenly, something seemed to rouse him to the realities of life, and shaking off his inertia, he called a name, 'Parameswara!'

From the other side of the courtyard, a Nair yeoman armed with sword and shield, like the Royal Bodyguards of those days, immediately appeared before the Brahmin and stood to a side with the utmost respect, waiting for his orders. The Brahmin turned to him.

'I do not think it advisable to stay in these parts any longer. What are we to do? Why not proceed to Trivandrum?'

'If we return to Trivandrum without going to Bhoothapandi, the purpose of our trip will be unfulfilled.'

'When the news regarding my uncle's illness has reached me, is it not my duty to hasten there immediately? What good are we going to gain by staying here? Without men and money, nothing can be done, and we have neither. We have enlisted the sympathy of but one solitary Pathan!'

'More people will certainly join our side. They have not been identified mainly because of our indolence.'

The Brahmin's face became livid with rage and vexation, as the word 'indolence' passed the other's lips.

'What am I to do? Since that Evil Genius has come to Padmanabhapuram, it has not been possible to assemble men of influence here. But I have an idea. You must go to Bhoothapandi and try to see Arumukham Pillai. I shall proceed straight to Trivandrum.'

The other seemed to frown upon this proposal. He was not in favour of parting from his master. So much was clear from his next words.

'I am of the opinion that it will be better that I too come to Trivandrum and then proceed to Bhoothapandi. These solitary trips are not very healthy. It is too early to forget the incident at Kalliankadu. There should not be another occurrence of the kind.'

'What is the use of shirking danger? You can proceed to Bhoothapandi even now. There can be nothing worse than the danger that threatens us at present.'

'Such commands are extremely painful to us. It is better to go to Keralapuram and proceed from there to Trivandrum with sufficient escort. But . . . even the morning ablutions have not been attended to . . .'

'I am going to Trivandrum straight. After enquiring about uncle's health, the other things can be settled. In the meantime, you must go to Bhoothapandi and pacify the Madura people . . . What's that?' The

Brahmin sprang to his feet.

Immediately, Parameswaran Pillai sprang towards the doorway, and after one glance at the road, rushed back in haste, with an anxious face. 'Jump over the wall . . . quick . . . some ten to twenty lancers are coming this way . . .'

The news, whatever its alarming import, did not seem to shake the Brahmin's fortitude, in spite of the fear and anxiety throbbing in the tone in which it was conveyed to him. He slowly walked out of the doorway and vaulted over the outer wall with ease, followed by his faithful bodyguard. The lancers had by this time reached the southern gateway. Altogether there were fourteen of them under the leadership of the redoubtable Velu Kurup, who enjoyed in these days an unenviable notoriety for unexampled courage and cruelty, so much so, that his name had become synonymous with terror throughout the State. Everyone of the party carried a long spear in addition to the short sword and shield.

The leader Velu Kurup was a short thickset dwarf, ebony black in colour, with a low forehead, uneven protruding teeth and fierce bloodshot eyes that shone like crimson coals. The evil light that invariably shone in them and the unusual width of his shoulders, gave him the appearance of some savage animal, that has become extinct in the world. The trusted servant of Sri Padmanabhan Thampi, he knew no higher God than his hard-hearted master, and acknowledged no higher principles than his orders.

Entering the palace compound, the lancers conducted a hasty search through all the rooms from attic to cellar, and finding their quarry flown, crossed to the southern gate and looked for tracks in the mossy undergrowth that surrounded the palace. Following the faint trail for some distance, their pains were rewarded by the sight of the flying figures in front; at which there arose a wild shout of triumph from the pursuing throng, like the mad bay of hungry wolves.

Like timid rabbits pursued by hell-hounds, the Brahmin and his bodyguard flew over thorn and thicket, indifferent alike to physical pain and bodily fatigue, spurred on by the instinct of self-preservation. Dodging between trees and towering rocks, stumbling over hillocks and hidden ditches, on the unseen wings of fear, they reached the open spaces on the slope of the Veli Hills, when they saw before them a wildly attired member of the lower classes, known as Channars, gesticulating to them. Near him stood the stump of a super-annuated jack-tree, bare of leaves and boughs. By some freak of nature, its trunk had been hollowed out in the nature of a cylindrical room, and this the Channan pointed out to the fugitive pair. When the two were safely concealed within this, the Channan began to run to the west.

Intent on following the barefoot track, the pursuing party of lancers never paused near the tree-trunk but followed the footsteps that continued to the west, as planned by the unknown Channan. Satisfied that the lancers had passed out of sight, the pair came out of the hollow tree-trunk, and doubled back on their own traces, till they reached a clump of palms, where some more of the Channars were idling away their time. Of them they enquired whether there were any respectable Nair families in the neighbourhood, and proceeded in another direction on the information received.

Meantime, the lancers were in full cry. The leader was seen to exhort his followers not to slacken speed till the fugitives were run to earth, to which many a bloodthirsty villain responded in high glee, 'If we are men, his head shall adorn our spears before long.' But after an hour or so of continued running, they found that the tracks suddenly stopped and that they had been chasing the proverbial wild geese. While they were debating within themselves as to the next step, a burst of wild music suddenly smote their ears and they turned round. To the accompaniment of his own senseless song, a fantastic figure clad in filthy rags was performing mad capers before them.

Vexed beyond words at the futile termination of their murderous quest, Velu Kurup was ready to take offence at the slightest word, and turning to the Channan, he asked whether two people had passed that way. But the mad fellow did not seem to hear him. Instead, the wild song continued. And then, it seemed that the rich resonant voice of the demented dancer put some vague fear into the heart of Velu Kurup. Nevertheless he addressed the madcap, 'Stop that song, you rascal and answer me . . .'

Even this burst of anger did not seem to penetrate into the diseased intellect of the Channan. Only, he struck a different tune and suiting his pace and action to the funny rhythm of his composition, he sang about a fire-eating devil on the top of that particular hill. Velu Kurup could not brook the fellow's impudence, and flying into a tantrum of rage, raised his foot and struck the madman across the cheek, when lo! . . . from nowhere, steel-tipped arrows began to rain upon him and his party, putting them to instant flight, in preference to an untimely end. For, two of them had already dropped dead on account of the unerring missiles of death.

When the lancer's angry foot struck him across the cheek, for a moment, the Channan's idiotic face seemed to clear to give place to a paroxysm of rage. But with rare strength of mind, he controlled the unbidden rise of temper, and continued his wild capers till the last of the lancers had vanished round the corner. Then he paused to look about him, and saw emerging from the shadow of another tree a long limbed Nair youth, carrying a gaily painted long-bow and a sheaf of arrows, like some legendary hero stepping out of the pages of some mythological book. The newcomer seemed to be possessed of incredible strength, for, in spite of his slender figure, he tossed aside the corpses of the dead lancers with his foot with ridiculous ease. Having collected the innumerable arrows that lay about the place, he held a brief conversation with the mad Channan whom he seemed to know, and vanished into the woods as quietly and as mysteriously as he had appeared.

—Translated from the Malayalam by B.K. Menon

The village before time

V.K. Madhavan Kutty

I was born in a little village in the interior of the old Palghat taluk, in central Kerala.

The majority of the villagers were Nairs. There are various types of Nairs—the Kiriyath Nairs, the Athikurissi Nairs, the Veluthedan Nairs and so on. Each group lived in their own special island in the village. Indeed, the entire village was a conglomeration of little islands, for the members of each caste lived in their own particular space, performed their own prescribed duties and reaped the fruit of their own actions. No one desired a reward greater than calmness of mind.

At a time when the Government and the ruling front were making attempts to install electricity in every nook and corner of Kerala, my village took pride in declaring that they were wrong to do so. Two electricity poles had been planted in the centre of the village, south of the Bhagavathy temple. On some nights, pinpoints of light came alive on them, flickered for a while like glow-worms and went out. Meanwhile, the village continued to foster its ancient lifestyle in most aspects.

The Panchayat Board in office at the time of Independence built only one road through the village. This has now become a narrow lane full of potholes. The road was named 'Panchayat Road' since there was at the time no one in the village worthy enough to give it his name. Had it been named after some village celebrity who had died, the relatives of other deceased celebrities would have protested.

The signboard that used to say 'Panchayat Road' has now disappeared. But there is a stone trough nearly a hundred feet long at the point where the road begins and the words 'Donated by Valia Veettil Kunji Amma' can still be seen clearly engraved on it. It used to hold water for the cart-drawing bullocks that passed that way. Cart-

This extract is taken from *The Village Before Time*, published by IndiaInk.

drawing bullocks are now a thing of the past. The well that used to be on the roadside near the trough has been filled up with mud. And the trough itself, dry and empty, no longer has the dignity or worthiness that a thing so old should possess. People waiting for a bus sometimes sit on the edge of the trough with their legs drawn up, or stand beside it, resting their umbrellas casually on the rim.

Kuttiraman Nair, who used to be the President of the Panchayat Board at the time the road was built, lived at the end of the road. This does not imply that the road was laid right up to his house because he was the President or anything like that. The road led to the Nair thara, the quarter where most of the Nairs, the dominant caste in the village, lived. If you walked along the road past the Nair thara and the fields, you came to the Ezhava thara.

The arrival of Abraham, the newly appointed village postman, was an event of note. It was the first time the villagers had set eyes on a Christian. Curly-haired Abraham with his dark, thick eyebrows and light eyes instantly became the centre of everyone's attention.

At first, the Nairs would not accept letters from his hands. The situation changed only when Purayath Narayanan Nair declared that the touch of a Christian would not pollute. Narayanan Nair claimed that while working in Kottayam, he had seen the local Nairs there entertain Christians in their homes. All the same, Abraham was not allowed to enter the Nair houses in our village and if he was offered tea or water, he had to pour it into his mouth without letting the glass touch his lips. He was, however, excused from inverting the glass when he finished, as local custom demanded of the lower castes.

Every Sunday, Abraham walked sixteen miles to church in Palghat. He came back in the afternoon after lunching on mutton chops and biriyani in the Komala Vilas Military Hotel. It was rumoured that he drank two drams of whisky before lunch. Such things were not available in the village.

Abraham lived in a rented room near the Post Office and cooked his own food. He was the first outsider to come to the village and settle down there.

Damodaran Nair wanted to find out whether Abraham was a Catholic or a Protestant. Ascertaining the different religions and castes people belonged to and understanding the differences between them was always a matter of deep interest to Damodaran Nair.

'You mean Christians have castes as well?'

'Of course, and they're quite rigid about them.'

'Oh God! Abraham is a Nazrani, that's all we need to know, Damodaran Nair.'

People would crowd in front of the Post Office when the mail arrived, hoping for letters or money orders from children and relatives. Abraham would open the postbag and sort out and arrange the letters. He would then hand over a locked, sealed leather bag to the Post Master. By the time the Post Master verified the number of money orders and the cash to be paid out, Abraham would have the letters stamped and read. He would then take the money orders from the Post Master, stamp them and call out the names one after another. Those with prior information would be waiting expectantly. Most money orders were collected directly from the Post Office by the addressees and the rest were sent to their respective destinations in the afternoon.

Abraham was usually given a tip when he took a money order to a Nair house. Although he was not particularly happy to receive it, he never expressed any displeasure. However big the sum of money he handed over, he received no more than a rupee. As he took the money and put it in his pocket, he would say to himself, 'Why couldn't they have come to the Post Office to collect this?'

The Nairs thought it beneath their dignity to collect their money orders from the Post Office. They thought it equally demeaning to write or receive postcards. 'A letter should be a proper letter,' said Chandu Nair once. 'Only the writer and the recipient should know its contents.'

'Who would want to read a postcard, Chandu Nair, and what harm if they did?'

'Why should they? It's best to use envelopes. Cards are below our status, they're meant for inferiors, for mlecchas.'

There were two kinds of people in Chandu Nair's world—Nairs and mlecchas. It was said that he once returned a letter to the Post Master because the honorific 'Maharaja Rajamanya Sir' had not been prefixed to his name. The fact that he was a titled Nair was something Chandu Nair never forgot and never allowed others to forget.

When Abraham was appointed postman, Chandu Nair tied a little basket to his gate. Not because he thought it fashionable to do so, but because he wanted to avoid accepting a letter directly from Abraham's hand. On average, Chandu Nair received no more than one letter every other month.

Soon after Abraham came to the village, he bought a piece of land facing the Post Office and built himself a little house. He planted tapioca behind it. Later, he bought another piece of land near the first one and then a small mango grove. The villagers watched the tapioca grow and flourish. The Nairs consoled themselves, 'Only Christians eat that stuff.'

In a year's time, Abraham's elder brother and family joined him. Two years later, Abraham married Thresiamma from Kottayam and gradually, there were eight Christian families in the village.

When Thresiamma arrived, the villagers watched curiously as she got down from the bus with her box and bag and followed Abraham to their house. She was a pretty, curly-haired young girl. She wore a long blouse and a mundu, the traditional Christian dress. Her jewels must have been worth five sovereigns.

'Good-looking girl, pity she's a Christian,' remarked a foolish Nair, fortunately out of Abraham's hearing.

The Christians thus established a new island in the village. Ten years later, they built a church, and a bishop came to consecrate it. By that time, Abraham had become the President of the local Christian Welfare Society. Affectionately known as 'Avarachan', he was now an accepted member of the village.

The branch Post Office had been elevated to a Sub-Post Office and an additional postman appointed as Abraham's assistant. The fact that this assistant was a Nair touched a corner of Abraham's heart with secret delight.

It was Abraham who imported rubber plants to the village.

By the time the Kerala Congress, a political party dominated by the Christians, was formed, Abraham had united with Jesus. The Kerala Congress had its own flag and signboard but could not find a candidate to contest the elections. Abraham's brother, Thomachan's constant lament was, 'If Avarachan were alive, he would have been elected unanimously.'

The influx of new inhabitants to the village continued. Tapioca and rubber became part of the landscape of the village.

The conflict for votes between the Nairs and the backward classes continued. The value of Nair votes diminished gradually and low caste Hindus began to realize that their votes were not polluted.

Islands of religion took shape in the village in addition to the islands of caste.

—Translated from the Malayalam by Gita Krishnankutty

Chemmeen

Thakazhi Sivasankara Pillai

Chemban Kunju was a lucky man. No one on the seafront got the haul that he brought home. His haul was often twice as large as that of the others. When he cast the net, it never went wrong. It was a matter of great wonder.

In the evening when he counted the cash, Chakki would say, 'We must give away the girl now.'

Chemban Kunju never gave it a straight answer.

'What are you thinking of? She can't hang around like this indefinitely,' Chakki would continue.

Chemban Kunju kept quiet. As long as he made good money, it didn't appear as a big problem to him. He could do something about it the moment he made up his mind.

Chemban Kunju acquired all the accessories necessary for a boat. Now he could go to sea at any time of year. He had everything.

Pareekutti's curing yard almost shut down. He was not getting any work to speak of. He had no money. His father, Abdullah Muthalali, came and blamed him for his state of affairs. He said that Pareekutti had given away all his money to a fisherwoman on the seashore. Karuthamma overheard the accusation.

She pressed her mother with the need to return Pareekutti's money. She told Chakki what she heard Abdullah Muthalali tell his son. What could be more humiliating? In fact, hadn't Pareekutti taken his capital and given it to a fisherwoman?

'We shall pay it all back, wait,' was Chemban Kunju's reply when Chakki brought up the matter.

Then Chemban Kunju began even more grandiose plans! He must have two boats and nets. He must have land and a house. He must have money in his hands.

This extract is taken from *Chemmeen*, published by Jaico Publishing House.

'And then should one work all one's life? Like Pallikunnath, one must retire and enjoy oneself,' he said.

He was determined to fatten up Chakki a bit.

'Oh yes, you think I am going to put on weight now?' Chakki said.

'Never mind all that. You will put on weight.'

Never before had Chakki heard Chemban Kunju talk of enjoying himself. He had developed a new concept of living.

'Well, how are you going to enjoy yourself in your old age? Where did you learn this? You must have learned it somewhere,' she said.

'Of course you can have fun even in your old age. Go and look at Pallikunnath. You should see him enjoying himself. Let me tell you,' Chemban Kunju said, 'that woman Pappikunju is your age. But she is well preserved. You should see her with her hair combed back neatly, her lips red and the caste mark on her forehead. She is like gold to look at. That fisherman and his wife are like a young couple.'

'So should I also dress up like a young girl?' Chakki asked.

'And why not?'

'Won't you be ashamed?'

'What is there to be ashamed of?'

'No, I can't,' said Chakki shyly.

Chemban Kunju described the life of Kandankoran. 'Let me tell you something. One day when I went there, I saw them, like a young couple, in each other's arms, and kissing. I was quite embarrassed.'

'Disgraceful,' said Chakki.

'What is so disgraceful about it? They are like young people laughing and playing all the time,' Chemban Kunju said.

'Haven't they any children?'

'Only one boy.'

Chemban Kunju looked at Chakki and said, 'I want to fatten you up a bit like Pappikunju and we must also have some fun like young people.'

In fact, Chakki also had such longings. To be held in his arms and to be kissed. But she wouldn't say it.

'You should put on a bit yourself,' she said.

'I will also improve in health,' Chemban Kunju said. 'And it is only then that we shall come to the rest.'

'It will all come to pass by the grace of the goddess of the sea,' he said. 'When we have land and a home, when we can live even without having to work—well, then we can enjoy ourselves and have fun like young people. By then we will have given away the girls in marriage.'

But she wasn't beautiful like Pappikunju, protested Chakki. Chemban Kunju felt for certain that even that wouldn't be so when the time came.

'But what if I die by then?'

'Go away, silly. Don't say such things.'

Then one day the colour of the sea changed. The water looked red. The fishermen believed it was the time the sea goddess had her periods. For some days after that there would be no fish in the sea. After two or three days of idleness Chemban Kunju could not keep quiet. He wondered why he should not go farther out into the sea, beyond the horizon as the fishermen said, and look for fish.

He called his men to the boat and discussed the matter. None of them would give him an answer there and then. It was very rarely that the fishermen of that coast had gone to sea at such times. When the goddess of the sea had her periods, they didn't go out fishing.

'If you won't come, I am going to let you starve. I cannot afford to give you any maintenance,' Chemban Kunju told them sharply.

That period of deprivation continued for some time. Everyone slowly went through his savings. Some launched their boats and tried their luck, but there wasn't even the smallest fish to be had. The workers bothered the boat owners for help and advances. But even the owners had nothing left.

Achakunju, who made up his mind to get his own boat and net, was the one in the greatest need. He had children to feed.

One day he had nothing left. The day before he had cleaned up whatever little dried fish and odds and ends there were left in the house. The fisherman and his wife began to quarrel. Achakunju got angry with his insubordinate wife and gave her two slaps and went out of the house. It was she who had to stay home and bear the burden of the children. Could she walk out of the house?

Nallapennu cursed Achakunju. 'You are walking out of here so that you can go to the teashop and have your fill!' she said.

Nallapennu waited for him till evening. Finally she took her brass tumblers and went to Chakki. She said she would like to mortgage them to Chakki or sell them for a rupee. Chakki took them and gave Nallapennu a rupee.

Lakshmi, who heard of this, arrived with her child's earrings. Then other women came with their possessions. Chakki began to feel worried. She did not have money to dispense like that, yet nobody would believe her if she said she had no money. Kalikunju, who had toiled and saved for a year to get a brass bowl, came to Chakki with it.

'If all of you come like this, what will I do? I haven't any money buried away,' Chakki told her.

Kalikunju had come because her children were starving. She did not expect such words or treatment from Chakki.

'Everybody wants Chemban Kunju's money. When he is in trouble, everyone lets him down,' Chakki said.

'What did we do?' Kalikunju asked.

'Nothing. But there is no more money here.'

'Why are you talking as if you don't know me?'

'Why are you getting impertinent?'

And so there began a battle of words. Karuthamma cut in to make the peace. She was afraid that if a real quarrel developed her story would be brought into it. Karuthamma touched Kalikunju's feet and begged her to stop. Disappointed, Kalikunju left with her brass bowl.

'What is this, Mother, losing your head like this?' Karuthamma asked.

'And why shouldn't I?'

'Since we got the boat and net, you and Father both seem different people.'

That evening, while Chemban Kunju was having his supper, Chakki gave him the news of the village, the story of their starvation. In no home had the kitchen fires been lighted.

'Let them starve. Let them all starve,' Chemban Kunju said.

Karuthamma was shocked.

'Let them suffer. When they get money again, these people will dance and make merry. Then they will go to Alleppey and eat extravagantly. Even if the wife normally has nothing to cover her, they will go in for gold-embroidered finery as soon as money comes into their hands. They don't walk the earth at such times. Now let them count the stars.'

'A fisherman need not save,' Chakki said, stating an old truth.

'Then, let them not,' Chemban Kunju said. 'And they will suffer like this. And teach it all to that girl, to starve like this.'

'Oh—you are, of course, a wise man!' Chakki said with a smile.

'Yes, I am a wise man. I have cash in my hands.'

'Don't tell me that,' Chakki said. 'That Pareekutti boy has had to shut down his curing yard. And the girl is hanging about unmarried, in the full bloom of her youth.'

Karuthamma wanted to add, 'Pareekutti, too, ought to starve, shouldn't he, Father?'

As the hard times in the village continued, Chemban Kunju and Chakki managed to collect a lot of odds and ends—brass pots and pans, even bits of gold—at bargain prices. They would come in handy for Karuthamma's marriage. One day Chakki bought a nice bedstead. When her husband came home she told him, smiling and somewhat shyly.

'I have bought a bedstead,' she said.

'Well, why did you buy it?' Chemban Kunju asked with the same sort of smile.

'What is a bed for? To sleep on.'

'And who will sleep on it?'

'When your daughter's bridegroom comes, it is for them.'

'Is that so?'

'And for who else? Not for an old man and his woman.'

'All right, then I shall have a nice mattress made for myself, just like the one I saw at Kandankoran's,' Chemban Kunju said as if he wanted to believe it.

'Then you should have a wife exactly like his to sleep on it,' Chakki said.

'I shall make you into one like that.'

One morning when Chemban Kunju woke up, he found Ramankunju waiting for him. Chemban Kunju welcomed Ramankunju and asked him to sit down. Ramankunju was a boat owner of the seafront. He had two boats. All his property had been mortgaged. For a short while Chemban Kunju had worked for Ramankunju.

Now Ramankunju wanted some money to pay maintenance wages

for his starving workers. He already owed Ouseph money and he felt embarrassed to ask for more.

'Those who have been standing by us and depending on us are starving. There is no work to be had at sea. How can I watch this sight?' Ramankunju said.

Chemban Kunju agreed that it was true.

'Yes, of course, it does not become a boat owner of your standing,' he said.

Without the slightest hesitation Chemban Kunju agreed to give Ramankunju the money.

'How much money do you need?'

'A hundred and fifty rupees will do.'

Chemban Kunju counted the money and gave it to him.

'Are you not giving any maintenance allowance to your workers?' Ramankunju asked.

Chemban Kunju scratched his head and said, 'How can I do that? I am also a worker. Can a squirrel open his mouth as wide as an elephant?'

When Ramankunju had gone, Chemban Kunju went to Chakki and laughed aloud like a madman. She had never seen him so happy and excited.

'What is this? Are you mad?' Chakki asked.

'What do you know, silly?' he said. 'His miserable boat is going to be mine within six months. This is the advantage of having money in your hand.'

When Chemban Kunju's workers began to worry him for some maintenance allowance, he asked, 'Are you ready to work?'

They said they were ready.

'Then we will go far out into the sea to look for fish,' Chemban Kunju said.

'How can we do that? Go far out into the sea at a time such as this?' they asked.

Chemban Kunju had another trick in reserve. All right, he would engage others for the work. After that he would keep those very people to work for him.

'I have a boat and its accessories. And I can't afford to stay idle. I am losing a lot of money,' he said.

Two or three days later, very early one morning, Chakki and Karuthamma saw the boat speeding westward far out into the sea. Only then did they realize what had been happening. That day the women and children of some thirteen families waited by the seashore. They waited anxiously and prayed. The old ones looked at the sea and said that the currents looked vicious. They thought there were whirlpools in the sea beyond.

Even after dusk the boat did not return. On the seashore one could hear weeping and crying. By nightfall the entire seafront had gathered there; everyone stood looking west toward the sea.

It was a windless cloudless night. The stars shone brightly. The sea was calm. Far away in the distance someone thought he saw a speck on the sea. It might well be the boat. But it wasn't. There was no sign of the boat.

Fisherman Kochan's old mother beat on her chest and asked Chakki to bring her only son back. Vava's wife, who was carrying a baby, did not blame anybody; she just cried. The seafront was a picture of misery.

When it was nearly midnight, shouts were heard.

'The boat is coming,' someone cried out.

The boat was speeding toward the shore like a bird.

The boat had a shark in it. They had caught another but they couldn't manage to bring both.

Chemban Kunju cut the shark to bits and distributed it to the women to take inland for selling. He told them they could give him the money after they had sold it. Kalikunju, Lakshmi and the others got their share. Thus in many a home the fires were lighted in the kitchen that night.

Two days later they again went right out to sea. That day, too, Chemban Kunju returned triumphant. Even when the sea seemed barren, Chemban Kunju could make money. The old ones were defeated and kept quiet. The women said that they could eat now, thanks to Chemban Kunju.

Some of the other boat owners also went out fishing beyond the horizon.

After the hardships everyone hoped there would be bright days ahead when the chemmeen (shrimp) were plentiful. The year before, the *Chakara* had been to the north of Alleppey. By all accounts, therefore, this year it should be at the Nirkunnam seafront. In any case, to avoid bad luck, they must get ready for it. That meant that the boats and nets had to be repaired, mended and kept in good trim.

Ouseph and Govindan, the moneylenders, came out to the seashore, their pockets bulging. Everybody was in need of money. The fishermen agreed to any terms. The traders who owned the curing yards made friends with the big fish merchants of Alleppey and Quilon and Cochin, and their agents. The seafront soon reflected the affluence of borrowed money.

There were also small traders who went from home to home lending money to the womenfolk. They gave advance money for the fish that would be dried and stored. One young trader was stabbed by a fisherman in his hut because he tried to molest his wife.

Chemban Kunju saw Ramankunju from time to time. Ramankunju feared that Chemban Kunju would ask for the return of his money. But not only did Chemban Kunju not ask for his money, he even offered him more, if Ramankunju needed it.

Pareekutti made no preparations for the *Chakara* season. His father had asked him to close down his curing yard. It was Abdullah's opinion that Pareekutti should take up some other work elsewhere. But Pareekutti would not leave the seafront.

Abdullah was surprised and asked, 'What is this?'

'Father, you brought me to the seafront and left me here to trade in fish when I was a little boy. I don't know any other vocation,' Pareekutti said.

'How did you manage to squander all your money?'

Pareekutti had to answer. 'Father, in business you may profit or lose. Sometimes you don't even have your capital left,' he said.

'What if you lose still further?'

'What you have decided to bequeath to me as my rightful share is all that I ask for. You needn't give me anything more,' Pareekutti said.

'But I have nothing of real value to give you,' his father said.

Abdullah had many responsibilities. Although he was once a rich man, he had lost everything. He had a daughter to give away in marriage. Abdullah described all his problems. Even then Pareekutti wouldn't change his mind.

Karuthamma noticed that Pareekutti was not preparing for the *Chakara* season. He hadn't made ready the vessels for boiling shrimp. He wasn't buying the coir mats to dry the fish on or the baskets to contain them. She told her mother that it was time to return the money to Pareekutti. If they felt grateful for the help he had given them, the money had to be returned.

Chakki in turn shouted at Chemban Kunju. Not only did it not work, but Chemban Kunju became angry. Karuthamma was convinced that Chemban Kunju would never give Pareekutti his money.

'I am afraid I can't bear this burden,' she said to her mother.

For a moment her mother didn't get the point.

'What burden are you carrying?' she asked.

Karuthamma burst into tears. Chakki comforted her. But Karuthamma was obstinate.

'I am going to tell Father everything, everything—then I know he will find the money.'

Chakki was terrified.

'Don't say anything, my child!'

If Chemban Kunju knew only as much of the story as Chakki did, what would happen? Chakki couldn't imagine it. When she heard Karuthamma's words, Chakki realized that there was more involved than she herself knew.

—*Translated from the Malayalam by V.K. Narayana Menon*

Grandmother's funeral

Jeet Thayil

What stories you must know, there in your closed dominion,
quiet narratives composed for the doomed enclosures
of bone, hair and fingernail fragments; the ancient
hoops of gold removed from your ears and wrists.
The light drowns to a shoreline uncertain and unseen
from this dim church, whitewashed on a hill in the lush south.
The congregation stands entranced, our white shirts and mundus
starched, sung aloft on ancient rhythms, the talismanic glow
of hymns repeated in a tongue all of us remember and nobody
understands; some words promise an impossible redemption:
barachimo, deyvam, shudham, slomo. Evening censers
glow in the patriarchs' palms, pass the smoke
from hand to hand and end to end of this heaving room,
where Syriac, the first figure of faith, waits
with his fierce accountings; your ally in the conundrums
of Christ, the mother, her open heart in the calendar.
The two single beds in the hall where you and your husband
lived your lives in chaste matrimony, a wedlock holy as hands,
perfected your many children, the young dead become legend,
oversaw your strict enunciations of shekels, rice and prayer.
Then the slow erosions of memory, your tidy acres overgrown,
the ungentle stripping of names, faces, an ignoble disrobing
for the writer you were, grace, the first of our long line.
Crawling to eternity, alone inside the one house
generations of sons and daughters embarked from, you faced
the curse of longevity visited on the women of this tribe
with a wilful retrieval of dignity: the clenched refusals
of food and water, the final naysaying to the sanctification
of all who lived to your great age: a life-affirming No
that resounds still through the halls of your ruined house.

In search of doubting Thomas

William Dalrymple

The rains come to the South Indian state of Kerala for long months at a time. It is the greenest state in India: hot and humid, still and brooding. The soil is so fertile that as you drift up the lotus-choked waterways, the trees close in around you as twisting tropical fan vaults of palm and bamboo arch together in the forest canopy. Mango trees hang heavy over the fishermen's skiffs; vines creep through the fronds of the waterside papaya orchards.

In this country live a people who believe that St. Thomas—the apostle of Jesus who famously refused to believe in the resurrection 'until I have placed my hands in the holes left by the nails and the wound left by the spear'—came to India from Palestine after the Resurrection, and that he baptised their ancestors. Moreover, this is not a modern tradition: it has been the firm conviction of the Christians here since at least the sixth century AD, and in all likelihood for hundreds of years before that.

Certainly, in 594 AD, the French monastic chronicler Gregory of Tours met a wandering Greek monk who reported that in southern India he had met Christians who had told him about St. Thomas's missionary journey to India and who had shown him the tomb of the apostle. Over the centuries to come, almost every Western traveller to southern India from Marco Polo to the first Portuguese conquistadors reported the same story. Indeed, the legend of St. Thomas led to the first ever recorded journey to India by an Englishman: according to the Anglo-Saxon Chronicle, King Alfred (he of the burned cakes) sent Bishop Sighelm of Sherborne 'to St. Thomas in India'; years later the bishop returned, carrying with him 'precious stones and the odiferous essences of that country.'

The stories that the travellers brought back with them varied little in their outlines: all said how in India St. Thomas was universally believed to have arrived in AD 52 from Palestine by boat; that he had travelled down the Red Sea and across the Persian Gulf, and that he landed at the great Keralan port of Cranganore, the spice entrepot to which the Roman Red Sea merchant fleet would head each year to buy pepper and Indian slave girls for the Mediterranean market. In Kerala St. Thomas was said to have converted the local Brahmins with the aid of miracles and to have built seven churches. He then headed eastwards to the ancient temple town of Mylapore, on the outskirts of modern Chennai. There the saint was opposed by the orthodox Brahmins of the temple, and finally martyred. His followers built a tomb and monastery over his grave which, said the travellers, was now one of the principal pilgrimage centres—for Muslims and Hindus as well as Christians—in southern India.

Although the historicity of the legend is ultimately unprovable, the modern St. Thomas Christians, as they still call themselves, regard this tradition as something more than a myth: for them it is an article of faith which underpins not only their religious beliefs but their whole identity and their place in Indian society. Moreover they are agreed—as, amazingly, are many of their Hindu neighbours—that St. Thomas is not dead: that he is still present in Kerala, guarding over his followers and guiding his church.

This was a conviction that I came across all over southern India when I travelled through the region this January, making a BBC documentary on the legend. It was particularly palpable at the small 'Miracle Church' of Putenangadi, south of Kochi. At a time when in North India the violent conflict between India's Hindus and Christians was making headlines across the world, members of both faiths could be found side by side crammed into the same church, all quite convinced that St. Thomas was personally present in the building, and that he could not fail to answer the prayers of his devotees. At the back of this church I came across an old Hindu woman named Jaya. I asked her why she, a Hindu, chose to come and pray in a Christian church.

'So that I can be relieved of all my troubles,' she replied. 'I believe that St. Thomas can do that. It is that faith that brings me here. If there's anything I need, I ask St. Thomas for it.'

'But as a Hindu why would you come to a Christian church?' I asked. 'Why not go to the temple?'

'Because I have faith,' she repeated simply. 'When I have difficulties,

St. Thomas solves them for me. Of course, I go to the temple too. But any big problem I have, I come here and I pray, and my prayers are always answered.'

I asked her what she asked St. Thomas for.

'I had a lot of trouble constructing a home for my family,' she replied. 'I came here and prayed and slowly things sorted themselves out. I also had other problems at home—but that has changed. Today I have what I need: I don't live in luxury but I don't want for anything . . .'

'So do you believe that St. Thomas is somehow alive and looking after you?'

'For me St. Thomas is definitely alive,' she said. 'He's not dead. At all times he is in my thoughts and often he appears in my dreams. That's why I come here. Today I didn't really have the time, but I made the time to come. I feel very uneasy if I don't come and pray here every Friday.'

'So you've actually had a glimpse of him in a dream?'

'I have him in my thoughts always,' repeated Jaya. 'Whenever I pray to him, he comes and answers me. Every evening when I light the lamp in my home, I call to him.'

Later, Jaya introduced me to her Christian friend, Miriam.

'In my experience, praying to St. Thomas here is always effective,' said Miriam. 'Whatever I need I pray for and my prayers are heard and answered. I pray for good health and strength. I pray to be delivered from any enemies. I don't pray for money or wealth—I simply put myself in St. Thomas's hands and ask that he protect me. You see, I didn't get married because I didn't want to. So now I come and pray here because I'm on my own. I look to St. Thomas for his protection and he has blessed me until today.'

'So St. Thomas is your protector?'

'I have no one else,' she replied. 'St. Thomas is the apostle of India. This church is built in his name. Of course there is God, but it is St. Thomas's name that we call. Before I go to bed every evening, I pray to St Thomas and it gives me courage and strength. He is all I have.'

*

The trail of St. Thomas's journey to India begins thousands of miles from Kerala in the deserts of the Middle East.

In the late sixth century, the Byzantine Empire was beginning to crumble under a wave of attacks. The great classical cities of the East Mediterranean were slowly falling into ruin and decay. As their libraries and universities were burned down or deserted, many of the most important manuscripts were preserved in the library of a remote monastery in the deserts of the Sinai, now known as St. Catherine's. The great walls of St. Catherine's, and its sheer isolation, preserved it from attacks for centuries. Protected from their enemies, the monks were able to accumulate one of the greatest treasuries of icons and illuminated manuscripts in the Christian world.

When the first European travellers began penetrating this region, they were astonished to find in the monastery a library of unmatched richness containing lost works by great classical authors and the oldest extant copy of the New Testament. But perhaps the strangest discovery of all was a previously unknown early Christian text dating from the fourth century AD. The manuscript was entitled the *Acts of St. Thomas*.

The manuscript told a strange story that had been completely forgotten in the traditions of the Western Church. According to the *Acts*, St. Thomas was Jesus's twin (the Syriac for Thomas—*Te'oma*—means twin, as does his Greek name *Didymos*); like his brother he was a carpenter from Galilee. After Jesus's death, according to the *Acts*, the apostle had been summoned to India—and his martyrdom—by the mysterious King Gondophares.

Nineteenth-century biblical scholars were at first very sceptical of the *Acts of St. Thomas*. They correctly pointed out that the story contained many clearly apocryphal Gnostic elements, and that the earliest surviving version of the text, which had been written in fourth century Mesopotamia, dated from at least two centuries after the events described; indeed, up to the beginning of this century the document was sometimes dismissed as a pious romance. Nevertheless, over the last hundred years, as research has progressed both into ancient Indian history and the links between India and the Roman Middle East, there have been a series of remarkable discoveries which have gone a long way to prove that the story contained in the *Acts* seems to be built on surprisingly solid historical foundations.

Firstly, British archaeologists working in late nineteenth-century India began to find hoards of coins belonging to a previously unknown Indian king: the Raja Gondophares, who ruled from AD 19 to AD 45. If St. Thomas had ever been summoned to India, chronological logic demands that it would indeed have been Raja Gondophares who would have done it, just as the *Acts* had always maintained. Moreover, the fact that the Acts had accurately preserved the name of an obscure Indian raja, whose name and lineage had completely disappeared from the face of the earth, implied that it must contain at least a nucleus of genuine historical information dating from the first century.

Archaeological discoveries have since confirmed many other details of the story, revealing that maritime contacts between the Roman world and India were much more extensive than anyone had previously realized. In the 1930's, Sir Mortimer Wheeler discovered and excavated a major Roman trading station on the South Indian coast, while other scholars unearthed references showing that at the time of Thomas, the trick of sailing with the monsoon had just been discovered, reducing the journey time from the Red Sea to India to just under 40 days. Indeed, according to a previously overlooked remark by Strabo, in the mid first century, no less than 200 Roman trading vessels a year were making the annual journey to the bazaars of Malabar and back again. More intriguing still, analysis of Roman coin hoards in India has shown that the Roman spice trade peaked exactly in the middle of the first century AD, building up under Augustus and building to a climax under Nero. All this showed that if St. Thomas had wanted to come to India, the passage from Palestine, far from being a near-impossible feat, would in fact have been easier, more frequent and probably cheaper than at any other time in the next one thousand five hundred years—until Vasco da Gama discovered the sea route to the Indies in 1498.

Scholars discovered further conformation of the *Acts* in the practices of the St. Thomas Christians themselves. Since the Second World War, theologians have become increasingly aware of the Jewishness of Jesus and his first disciples in Jerusalem: it has become apparent, for example, that the very first Jerusalem Christians would have carried on going to the temple, performing sacrifices, obeying the Jewish food laws and performing circumcisions on their children. If St.

Thomas had carried Christianity to India, it is likely that he would have carried with him a distinctly more Jewish form of the religion than that brought to Europe by St. Paul. Hence the importance of the fact that some of the St. Thomas Christian churches to this day retain Judeo-Christian practices long dropped in the West, such as the celebration of the solemn Passover Feast. Hence also the significance of the fact that the St. Thomas Christians still use the two earliest Christian liturgies in existence: the Mass of Addai and Mari, and the Liturgy of St. James, once used by the early Church of Jerusalem. More remarkable still is the fact that these ancient church services are still at least partly sung in Aramaic, the language spoken by both Jesus and St. Thomas.

*

The more you investigate the evidence, the more you are irresistibly drawn to the conclusion that whether or not St. Thomas did himself come to India, he most certainly *could* have come, and if he didn't personally make the journey, then it seems certain that some other very early Christian missionary *did*, for there is certainly evidence for a substantial Christian population in India by at least the third century. And if there is no documentary proof finally to clinch the case, then there is at least a very good reason for its absence: for the entire historical documentation of the St. Thomas Christians was reduced to ashes in the sixteenth century—not by Muslims or Hindus, but by a newly arrived European Christian power: the Portuguese.

As far as the Portuguese colonial authorities were concerned, the St. Thomas Christians were heretics, an idea that was confirmed by their belief in reincarnation and astrology, and the Hindu-style sculptures of elephants and dancing girls found carved on their crosses. Notions that they might also have maintained early Christian traditions predating the arrival of the faith in Europe were dismissed out of hand. The Inquisition was brought in, and the historical records of the St. Thomas Christians put to the flame.

Yet the old stories did survive, locked in a place that the Inquisition could never touch: in the minds and memories of the Christians of the most inaccessible Keralan backwaters. For in their songs and dances, passed on from father to son and teacher to pupil, the St. Thomas Christians preserved intact many of their most ancient traditions. Scholars now believe that if the answer to the riddle of the legends of St. Thomas lies anywhere, it is in this rich and largely unstudied oral tradition.

The man who has done more than anything to preserve this ancient Keralan heritage of St. Thomas songs and dances is a plump Catholic priest and village school teacher named Fr. Jacob Vellian. Working in isolation, in his spare time, with very little help and pitiful resources, Fr. Jacob has since 1973 single-handedly travelled from village to village in Kerala, systematically collecting the Christian songs and dances which talked of St. Thomas's travels and exploits. On two occasions, hidden in remote villages, he stumbled across ancient palm leaf books, which preserved other fragments of the songs and ballads in tiny one millimetre high Malayalam lettering: the oldest surviving documentation of the St. Thomas Christians.

There were, he discovered, still current in the Keralan countryside, literally hundreds of songs recording the deeds of St. Thomas, as well as two ancient full-length ballads, the older of which, *The Margam Kali Pattu* or *Song of the Way* was of epic proportions. Both of these ballads certainly predated the coming of the Portuguese and both, from their very archaic language, showed every sign of dating from the very earliest centuries AD. In many cases the two ballads had become hopelessly intertwined and it was a job of considerable complexity to unravel the two, quite apart from writing down the correct musical accompaniment and the choreography that went with them.

Almost everywhere Fr. Vellian found the oral tradition on the verge of extinction, with the young people unwilling to carry on the job of learning by heart the complex stanzas of the ballads. In several places he was able to record lost fragments of the epics just weeks before the last of the *ashans* (or village bards) died, taking their songs to their grave.

'Over the years I have tried to meet with every Christian *ashan* in Kerala,' Vellian told me. 'Most of them were illiterate: isolated old men who were only barely aware of the importance of what they were clinging onto. Some had a few disciples and were very eager to teach what they knew; others had none. But no one was trying to write down what they had preserved. No one was promoting them or rewarding them for their work. As a result, much must have been lost. No one *ashan* knew the whole of the two longest ballads: some knew twenty per cent; some seventy per cent. But the fourteen sections that we now have seem to be the whole of *The Song of the Way*, and the job now is to study this—and to make sure it is passed on.'

To that end, Vellian has been building on another, almost lost Keralan tradition: the Dancing Nuns of Malabar. Fr. Vellian has spent the last few years training the nuns of Kerala to dance the ancient dances of St. Thomas, and all over Kerala groups of wimpled sisters can now be seen swaying uncertainly to the beat of the tabla as they attempt to master the dances which tell of the apostle's travels. In this way, what may be the last surviving link with the tradition of the apostles is now being preserved by a group of South Indian Whoopy Goldbergs. For all the unintentional comedy of this, Fr. Vellian is adamant that the oral traditions of Kerala have accurately preserved a series of texts that may well hold the vital clues which could help prove the St. Thomas legend.

'The palm leaf documents that we have collected show how accurately the bards have preserved the text,' he says. 'Here or there a word may have changed in the three hundred years since the earliest of these texts was written down, but by and large the versions we have collected in the fields are consistent both with each other and these palm leaf texts. These traditions are an authentic and incredibly valuable and ancient source of Christian history, and should be respected as such.'

Vellian is, of course, right. For while Christianity has never been a major faith in India, it is a religion with deep roots in the soil, and one which has clung on with incredible tenacity, despite all the odds. Above all, the Church here has remained faithful to the tradition of St. Thomas's journey from Palestine to India. It is a story long forgotten in a West which has come to regard itself as the true home of the faith, forgetting that in its essence Christianity is not a Western but an Eastern religion.

Before leaving Kerala, I asked Fr. Vellian whether he really believed that his work would eventually provide some conclusive evidence to prove St. Thomas's journey.

'In the end *we* are the evidence,' said Vellian. 'We have a very ancient, unbroken tradition in the community that St. Thomas was the founder of the Church in India. Our traditions are unanimous that he came here, and that is something we have held onto, despite persecution, for seventeen hundred years. Our spirituality is very close to that of the early Church and we believe our Church is as old as any Apostolic Church in the world. Our songs and traditions are quite clear about this. In the end, it is these traditions that we base our belief on: not something on paper or stone, which is secondary. In the end, it is our fidelity to St. Thomas that is most important to us.'

The blue light

Vaikom Muhammad Basheer

This is the story of one of the amazing incidents of my life. No, not just an incident. It is better to call it something out of the ordinary, something supernatural which took place. I have tried to understand it by using scientific logic. But I have not succeeded. Perhaps you may be able to do it—analyse it. I call it an amazing happening . . . yes, what else can I call it?

This is what happened.

The day, the month and the year do not matter. I was in search of a house. That was nothing new. I am always in search of a house. I never get a house or a room that I like. The place where I stayed I found had a hundred faults. But to whom could I complain? If I didn't like it I could just go away. But go where? And so I lived there full of resentment. How many houses there had been, how many rooms, with which I had been dissatisfied! It wasn't anybody's fault. I did not like them. So I left. Someone else would come in my place and he or she would like it. That is the character of rented houses.

Those were the days when there was a scarcity of rented houses. What could once be rented for ten rupees could not now be got for fifty. And so I wandered about in search of a house and there it was!

It was a small one-storeyed house. Far from the bustle of the town; somewhere near the municipal limit. There was an ancient board—'To let.'

I liked it on the whole. Upstairs there were two rooms and a balcony. Four rooms on the ground floor, and a bathroom in addition. There was also a kitchen and running tap water. Only there was no electricity. There was a well in front of the kitchen. Nearby, in a corner of the compound, was a lavatory. The well was an old one with a low stone

This story was published in *Malayalam Literary Survey*, published by Sahitya Akademi, Trissur.

wall round it. There were plenty of trees in the compound which was walled in on all sides. One great advantage was that there were no neighbours. The house abutted on a main road.

I was surprised and delighted. Why hadn't anyone taken this house? I had by luck caught hold of a lovely woman when lovely women were hard to come by. I must hide her with a veil! This was the feeling the house evoked in me. I was excited. I ran about and got busy. I borrowed money. I paid two months' advance rent and obtained the key. In short, I moved into the house. The same day I bought a new hurricane lamp.

I swept and cleaned all the rooms, the kitchen and the bathroom. There was plenty of rubbish all over. And a great deal of dust. I washed and cleaned the rooms once again. Then I took a bath. I felt contented. I went and sat on the wall of the well. I was happy. I could sit and dream. I could walk about in the compound. I had to plan a garden in the front yard. It would be mostly rose bushes; a few creepers of jasmine. I wondered whether to appoint a cook—no, that would be a bother. In the morning after I had taken a bath I could go to the tea shop with a thermos flask so that I could bring back tea. I would arrange with a hotel to give me lunch at noon. I could ask them to send me the evening meal. Then I must meet the postman and tell him that I had come to stay here. I must also ask him not to tell anyone that the house was no longer empty . . . Nights of lonely beauty, days of lonely beauty; I could write a great deal . . . Thinking of all this I looked into the well. I could not see whether it had water. There were plenty of bushes and undergrowth covering the surface. I picked up a stone and dropped it in the well. *Ploom!* There was a splash and an echo. There was water in the well.

It was eleven in the morning.

I had not slept a wink the previous night. I had settled my account with the hotel in the evening. After this I had met the house owner. I had folded and tied up my canvas bed. I had packed my gramophone and records. I had packed my trunk, my papers, my books, the easy chair, the bookshelf—all my worldly goods. At dawn I had set out with the things in two carts.

I shut the doors of my new house and locked the front door. I stepped onto the road and shut the gate. I put the key in my pocket and walked on with a sense of pride. I thought to myself, with whose song should I inaugurate my house-warming tonight? . . . I have with me more than a hundred gramophone records; they are in English, Arabic, Hindi, Urdu, Tamil, Bengali. There is nothing in Malayalam. There are some who sing well in Malayalam. One can buy records of their music; but the music score is bad. When will Malayalam have a good music director? Such as Pankaj Mullick or Dilip Kumar Roy? I asked myself, whose record shall I play first tonight? Pankaj Mullick, Dilip Kumar Roy, Saigal, Bing Crosby, Paul Robeson, Abdul Karim Khan, Kanan Devi, Kumari Majumdas Gupta, Khurshid, Juthika Ray, M.S. Subbulakshmi . . . I thought of ten or twenty names. Finally I decided. There's a song which goes 'Here comes the wanderer.' *Door desh ka rahnewala aya*, it begins. Who sang that? A man or a woman? I couldn't recall. I decided to look it up. I walked on.

First I met the postman and talked to him. When I told him of the house I had occupied he said with a touch of fear, '*Ayya*! Sir . . . in that house . . . a violent death took place there. No one stays there. That's why that house has remained vacant all this time.'

A house where there had been a violent death? I was somewhat taken aback. I asked, 'What kind of violent death?'

'Isn't there a well in the yard? . . . someone jumped into it. After that there has been no peace or quiet in that house. Many people stayed there. At night the doors would shut with a bang. The water taps would start running . . .'

Doors would shut with a bang! Water taps would run! Amazing, both the water taps had shackles and locks. The house owner had told me that people used to jump over the wall and have a bath there, so the taps had been kept locked! I should have asked him why the taps inside the closed bathroom had also been kept locked . . . I hadn't thought of it then.

'The ghost will hold you by the throat, strangle you! Didn't anyone tell you this, sir!'

I thought to myself, splendid . . . and I have paid two months' rent in advance! I told him, 'Oh, that's nothing serious. One magic incantation will take care of it. Anyhow, see that letters and so on reach me there.'

I said this bravely. I am neither courageous nor cowardly. I fear what most people are normally afraid of. So perhaps I should be considered a coward. What would you have done under such circumstances?

I walked on slowly. I wondered what I should do. I never create situations just for the sake of the experience. But when an experience comes your way uninvited what can be done then?

I stepped into a hotel and drank tea. I didn't feel like having a meal. It was as if my belly was on fire. I talked to the hotelkeeper about my food being sent to the house. When he heard the location of the house he too said, 'I'll send you food there during the day, but at night . . .! The boys will not go there. A woman jumped into that well and drowned. She'll be somewhere around the place! Sir, aren't you afraid of ghosts?'

A good half of my fear left me. It was a woman, was it? I said, 'Oh, that's nothing serious. And I have the right magic incantation!'

I did not know any magic incantation. But then it was a woman and, as I said, half my fear was gone. From there I went to a bank nearby. I had two or three friends who were clerks there. I told them the news. They were angry with me. 'You did a foolish thing. That house is haunted by a ghost. It harms men especially.'

So the ghost hated men. That was nice!

One of them said, 'Couldn't you have talked to one of us before you leased the house?'

I said, 'Who knew about all this then? Let me ask you one thing. Why did that woman jump into the well and kill herself?'

'Love,' another friend replied. 'Her name was Bhargavi. Age twenty-one. She passed her B.A. Even before that she was in love with a chap—deeply in love. But he married another girl. On the night of the wedding Bhargavi jumped into the well and killed herself!'

Most of my fear left me. So, was that the reason for her enmity towards men?

I said, 'Bhargavi won't harm me.'

'Why not?'

I said, 'I know a magic incantation!'

'Ah, let's see . . . You'll shout and cry in the night!'

I said nothing to that.

I returned to my house. I opened the doors and windows. Then I went down and stood near the well.

'Bhargavi Kutty!' I called out in a low voice. 'We have not met. I have come to stay here. In my opinion I'm a good man; a confirmed bachelor. I've heard a number of complaints about you, Bhargavi. It seems you do not let people stay here. You open the water taps at night. You bang the doors shut. You hold men by the throat and try to strangle them . . . These are the kinds of things I hear. What should I do now? I've paid two months rent in advance. And I like this place very much.

'I want to sit and work here. That is to say, I want to write some stories. Incidentally, let me ask you something. Bhargavi Kutty, do you like stories? If you do I can read out all my stories to you, Bhargavi Kutty. Shall I? . . . I've no quarrel with you, Bhargavi Kutty. The reason being that nothing has happened between us . . . I dropped a stone into the well thoughtlessly. Nothing like that will happen again. Forgive me. Do you hear me, Bhargavi Kutty! I have with me a very good gramophone. And some two hundred excellent songs. Are you fond of music?'

Having said this much, I kept quiet. To whom was I talking? . . . to an open-mouthed well ready to swallow anything?—To the trees, the house, the atmosphere, the earth, the sky . . . to whom? Was I talking to my disturbed mind? I said to myself, I am talking to a creature of my mind. Bhargavi. I had not seen her. A young woman who had been twenty-one years old. She had loved a man deeply. She had wanted to live as the wife of this man, as his life-long companion. She had dreamt of her life with him. But that dream . . . yes, it remained just a dream. She became disillusioned, felt unwanted . . .

'Bhargavi Kutty!' I said, 'you should not have acted that way. Don't think I am blaming you. The man you cared for did not love you enough. He loved another woman more. He married her. So life became bitter to you. Quite so. But life is not full of such bitterness. Let that go. As far as you are concerned history will not repeat itself.

'Bhargavi Kutty, don't think I am blaming you. Did you really die for love? Love is the dawn of an eternal life. Silly girl that you were, you knew nothing about life. That is what this enmity of yours to men proves. You knew just one man. Let us agree that the particular man harmed you. But was it right for you to look at all men through tinted glasses? If you had not committed suicide but had lived on you would have realized that your attitude was wrong. There would have been men who would have called you a goddess and worshipped you. But as I said, in your case history will not repeat itself.

'Anyhow, you must not harm me. This is not a challenge. This is a request. If you strangle me to death tonight there will be no one to ask you why—not that one can take revenge on you. There will be no one to do it for I have no one.

'Bhargavi Kutty, do you understand my situation? We are both staying here. That is to say, I intend staying here. The well and the house belong to me by right. Let that be. You may use the four rooms on the ground floor and the well and we shall share equally the kitchen and the bathroom. Do you like this arrangement?'

I was satisfied. Nothing happened.

It was night. I went to eat my meal and returned with the thermos flask full of tea. I switched on my electric torch and lit the hurricane lamp. The room was steeped in yellow light.

I went downstairs with my torch. I stood still in the darkness for some time. My object was to lock the water taps. I opened all the windows. Then I went near the well and the kitchen. I decided that the water taps should not be locked.

I shut the doors and secured them and went upstairs. I drank some tea. I lit a beedi and sat on the chair for a little while. I was about to start writing when I felt as though someone stood behind my chair . . . Bhargavi!

I said, 'I dislike anyone looking on when I am writing.'

I turned round . . . wasn't anyone there?

Somehow I did not have the inclination to continue writing. I got up and paced back and forth across the two rooms. There was no breeze. Outside, even the leaves on the trees did not stir. When I looked out through the window . . . there was a light!

I could not make out whether the light was blue or red or yellow . . . I saw it only for an instant.

Oh, that's an illusion, I told myself. I could not swear that I had seen the light or that I had not seen it. But then, if I had not seen it, how could I have imagined it?

I paced up and down for a long time. I stood near the window for a while. I saw nothing different. I tried to read but I could not concentrate. I thought I might as well sleep early and made my bed.

I put out the lamp. I suddenly felt like listening to some records.

I lit the lamp again. I opened up the gramophone. I fixed a new needle to the sound box. I wound up the machine.

Whose song should I play? The world was silent. But there was a hum all round. The humming resounded through my ears. I did not feel afraid. But there was a thrill, a vibration, which went through me. There hung suspended in the air a frightening silence which I wanted to shatter into a hundred thousand bits. Whose song would do that? I searched among the records and finally picked up one by the black American singer Paul Robeson. He sang through the machine. The sweet, sonorous, manly voice sang, 'Joshua fought the battle of Jericho.'

That was followed by Pankaj Mullick: '*Tu dar na Surabhi . . .*' (Surabhi, you have nothing to fear . . .)

After that the soft, melodious, feminine voice of M.S. Subbulakshmi: '*Katinile varum geetam . . .*' (The song wafted by in the breeze . . .)

M.S. Subbulakshmi's song came to an end.

After the three songs I felt a sense of peace. I sat in the stillness for some time. Then I decided to call on the great Saigal. He sang in that low voice full of sweetness and pathos. '*Soja Rajkumari . . .*' (Sleep, Princess).

That song too came to an end.

'That's all; we will resume tomorrow,' I said, and closed the gramophone. I put out the lamp, lit a beedi and lay down. Next to me was the electric torch and my watch.

I had closed the door to the balcony before I lay down. It must have been about ten o'clock. I lay listening.

I could hear nothing but the soft *tik-tik* of the watch. The minutes and hours moved on. There was no fear. What I felt in my mind was a cool . . . a cool alertness. This was nothing new for me. In my twenty years of solitary life I have had many experiences, the meaning of which I have not been able to fathom. And so my attention shuttled between the past and the present. In between I listened . . . for knocks on the door . . . the noise of running water from the pipes. Would I feel the pressure of being strangled? I listened till three o'clock.

I heard nothing. I experienced nothing. Absolute calm. I slept. I had no dreams. I got up the next morning at nine.

Nothing had happened!

'Bhargavi Kutty, many thanks . . . I understand one thing now. People are finding fault with you, Bhargavi Kutty, for no reason at all! Let them say what they like, don't you think so?'

Days and nights passed thus. Most nights when I was tired of writing I would put on records. Before each song I would announce the name of the singer and the meaning of the song. I would say, 'The next song is by the Bengali singer Pankaj Mullick. It is a sad song which evokes memories of days gone by. Listen to it carefully. *'Guzar gaya woh zamana kaise . . . kaise . . .'* (How those days have gone by . . . vanished . . .)

Or else I would say, 'The next song is by Bing Crosby, "In the moonlight", which means—you're a graduate, excuse me.'

I would say all these things to myself. Two and a half months passed thus. I nurtured and brought into being a garden. Whenever flowers bloomed I would announce that they were for Bhargavi Kutty. During this time I wrote a short novel. Many of my friends visited me. Many of them stayed the night with me. Before they went to sleep I would quietly go down and speak in a low tone into the darkness. 'Look Bhargavi Kutty, some of my friends are staying here tonight. Please don't strangle them to death. If anything like that happens the police will catch me. Please be careful . . . good night!'

Ordinarily, before I left the house I would say, 'Bhargavi Kutty, look after the house. If any thief comes you can strangle him to death. But don't leave the dead body here. You must take the corpse some three miles away! Otherwise we will be in trouble.'

At night when I returned after the late cinema show I would call out: 'It's me.'

All this was during the first few months of my stay. As time passed I tended to forget Bhargavi. That is to say, I did not talk to her much. I would occasionally remember her, that was all.

On this earth . . . since the beginning of man in this world . . . countless, hundreds of thousands of men and women have died. They have become one with the earth, with the dust of the earth. We all know this. Bhargavi survived as a memory of them all; that is how I thought of her.

Then something happened one night.

It must have been about ten o'clock. I had been writing a story since nine. It was a highly emotional piece. I was writing feverishly. I felt that the light was gradually dimming.

I took up the lamp and shook it. There was no kerosene at all, even then I thought I could write one more page. This was not a clearly thought-out intention. My entire attention was on the story I was writing. When the light dimmed what would one's natural reaction be? To find out if there was enough oil, as I had done. Then I turned up the wick. I went on writing. Again the light became dimmer. Again I turned up the wick. I continued writing. Again the light dimmed. Again I turned up the wick. As this went on the wick of the lamp became a glowing object four inches long and half an inch wide.

I switched on the electric torch and lowered the wick of the lantern completely. I need hardly say that the lamp went out.

I asked myself, 'How does one get a light?'

I needed to get kerosene. I remembered that I could go to the bank. Those clerks stayed in a portion of the building. I could borrow some kerosene from their stove. I picked up the torch and the empty kerosene bottle, locked the door, went downstairs and closed the front door. I stepped outside, closed the gate and walked along the road. There was a misty moonlight. The sky was overcast.

I walked fast.

I reached the front of the bank building, looked up and called one of the clerks by name. After I had called twice or thrice, one of them came down and opened the side gate. We walked along the side of the building and climbed up the back stairs. Here I found that the three of them had been playing cards.

When I told them about the kerosene one of them laughed and asked me, 'Couldn't you have asked that Bhargavi to fetch you kerosene?'

I said nothing though I too laughed. While one of them was taking some kerosene out of the stove it started raining.

I said, 'You must give me an umbrella also.'

They said, 'Never mind an umbrella, we don't even have a bare stick to make up one. Let's play cards. You can go when the rain stops.'

And so I played cards. My partner and I lost three rounds which was mainly because I could not concentrate. My mind was on the story I was writing. It stopped raining at about one o'clock. I picked up the torch and the bottle of kerosene. The clerks got ready to go to bed. When I went down the stairs and reached the road they switched off the light.

There was no movement on the road, nor any light. I walked on. There was no light anywhere. I turned the corner and approached my house. In the dim moonlight the whole world appeared steeped in misty wonder. I do not know what thoughts passed through my mind. Perhaps I thought of nothing in particular. I walked along the deserted and silent road with the torch switched on.

I reached the house, opened the gate and went in. I opened the front door, entered and closed it. I had no reason to think that anything out of the ordinary had happened upstairs. But I must mention one thing—my mind was full of a strange sadness for no reason whatsoever. I wanted to weep. I can laugh easily. But I find it difficult to weep. No tear, not even a drop usually comes out of my eyes. When I wanted to weep I would feel a strange sense of divinity. I felt it then.

I went up the stairs in that frame of mind. And then . , . an unusual sight met my eyes. My subconscious recorded it. This is what had happened. When I had closed the door and left, the lamp had gone out completely for want of oil. The room had been dark. After that it had rained for a while. About three hours had passed. But now there was light inside the room. It could be seen through the chinks in the door . . . This was the light my eyes had seen and my subconscious had registered. But this, this mystery, was not recognized by my conscious self.

As usual I took out my key. Then I focused my torchlight on the padlock. The lock gleamed like silver . . . or is it more correct to say that the lock smiled in the light?

I opened the door and went in; then I saw everything. That is to say, my entire being realized with a start what was happening. I did not tremble in fear. I stood there stunned. I felt a kind of warmth go through me and I sweated.

The entire room and its white walls were illuminated with a blue light. The light came from the lamp . . . two inches of blue flame . . . I stood there struck with amazement.

Who had lit the lamp which had gone out for want of kerosene? Where did this blue light come from?

—Translated from the Malayalam by V. Abdulla

Dinesh Khanna

Fool's paradise?

Ammu Joseph

'Myths about our matrilineal society need to be broken,' said a journalist participating in a workshop in Shillong in September 2001. I sat up. Was I in Meghalaya or Kerala?

This was only my second visit to the northeastern region of India, which is about as far as you can get, within the borders, from Kerala on the southwestern coast. During my brief encounter with Assam two years earlier I had been struck by the unexpected similarities in climate, vegetation, food and clothes between states situated at diametrically opposite ends of the subcontinent. This time, too, on the drive up to Shillong from Guwahati, I was strangely reminded of my imaginary homeland.

On both occasions I was vaguely aware of other possible parallels between these farflung corners of the country, among them the matrilineal tradition associated with some local communities. And now here I was in the idyllic setting of a northeastern hilltop, listening to a conversation that could just as well have been taking place on a southwestern seafront.

The animated discussion sparked off by a question about the position of women in the northeastern states, posed by a journalist from Kolkata, was reminiscent of many a past exchange between Malayalis and non-Malayalis on the position of women in Kerala. I listened with a sense of déjà vu as the northeasterners attempted to clarify that only a few tribes in the region were matrilineal and that even among the Khasis of Meghalaya, the largest and most prominent of these communities, the system did not necessarily vest power—even over inherited property—in the hands of women.

They highlighted the fact that public life in the region continued to be male-dominated. Even among the Khasis, they said, women were not allowed to participate in traditional institutions of local governance, such as community-based darbars or village authorities.

The legislative assemblies of all the seven states were predominantly male, with women's participation in electoral politics continuing to be very low across the region. Speaking as they were in a forum of journalists, they also called attention to the negligible presence of women in the embattled northeast-based media.

I listened with a growing sense of been-there-heard-that as local journalists acknowledged that women in most communities of the northeast customarily enjoyed a degree of physical and social mobility unknown in many other parts of the country and did not suffer some of the gross forms of gender-based oppression and discrimination that are commonplace elsewhere. However, they pointed out, this reality could not be used to generalize about gender equality and the empowerment of women in the northeastern states. As a young journalist from Shillong put it, 'Freedom and empowerment are different things.'

It was all such familiar ground. Listening to women journalists from different parts of the northeast, I could hear echoes from my conversations with girls and women in Kerala, including women journalists, at various points during the 1990s. Just a few years earlier, a young journalist in Thiruvananthapuram had told me quite emphatically: 'Equality and freedom are elusive for women in Kerala.'

It is obvious, of course, that there are a number of significant differences in the situation of women in the northeastern states, on the one hand, and Kerala, on the other.

One is the question of mobility. Women in the northeast, especially those who belong to tribal communities, generally acknowledge their relative freedom of movement and association (including with the opposite sex). But for women in Kerala mobility remains a major problem, despite the fact that Malayali women, especially nurses, can be found working all over the country and, indeed, the world. This apparent contradiction is, in fact, an integral part of the complex reality of the lives of women from the state.

It is only natural, I suppose, that the most vociferous complaints about the absence of freedom and mobility are voiced by young women. For instance, a group of adolescent girls in Kochi who spoke to me in 1996 conceded that girls in Kerala were allowed and even encouraged to go to school and extra tutorial classes. But, they pointed out, they were expected to return straight home after classes. They claimed that there was little question of their being allowed to go anywhere else except in the company of other family members, whereas their brothers were free to roam about whenever and wherever they pleased.

The girls were clearly unhappy about their lack of swaathanthriam (freedom). They were irked by the fact that 'boys have more adhikaaram (authority) and more avakaasham (rights).' According to one teenager, boys were not only more mobile than girls of their own age but they were actually more free to come and go than adult women of her community, who usually required permission from male family members—sometimes even their own sons—to go beyond the neighbourhood.

The issue of mobility was also raised during a workshop for women writers in Malayalam that took place in Vizhinjam, near Kovalam, in 1999. Talking about the 'domesticity' associated with much creative writing by women, which sometimes resulted in their work being unfairly dismissed as 'kitchen literature,' several well-known poets, short story writers and novelists pointed out that the world they wrote about was the world they inhabited. According to them, societal restrictions on women's mobility could not but circumscribe their exposure to the wider world and thereby, their experience of life outside their immediate environment. A critic suggested that women's lack of mobility could be said to constitute an invisible but influential form of censorship, impinging as it often did on what they were able to write about.

The surprisingly few women in journalism in Kerala also reported difficulties arising from restrictions on their movement. In the first place, they said, the timings associated with media jobs made journalism an unpopular career choice for women in the eyes of families and communities, at least within the state. They pointed out that it was not easy for women journalists in Kerala to participate fully and freely in the profession when most parents and other family decision-makers preferred to have them home before nightfall. According to them, they faced similar attitudes at the workplace, with editors and managements generally assigning them to work that did not involve late hours or much moving about.

Closely tied up with mobility is the question of 'character' and 'reputation,' which clearly continues to dog women in the state. The manifestly strict segregation of the sexes that persists in much of Kerala society even today is another area where customs in the hilly northeast and the coastal southwest of the country appear to diverge.

Young women in Kerala are obviously aware that the restrictions they are routinely subjected to are meant primarily to safeguard their apparently all-important reputations. They suggest that as far as society is concerned the most valued attribute in a girl is what is known as 'good character,' best demonstrated by socially acceptable behaviour (swabhaavam). According to a group of high school students in Kochi, the bane of their lives was gossip, the threat of which made their otherwise sensible and reasonable parents keep an uncomfortably tight rein on them. They chafed at the resulting curbs on their mobility, as well as the austere dress code to which they were expected to conform.

The writers, too, spoke of the pressure to safeguard their reputations, especially in a social context where, as one of them put it, 'People look for personal elements in whatever women write.' A number of them pointed out that women writers were accepted and even feted as long as their writing conformed to socially accepted norms. According to a critic, gender-based double standards were rife in Malayalam literature. 'Writing by women which reinforces or is, at least, uncritical of prevailing societal norms is praised, while works by women that critique patriarchal values and promote the concept of women's identity as individuals provoke censure,' she said. 'Men who write differently are honoured, but women who dare to do so are isolated—either by ignoring them or by singling them out for negative criticism.'

The writers also talked about the difficulties of writing about certain subjects, given the predominantly conservative social environment in the state. According to one writer, if a few women writers in Malayalam had managed to achieve a certain measure of freedom as writers, they had invariably done so by opting to lead relatively reclusive lives, avoiding the public sphere and choosing not to participate even in literary fora. Few of the writers refuted the allegation that the literary establishment had a tendency to brand women who conveyed unconventional ideas on sensitive subjects, such as the human body and bodily functions, sex and sexuality, and male-female relationships. According to them, both critics and publishers commonly upheld what they considered 'decent' writing while resisting writing that questioned or otherwise threatened traditional—read patriarchal—'family values'.

The journalists I interviewed also spoke at length about the professional hurdles placed in their path by the social conservatism that still characterises Kerala society. Many pointed out that they faced difficulties in cultivating sources of news and information who, by and large, remained male since men continued to occupy positions of authority in most fields of activity. They said the problem was exacerbated by the fact that social interaction between the sexes continued to be limited and constrained despite the spread of education and progress in other aspects of development.

A number of them also complained about having to contend with unnecessary gossip and innuendo in the course of their working lives. According to them, even the most innocuous behaviour—such as chatting with male colleagues, accompanying them to the canteen or accepting a ride from one of them—was likely to generate gossip that was liable to travel up to 'higher authorities.' A young journalist was indignant about the fuss that was kicked up in her media organization just because she stayed late in the office to complete a story. She alleged that rumours about her abounded after she once interviewed a literary figure in a hotel. 'I was just doing my job,' she said, 'but I had to deal with all kinds of speculation about why I had met him there.'

If freedom of movement and association is too nebulous a concept for its absence to be counted as a serious problem, the hard reality of dowry is surely not. The dowry system, which persists unabated and unchallenged in the state, despite women's access to education and employment, is widely viewed and condoned as an inevitable and inescapable reality in most local communities (however educated). While it is occasionally recognized as a source of financial strain, if not ruin, for families, it is rarely accepted as evidence of the devaluation of women in Kerala society. Nor is it acknowledged as a major source of psychological stress for young women.

Yet, according to adolescent girls in Kerala, the pernicious practice was one of the main reasons why they often wished they had not been born female. It is only too clear that the custom has an adverse effect on girls' image of themselves, their sense of self-worth and the attitudes and behaviour of others (including family members) towards them. With the sums involved spiralling out of control with little reference to family resources, there have even been media reports of girls committing suicide in despair over their parents' inability to drum up their dowries. It is a well-known fact that many of the apparently independent and intrepid young Malayali women working in different parts of the country and the world are busy saving towards their own dowries or those of their younger sisters.

Violence against women is, again, an issue that certainly cannot be dismissed as a trifling matter. It can no doubt be safely assumed that the experiences of women in the northeast and the southwest (as well as everywhere in between) converge with respect to this virtually universal aspect of human life. In any case, there is growing evidence that women in Kerala are no strangers to gender-based violence, both within and outside the home.

For example, the preliminary report of a recent, multi-site household survey on domestic violence in India has revealed that the prevalence of physical family violence against women in Thiruvananthapuram could be as high as 43 per cent. Pegging the prevalence of psychological violence against women within the home at 61 per cent in the state capital, the report suggested that this exceptionally high figure could be due, at least in part, to the relatively high reported rate of husband infidelity—higher, apparently, than in any of the other urban sites included in the survey.

Issues relating to gender-based roles and expectations within the family, sexual control, and dowry (in that order) were among the precipitating factors leading to domestic violence identified by the researchers, in Kerala as elsewhere. Significantly, some of the highest rates of dowry dissatisfaction and fresh demands for dowry were recorded in Thiruvananthapuram.

It is possible, as has been suggested, that the Thiruvananthapuram-based part of the multi-site study yielded unexpectedly high figures at least partly because of the superior methodology adopted by the project team in Kerala. Nevertheless, the fact remains that domestic violence is very much a part of the landscape in this part of the country.

Gender-based violence obviously abounds outside the home as well. The infamous Suryanelli case is among the best-known examples of what has apparently come to be known within the state as 'relay rape'. This particular instance involved the entrapment, confinement and multiple rape of a teenaged schoolgirl during a 40-day period in 1996, when she was held captive in different locations and raped over 100 times by at least 42 men, many of them well-known and influential members of society.

But the Suryanelli case, in which 35 of the accused were found guilty by a special court in September 2000 (only to be granted bail within a week by the high court), was reportedly only the tip of the iceberg: a number of similar so-called sex scandals came to light in its wake. Among them were the Kozhikode case, involving a powerful politician, in which a number of girls were trapped and sexually exploited in a racket revolving around an ice-cream parlour; the Pandalam case in which five college lecturers were accused of harassing a female student for over two months; and the Vithura case, in which a minor girl was repeatedly raped and a famous film actor was implicated.

Two notorious cases of sexual harassment also hit the headlines in Kerala at the turn of the millennium. The former state cabinet minister accused of sexual harassment by a senior Indian Administrative Staff (IAS) officer had reportedly harassed another female government employee, a member of the Indian Forest Service, a year earlier. An employee of Kozhikode University was not only sexually harassed by a stranger in a public transport bus but experienced further harassment and humiliation by policemen when she tried to lodge a complaint and, subsequently, by a university colleague who allegedly spread rumours that called her character into question. Both women suffered the consequences of daring to complain, while justice continued to elude them long after they decided to go public.

Sexual harassment on the streets (euphemistically known as 'eve-teasing') is also an ever-present reality in Kerala, as elsewhere. Virtually every adolescent girl I queried about this said she had experienced some form of sexual harassment in the public sphere. The problem was obviously so widespread that they had come to regard it as an inevitable aspect of their daily lives.

None of this is meant to suggest that Kerala is as bad as, or worse than, any other state in the country in this regard. Simplistic comparisons are particularly odious. The theme of my old and hitherto somewhat unpopular song is, rather, that the traditional portrayal of Kerala as a rare paradise for the female sex in an otherwise bleak subcontinental landscape presents only half the picture. And that the whole picture is far more complex, intriguing and indeed, enlightening.

There is clearly no denying the fact that Kerala's many commendable achievements in human and social development have had a beneficial impact on the women of the state in several important respects—most famously but not exclusively in terms of education.

But just as it would be absurd to conclude that women in the northeast are liberated because most of them get to choose their own husbands, it would be foolish to assume that women in Kerala are emancipated because nearly 88 per cent of them can read and write.

If the state's female literacy rate is a source of pride, especially when seen in relation to the national average of 54 per cent, its record in women's political participation (above the panchayat level) is not, with women members constituting just a little more than five per cent of the legislative assembly. If Kerala continues to be well ahead of the rest of the country in terms of the overall population sex ratio (1058 females per 1000 males), which corresponds to figures for the so-called developed world, it is certainly a matter of comfort and joy. But the dip in the sex ratio of the 0-6 age group revealed by the Census of India 2001, which is evident even in Kerala (963:1000), is plainly a matter for concern and inquiry.

Until recently, it was considered almost heretical to suggest that all is not as well with women in the state as development data seem to indicate. And that there is more to the status of women than literacy and education, work participation, fertility rate, and other conventional measures of women's advancement, not to mention the mythical matrilineal tradition.

Fortunately, there are emerging signs that this reality is now fairly widely accepted, even in official circles, both within the state and elsewhere. There are also encouraging signals that indicate formal recognition of the need to get beyond exclusive concern with the material conditions of women's lives and to focus attention on issues relating to the equally important question of the position of women in society. So there is hope yet for a future in which women in Kerala will be truly empowered and not merely living in a fool's paradise.

Where 'everything is different'

Abu Abraham

For me, as for most Malayalis, there is Kerala and there is India. The two are one, of course, but Kerala is so different from the rest of the country and so unique in its landscape, culture and history that a Malayali grows up having a mental distinction between Kerala, and the rest of India. This feeling of difference has nothing to do with any lack of identity with other parts of the country, nor do Malayalis feel any less loyal to India that is Bharat. Indeed, the Hindu traditions alone keep Kerala closely bound with the rest of India. After all, Shankaracharya did not come from nowhere. He was the product of a long process of cultural development and spiritual traditions that must have begun in Vedic times.

In geological terms, Kerala seems to be a later addition to the great Indian landmass. There is evidence that the inland towns of Kottayam and Tripunithura were seaports in the days when the Greeks sailed the Arabian Sea. The low-lying areas that now separate these places from the ocean were formed by currents off the coast, which swept the sand and silt flowing down the rivers, from east to west, into long banks parallel to the shore. In this manner, the backwaters and large lakes like Vembanad, stretching from Kochi to Kottayam, and the Ashtamudi at Kollam were formed.

The story of Parasurama, an incarnation of Vishnu, is a mythical version of the geological events of antiquity. Subramaniam, the peacock-riding son of Shiva, persuades Varuna, the god of the sea, to give Parasurama all the land he could cover with a throw of his axe, starting from the Western Ghats where he dwelt. Parasurama cast his axe, which landed near Kanyakumari, and the whole strip of land now known as Kerala rose from the sea. Parasurama then settled on this land some sixty-four Namboodri Brahmin families who had been faithful to the teachings of the Rig Veda and when he left, gave them sovereign rights.

Parasurama was the sixth incarnation of Vishnu, but it is a previous incarnation (the fifth) that Malayalis recall annually at the time of Onam, a festival that coincides with the harvest in late summer. Vishnu takes on the form of a dwarf, Vamana, and sets out to subdue the great Asura king, Bali or Mahabali, whose magical powers and popularity among the people had made the Brahminical deities jealous. Vamana asks Mahabali, known for his generosity and good government, for a gift of land, just as much as he could cover in three paces. When Bali innocently agrees, Vamana begins to grow until he is a giant, and his first stride covers the whole earth. Bali is thus forced to go to the infernal regions and returns to Kerala once a year to see how the people are faring. The Onam festival is an occasion for Malayalis to show, through feasting and dancing, how happy they are to welcome Bali again.

The story of Mahabali is regarded as a piece of mythological history representing the conquest of the native Dravidian culture by the Aryan teachers from the north, who brought with them the Vedic religion and the Sanskrit language and who, incidentally, introduced a caste system which never existed before. Caste, in a multitude of social divisions and cultural practices, later became the curse of Kerala.

The legends of Parasurama and Mahabali were, it is obvious, created by the Brahmin intruders to perpetuate their claim over the land as well as their social hegemony.

The later 'invaders' did not seek to dominate; they were traders. For at least two thousand years, the coastal ports of Kodungallur (Cranganore) and Kochi (Cochin) have seen the arrival of ships from West Asia and Europe, bringing travellers more varied and numerous than those who rode into India from the northwest. And unlike the experience of Punjab, these intrusions into Kerala were almost entirely peaceful.

From the days of Cleopatra, there is evidence of traders from the West coming to the Konkan and Malabar coasts. The earliest travellers were Arabs who were probably sailing to India in search of spices long before Cleopatra's time. The Greeks of Alexandria provide the first historical data on the Malabar coast. Later visits came from the Romans, the Muslims of Egypt and Iran, and the Chinese who renewed the European connection in the thirteenth century. They were followed by the Portuguese, Dutch, French, Danes, and finally the British, who presided over the native states of Travancore and Cochin along with Malabar (the northern part of Kerala) from 1791 onwards, when the East India Company's forces defeated Tipu Sultan's invading army and drove them over the Ghats and back to Mysore.

In many ways, these foreign contacts benefited Kerala and shaped its way of life and personality. As a result of commerce with the Western and Arab traders, Kerala developed a plantation system in the foothills of the Sahyadri mountains and a form of agriculture in the coastal areas based on cash crops. Kerala's economy is dependent on pepper, cardamom, rubber and tea and, of course, coconut, which provides coir and copra (dried kernel from which oil is extracted). The intensity of cultivation has made Kerala evergreen, with an elaborate system of canals through which, in the past, country boats carried goods for export to the little ports along the coast. The whole landscape is, in a sense, a reflection of its commercial history.

The coconut, incidentally, is not native to Kerala. Botanists think that it must have been brought from Indonesia either directly or via Sri Lanka. An old folk song of the Ezhava community says, 'Our ancestors of old, had their home in the land of Ceylon.' The fact that the Ezhavas of Kerala have been traditionally coconut cutters and toddy tappers emphasizes this connection. The origin of the Ezhavas (or Thiyas as they are known in Malabar) is obscure. But 'Thiya' is said to be a corruption of *dweepa* (island), suggesting that they were Sri Lankans.

As for toddy, its potency and flavour seem to have been appreciated by Malayalis and foreigners alike since ancient times. Marco Polo, in his account of his visit to the region, referred to a wine made out of sugar, but it could only have been arrack made from toddy, or sugarcane from which jaggery is prepared.

Marco Polo reached Kerala from China and, for such a widely travelled gentleman, his astonishment was great when he saw Kerala. He wrote: 'Everything is different from what it is with us and excels both in size and beauty. They have no fruit the same as ours, no beast, no bird. This is a consequence of the extreme heat. They have no grain excepting only rice. They make wine out of sugar, and a very good drink it is, and makes a man drunk sooner than grape wine. All that a human body needs for living is to be had in profusion and very cheap with the one exception of grain other than rice. They have no lack of skilled astrologers. They have physicians who are adept at preserving the human body in health. They are all black-skinned and go stark naked, both males and females, except for gay loincloths. They regard no form of lechery or sexual indulgence as sin.'

St. Thomas the Apostle is believed to have landed at Muziris (now Cranganore or Kodungallur) in 52 AD. His conversions created what is known as the earlier Christian community, the Church of St. Thomas or the Syrian Christian Church. Though there is no historical proof of St. Thomas' arrival, there is ample evidence of a well-established Church from the second century onwards.

St. Thomas, according to legend, preached the Gospel with great patience, and it was eight months before he could form his first congregation. During his stay in the Jewish quarters, he successfully converted the local raja, along with four hundred Hindus and forty Jews. He founded seven churches in towns along the coast. He is believed to have gone from Kerala to China and later returned to India, landing on the Coromandel coast where he was slain by hostile Hindus and buried in Mylapore, Madras. St. Thomas' conversions are recorded in a Brahmin account in the *Keralolpati*, according to which a certain Thoman 'who was an opponent of all Vedas' converted 'many prominent people in the land', including the reigning king, Bana Perumal.

Much before Christianity came to Kerala, it is possible that there was a Jewish community living in Kodungallur and Kochi. The Black Jews of Kerala (of whom few are now left because they have migrated to Israel) are believed, according to their own tradition, to be part of the diaspora (dispersal), arriving from Yemen and Babylon. The White Jews, who came from Iran and Iraq after the rise of Islam, dispute the claim of the Black Jews, describing them as local serfs who converted. The social customs of the Black Jews are no different from other Malayalis, whereas the Whites wear western clothes and prefer to remain as an alien community. There has been strict segregation between the two groups. They never intermarried and even in the common cemetery in Kochi there is a high wall that separates the Blacks from the Whites.

Marco Polo was not the only Italian traveller who recorded his impressions of Kerala. Nicholas Conti wrote in 1440 that Cochin was a city five miles in circumference. He remarked, 'China was a good place to make money in and Cochin to spend it,' though we are not told what attractions he found in the city. Marco Polo described how pepper was grown, indigo extracted, and mentioned calico, the cloth that got its name from Calicut (Kozhikode).

From Italian accounts of the fifteenth century, we get some idea of the Muslim and Christian communities. They speak of the wealth of the Muslim merchants who imported luxury articles like cloth of gold and silk in exchange for spices. Such accounts aroused the interest of the Portuguese. Until then, it was Venice that had a virtual monopoly of the spice trade to Europe. The Portuguese having decided on their imperialistic maritime adventures, presumably in order to gain prestige and power and not wishing to be overlooked by neighbouring Spain, sent a nobleman, Joas Peres Covilhao, on a reconnaissance mission in 1487. Covilhao died in Abyssinia on his return journey before he could give the king an account of his expedition. Nevertheless, the king went ahead with his plans for an expedition around the Cape of Good Hope, and Vasco da Gama sailed from Portugal in July 1497 with the banner of the Cross flying from his masthead. Successive Popes had given such adventurers rights over all territories discovered in Asia and Africa. The Portuguese, it appears, sincerely believed it was their duty to find new lands to be proselytized and turned over to the Roman Church.

Vasco da Gama was received by the Zamorin at a ceremonial durbar, which provided the strange spectacle of a European dressed elaborately in blue satin and velvet and a brocaded cloak, meeting a king dressed in simple clothes but adorned with glittering jewellery. Vasco da Gama, with his long beard which he had vowed not to cut until he returned to Portugal, made his entrance behind a band of trumpeters. He was accompanied by pages carrying gifts that included a gold chair on which the Zamorin obligingly sat to conduct the audience.

There is an elaborate and detailed description of the king, his dress, the jewellery and pearls around his neck and arms and in his pierced ears, and his long black hair, which was gathered up and tied into a knot at the top of his head. For such vivid descriptions we are indebted to the Portuguese chronicles of the time, for they give us a glimpse into life in Kerala as it was then.

The Zamorin did not show much enthusiasm for the Portuguese overtures for trade and business. Neither he nor the Arabs trusted them, and the Arab merchants had warned him of the ambitions of the Portuguese. Vasco da Gama then took five hostages and sailed away to Kannur, further north, where the local prince, a rival of the Zamorin, welcomed him. By manipulating the hostility between the princes, the Portuguese established their presence on the Malabar coast. In 1500, a large expedition of thirteen ships arrived from Portugal under the command of Pedro Alvarez Cabral, whose arrogance and brutality were typical of later Portuguese behaviour in Kerala. He began by seizing an Arab ship that was loading pepper, and the Arabs killed fifty Portuguese in the battle that followed. More and more ships began to arrive from Portugal and the Portuguese hold on the Malabar coast continued until 1571 when the Zamorin's forces made them abandon their effort to control the region.

The religious bigotry of the Portuguese was such that they persecuted the Jews according to the policy of their government back home. They offended the Christians who at first seemed to be their allies. When the Jesuits arrived in 1542, Francis Xavier travelled along the Kerala coast and through mass conversion among fishermen and untouchables in the Travancore state and Kanyakumari, established the first Latin Catholic church in India. They found, however, that the Syrian Christians were disinclined to embrace Roman Catholicism. While for fishermen, Christianity was an escape from caste, the Syrian Christians had experienced no such oppression, for they had lived from early times virtually as part of the larger Hindu community in customs, manners and culture.

In 1599, Alexis de Menezes, Roman Catholic Archbishop of Goa and Primate of all the East, arrived in Cochin with the intent of finally forcing the Syrian Christians to accept the Latin rite. He persuaded the Raja of Cochin to threaten punishment to any of his subjects who refused to submit to the Roman Church. The Portuguese burnt almost all the records of early Christianity, which they considered heretical writings. In the end, except for a small section of Christians who followed the Nestorian doctrines and whose bishops came from Babylon, the Syrian Christians bowed to Rome.

Then, in 1653, the Portuguese arrested at sea, off Cochin, a Nestorian bishop, Atahallah, travelling in disguise from the Persian Gulf. He was sent to Goa and handed over to the Inquisition, after which he was despatched to Lisbon and then to Rome, where he vanished. Atahallah, on his way from Lisbon to Rome, had sent a letter to Archdeacon Thomas, the leading Syrian Christian priest in Kerala, and it created a sensation in Cochin. Twenty thousand Christians marched to demand the bishop's release. The Portuguese blandly told them that he had drowned. The angry Christians then went to a church in Cochin outside which stood a leaning Cross on which they tied ropes. The huge crowd touched it and swore they would not accept Roman rule. The Cross stands even today as a historic monument—the Koonan Kurishu or Crooked Cross—marking the resurrection of an independent native Church on the Malabar coast.

There is one thing that should be said in favour of the Portuguese—they were not racist. They never ordered a colour bar. On the contrary, they encouraged soldiers and civil servants to marry women from Kerala. Malayalis, so long as they were Christians, had equal rights with Whites in the municipality they set up in Cochin. Converts were often given high military and civil posts, and some were even given titles. Francis Xavier's mass conversions among the low caste fishermen of Travancore were perhaps the first blows in the battle against untouchability. Caste was an all-pervading evil in Kerala until recently. When, a hundred years ago, Swami Vivekananda visited Kerala, he described the place as a madhouse. There was not only untouchability, but also 'unapproachability' and 'unseeability'. But today, due to a long tradition of free popular education as well as the continuous struggle of the lower castes, Kerala can almost claim to be a classless, if not casteless, society. The emancipation of the Ezhavas under the leadership of Sri Narayana Guru, who began his religious movement with the slogan, 'One God, one people, one religion', brought about the removal of most of the barriers that caste had set up against them.

The high literacy (almost a hundred per cent) as well as the new prosperity and egalitarianism that characterize modern Kerala have much to do with its being a coastal region with a long history of contact with other regions of the world, in the West as well as in the East. Foreign contacts kept the people alive to new ideas and ways of life. While they have been devoted to their cultural traditions and are to a large extent conservative in their social attitudes, Malayalis are at the same time cosmopolitan adventurers, travelling to different parts of the world to make a living and even settling away from home. The Gulf and the United States are their Meccas today and they have succeeded remarkably in the professions they have chosen.

The young Malayali today is privileged to live in a society that is going through a cultural renaissance, where the traditional arts are being revived and the Malayalam language being enriched with new writing. In literature and in films, Kerala has found a vast reservoir of talent that is speeding the new movement.

Kerala's peculiar history with its age-old tradition of religious tolerance (and even active help from Hindu rajas to other religious communities like Jews, Muslims and Christians) has had much to do with its present status, which is that of a highly educated, cultured and secular state. Religious and communal conflicts are so rare in Kerala that one can say, as Marco Polo said, that here 'everything is different'.

The first lessons

O.V. Vijayan

The rains were over, the skies shone, and Khasak readied itself for Onam, the festival of thanksgiving. Children went up into the hills at sunrise to gather flowers. For ten days they would arrange colourful designs in their yards with flower petals to welcome the deities of the festival. Ravi heard the children sing on the hillsides, and for a fleeting moment they touched him with the joy of a hundred home-comings. The moment passed, and once again he was the fugitive. A fugitive had no home, and a *sarai* no festival.

Ravi sought to share his fears with Madhavan Nair—the Onam recess would last a fortnight. Would the children come back to dreary routine after that spell of freedom?

'If I were their age, I wouldn't!' Ravi said.

'You lost your childhood somewhere along the way, Maash. I hope the children find it for you.'

As they parted Madhavan Nair said with some hesitation, 'There is one more pupil for you if you can take a risk.'

'A risk? Who's it anyway?'

Guilt and remorse made Madhavan Nair suggest it to Ravi. Some days ago Appu-Kili's mother Neeli was at his shop waiting for him to put the finishing stitches to a blouse he was making for her. She sat there bare-breasted, watching the dressmaker anticipate the contours.

'There, there!' she said suddenly. 'See, O Venerable Nair . . .'

On the other side of the square there were children at play. In their midst stood the cretin, taller than them and clad in conspicuous motley. Madhavan Nair remembered how she broke down as she pointed to Appu-Kili and said, 'Look at my son!'

This extract is taken from *The Legends of Khasak,* published by Penguin Books India.

It was just the other day that Madhavan Nair had made him that weird toga with scraps of cloth. He had scissored out a Gandhi and a sickle-and-hammer from discarded gunny bags, and stitched them on either side of the toga.

'If only you could tell the Maeshtar . . .' Neeli sobbed.

Madhavan Nair saw the tears fall on her bare breasts.

'I shall speak to the Maash, Neeli.'

'Not to teach my Appu but to stop him from roaming with children.'

When they reopened after the festival break, Ravi was pleasantly surprised to find the school had survived the vacation . . . Madhavan Nair arrived chaperoning Appu-Kili. The children crowded round the cretin who was neither man nor child. Ravi herded them back to their seats, taking care the dragonfly, the cretin's constant companion, was not lost. He drew the Parrot aside and asked him gently, 'Like to join the school, Kili?'

Madhavan Nair raised his hand to discipline the children, 'Quieten down, evil ones! You are upsetting my Parrot!' And to Kili, 'Didn't you hear what the Maash-Etta asked you? Speak, O Parrot of the Palms!'

Appu-Kili stood looking indifferent, his gaze on his toes.

'Why are you afraid?' Madhavan Nair reasoned. 'Isn't it our own school?'

That did not reassure the Parrot. The children in the school were all his playmates, they made signs of encouragement. From the benches came hushed invitations: *Come, Kili, come here, sit near me!* As Madhavan Nair turned to go, Appu-Kili let out a howl, 'Take me with you, Madhavan-Etto!'

'O avian!' the tailor despaired, 'you have put me to shame!'

Madhavan Nair took four coppers from his purse and asked one of the pupils, Alam Khan, to go and get some murukkus. He told Kili that the teacher would give him the murukkus if he sat quietly and did his lessons. Appu-Kili cheered up.

Ravi whispered, 'Madhavan Nair, my life is in peril. This prehistoric pet of yours . . .'

'Have no fear, Maash.'

Ravi found the child-man a place next to little Sohra.

'Sohra will take care of you, my winged being!' Madhavan Nair said, and added this parting advice. 'Study well, and become an engineer.'

'He will!' the class responded.

As Ravi turned to write out a sum on the blackboard, Sohra drew Kili close and passed him a sweet berry.

'Don't be afraid, Kili, I'm with you.'

During the Onam vacation cobwebs had gathered in the seedling house, and Ravi set apart a day for teacher and pupils to clean up the school. It became a war on the spiders. Adam drew a line on the floor with chalk and laid out the dead spiders. Appu-Kili picked up the biggest of them and tried to breathe life into it.

'Saar, Saar,' Kunhamina asked, 'how big are the really big spiders?'

Ravi pointed to the dome of the mosque, and said, 'That big.'

'Yaa Rahman!'

The spiders in the crevices of the walls were brown, and were only as big as an outspread palm. But outside, in the forests of the rain, they were born to power and splendour. Like the kings of old they revelled in the hunt. And in the teeming nights of fear they rose like stars of the nether dark . . . Ravi told the children the story of the spiders, how after they made love the female ate up her mate. The children could not believe that such bloody dynasties ruled over Khasak's peaceful grass and fern. Then Karuvu stood up and said the male spider was paying for his sins in an earlier birth. The children knew it was karma, the class was now unusually quiet.

The story of karma ended, but Ravi had set the children on a magic trail. They refused to do sums and recitations, and for the next two days Ravi did nothing but tell them stories of plants and animals. It was during one of these heady lessons that Kunhamina brought a hedge lizard to the classroom. The lizard made no attempt to escape.

'Hurt it, have you?' Ravi asked Kunhamina.

'No, Saar. Just doped it with castor sap.'

The lizard took a few unsteady steps on Ravi's table, then gave up, and looked around in ancient derision. Kunhamina had reckoned that Ravi would be pleased with the catch, but froze when she sensed his displeasure.

'Will it die?' Ravi asked Kunhamina. She wouldn't answer, but the rest of the class spoke. The castor sap, said Madhavi, was like the liquor they made in Khasak, it killed only when one had too much of it. Adam said hedge lizards were used in sorcery, he terrified himself with the thought of saturnine deities called up by the sorcerer. No child of Khasak was friends with the hedge lizard, said Karuvu, because it sucked the blood of children, sucked it through the air from afar. One realized it only when one watched the lizard's head suddenly turn crimson, the sign of the vampire.

There was more about the hedge lizard—the evil spirits exorcised by the astrologers went into exile riding the hedge lizard. They wouldn't say anything more as it was Khasak's secret.

Ravi and the children were engrossed in the stories and no one had noticed Kunhamina sobbing.

'Kunhamina,' Ravi said, 'I didn't mean to hurt you.'

That only made the sobbing worse. Tears brought the surma down in patches over her cheeks, and the silver anklets chimed as she moved her legs disconsolately under her desk. In the meantime the lizard recovered, and with one last look at everyone, stalked out of the classroom towards the hedges. Kunhamina smiled.

That day Ravi told the children the story of the lizards. In times before Man usurped the earth, the lizard held sway. A miraculous book opened, the children saw its pages rise and turn and flap. Out of it came mighty saurians moving slowly in deep canyons after the dull scent of prey, and pterodactyls rose screaming over their nesting precipices. The story was reluctantly interrupted for lunch; after hurried morsels the children raced back to school and huddled round their teacher. The pages rose and fell again . . . Long before the lizards, before the dinosaurs, two spores set out on an incredible journey. They came to a valley bathed in the placid glow of sunset.

My elder sister, said the little spore to the bigger spore, *let us see what lies beyond.*

This valley is green, replied the bigger spore, *I shall journey no farther.*

I want to journey, said the little spore, *I want to discover.* She gazed in wonder at the path before her.

Will you forget your sister? asked the bigger spore.

Never, said the little spore.

You will, little one, for this is the loveless tale of karma; in it there is only parting and sorrow.

The little spore journeyed on. The bigger spore stayed back in the valley. Her roots pierced the damp earth and sought the nutrients of death and memory. She sprouted over the earth, green and contented . . . A girl with silver anklets and eyes prettied with surma came to Chetali's valley to gather flowers. The Champaka tree stood alone—efflorescent, serene. The flower-gatherer reached out and held down a soft twig to pluck the flowers. As the twig broke the Champaka said, *My little sister, you have forgotten me!*

The children had gone home. Ravi closed his eyes, leaned back in his chair and abandoned himself to the charmed weariness. Around him rose the scent of incense, and the sound of bells and cymbals.

Vedan Uddharate Jagannivahate—the sloka celebrating the avatars of the Lord, evolute incarnations from fish to boar to man and deity resounded over everything.

The moment passed. Ravi, now awake, looked out. The sun was setting over Chetali's valley. The sunset filled the seedling house with the warmth of a sensuous fever.

Butter chicken in Ludhiana

Pankaj Mishra

When the rain stopped, I took a taxi to Kottayam. I went via Cochin, where I had planned to stop awhile and eat. But I had misremembered the distances between these places, with the result that I reached Kottayam very late in the evening.

The traffic was light: an occasional truck or car. There was an almost uninterrupted series of settlements along the road, mostly residential buildings, clean and well-tended, nestling amid banana and coconut trees, and completely without the desolating quality of roadside towns in the North. At larger settlements the road broadened instead of narrowing; no part of it looked encroached upon. And the women outside easily outnumbered men: mostly long-skirted, college-going girls with fresh flowers in their hair and books pressed to their bosoms, who giggled and pointed indecisively when asked for directions.

The road after Cochin—where I ate a hurried meal at Woodlands—suddenly deteriorated. The car lurched from side to side as it went over potholes; passing buses churned up thick clouds of red dust behind them. Then, just as suddenly, the road improved. The land here was hilly and less populated, the few houses were set well back from the road, and the vegetation was denser. Large fenced-in rubber estates lay on either side, with, sometimes, a shaded uninhabited-seeming bungalow on top of a hill. Teak forests and coffee plantations intervened to lend a few more shades of green to the scenery. Going endlessly up and down the twisting deserted road felt, in my fatigue-induced daze, like slowly penetrating to the core of an exceptionally lush and welcoming landscape.

At Kottayam, I checked into a hotel on the busy K.K. Road, quickly

This extract is taken from *Butter Chicken in Ludhiana: Travels in Small Town India*, published by Penguin Books India.

bathed, and then went out for a short walk.

I had noticed, while looking for my hotel, a number of new-looking readymade-clothes shops, their pastel interiors gleaming behind glass doors and windows, conspicuous in a street full of churches and old-fashioned, open-fronted shops. It was where I now went.

The shops—some called themselves 'boutiques'—were, as I had thought, new, and, without exception, deserted. I went into one with the bright name of 'Pretty Joanne'. The shop staff looked up with wide-eyed interest as I walked in. The interest turned into suspicion as I examined some outrageously gaudy 'designer' versions of the North Indian salwar kameez. Soon, one of them was breathing down my neck and demanding to know what I wanted.

'Just looking,' I said.

'But this is ladies boutique,' he said.

I hadn't known that. With as much dignity as I could muster, I made a quick exit.

I didn't go into any of the other shops, and merely observed them from the road, especially the people manning them, who, listlessly looking out from amid their brilliantly-lit enclosures, gave off a strange forlornness. It couldn't have been just the strain of waiting interminably for customers who never arrived. It was more the alienness of their setting: these shops which with their clean-cut lines, their dust-free interiors, their glass fronts, their air-conditioning, created an oppressively unfamiliar world for their inhabitants in a small place like Kottayam. It was something I thought I could recognize from the past. I had been living in Allahabad when its first 'fast-food' restaurant opened in 1987. The owner had been inspired by Nirula's of Delhi—inspired in turn by McDonald's of America—and he strove to recreate it in every way he could in Allahabad—down to the plastic vines and plants. But what at first looked strange and incongruous in Delhi was even more so in Allahabad. There were prospective customers I knew who would not dare to step inside the restaurant for fear of being intimidated and embarrassed. And the staff, most of whom were locals, had not ceased for months to give an impression of total unease in their alien Americanized surroundings, always looking, in their jaunty peaked caps and monogrammed uniforms, like people trapped in an overly elaborate and pointless masquerade.

In the morning, I called upon Mrs Mary Roy, famous litigant, and, currently, Principal of Corpus Christi School, Kottayam.

Mrs Roy, in a celebrated court case in the mid-eighties, had taken on the entire Syrian Christian Church, and won. She had contested the legality of a pre-independence Succession Act that denied women their rightful share in paternal property, allowing them only a pitiable fourth of the son's share. Amazingly, this Act, which stood automatically repealed after India became a republic in 1951 and promulgated its own Succession Act, had been allowed to govern property distribution for thirty-five more years. Finally, Mrs Roy took up the cudgels on behalf of Syrian Christian women, and filed a public interest litigation in the Supreme Court. That was in 1983. In 1986 came the historic judgement declaring the old Succession Act null and void.

The litigation attracted a fair amount of publicity, even if hardly as much as the coterminous Shah Bano case. Emerging from relative obscurity, Mrs Roy became for some time a national figure, her bold views on men, marriage, and feminism featured prominently in women's magazines.

And I first thought I had not properly realized the true extent of her fame when I tried calling her and found that she was as well-shielded from nosey journalists as any Bombay filmstar.

Three different voices interposed themselves between Mrs Roy and me. The first one told me that Mrs Roy was ill, and therefore unable to meet me. However, it asked for my hotel number in case, the voice said, Mrs Roy felt better and inclined to see me.

The call came ten minutes later. It was another voice this time, demanding to know, in not very clear English, my credentials.

I explained. I said I had come with an introduction from Mrs Roy's daughter, Arundhati—a Delhi-based filmmaker, whom I had briefly met through a mutual friend—and if Mrs Roy wasn't too indisposed, could I at least speak to her on the phone?

But this was almost instantly rejected, and the voice resumed its questioning. How did I know Arundhati? What kind of book was I writing? Why did I specifically want to meet Mrs Roy?

I patiently answered. Then the voice broke off without explanation. There was another call after just five minutes. It was the third

voice. The interrogation began anew. What was my book about? Why
. . .

I replied with weariness and a growing impulse to put the phone
down.

Finally, I was told to come round in an hour's time. I was given
directions to Corpus Christi school; I was warned not to pay more
than ten rupees to the autorickshaw driver.

Contrary to what I was told on the phone, Mrs Roy, when I was
finally ushered into her office, turned out to be in reasonably good
health. She was a large matronly woman in her late fifties, with
prominent black bags under her eyes, an affable manner, and an impish
smile that was startlingly like her daughter's. Unlike her three
assistants, she asked me no questions at all about myself. Perhaps, she
was satisfied by what she had been told by them. Perhaps—and this
seemed more likely after three hours in her company during which
she addressed me variously as Pankaj, Pradeep, Sunil, and Ashok—
she was simply incurious about someone who after all was only the
latest in a long line of interviewers.

She said she was going out to the bazaar for some urgent shopping.
Would I mind accompanying her? We could talk on the way, she said.

She wondered, as we walked out to the waiting car, why I was
interested in Kottayam. She said, 'It is such a backward small town.
Nothing happens here.'

But that was only a bit of instinctive self-deprecation before the
visitor. For soon after, in response to my mentioning the readymade-
clothes shops I had visited the day before, she said, 'Oh, Kottayam is
a very modern place. You'd be surprised. All these people are incredibly
rich. There is a lot of money in this town, even if it's not too apparent.'

And once we were out, and driving into downtown Kottayam, her
manner changed, became more expansive. 'Look,' she said, pointing
to a church, 'the church has some of the most valuable property in
Kottayam. Do you know there are about five hundred bishops in
Kottayam alone? They are always fighting each other because all of
them have such grand notions about themselves. They even dress like
the Pope!'

And when I made a remark about the number of women I had
noticed wearing salwar-kameezes, something that seemed to me an

interesting departure from traditional modes of dress, she said, 'But you know, this part of India was always very different in these matters. We had women going around bare-breasted before the British came and put an end to that. There was a whole agitation against the British on this issue.'

Later, as we waited for the girl who drove us to find some parking space, she said, 'Arundhati is thrilled by that girl. She came from a very poor background, but look at her now: how self-confident she is.'

I followed Mrs Roy on her shopping round. Despite what I had heard about her unpopularity, she appeared to be a well-respected figure. We went first to a large saree store where the men behind the counters rose to their feet as Mrs Roy walked in.

One of them, a tall, spry, spiffily-dressed young man, was her ex-student. We were introduced. His name was Vasudevan. He asked me what I was doing in Kottayam.

Just passing through, I said.

But there is *nothing* here, he said.

That was the second time in a day that I had heard this. 'But how can this be true?' I tried to protest, 'the largest-selling newspaper in India has its offices here. Then, it is the centre of Malayalam publishing. You have the Syrian Christian community here, so many denominations, so many churches. It is a *fascinating* place.'

Mrs Roy looked amused at my response. Vasudevan permitted himself a brief smile.

'That is all for tourists,' he said. 'For people who live here there is very little.'

Mrs Roy told me more about Vasudevan as he busied himself with her order. He was one of her success-stories. After graduating from her school, he had gone on to study at Sydenham College in Bombay. He had then come back to take charge of his father's saree shop.

The saree shop, she added in a lowered voice, had fallen on bad days lately. There were three floors in all when the shop first opened, and it had a monopoly on the wedding-saree business. Now, after the opening of Rehmanika in Cochin, it had gone into rapid decline. Just as it had decimated other saree-businesses in the region ten years ago, so it was being decimated by Rehmanika now.

I had been to Rehmanika on a previous visit to Cochin, attracted by its claim to being the largest saree store in Asia, and had come away quite impressed. It was gigantic all right, but it was also generous. Instead of being unceremoniously ejected, a casual stroller like myself had been presented with a soft-drink. In the air-cooled waiting space for impatient males, there had been a stack of the very latest magazines.

Vasudevan, overhearing me talk about Rehmanika, piped up: 'Do you know it is owned by a man from Kottayam?'

Mrs Roy turned to me and said, 'Didn't I tell you? People think big in this town.'

She asked Vasudevan to show me round the shop. He looked hesitant. The reason became quickly clear: there was nothing to see.

We went up unsteady wooden stairs to a dark hall full of dusty overturned furniture and musty smells. Vasudevan switched on the light. I looked. He waited. I thought hard of something to say.

Some time elapsed before Vasudevan said, 'This floor was operational until sometime back. Now we are trying to turn it into a readymade clothes section.'

'Oh,' I said.

We stood there in some embarrassment, both of us at a loss for words.

Then, as we were going down the stairs, Vasudevan said, apropos of nothing, 'Actually, I am from Bombay.'

But he wasn't. He had only studied there. I knew that already from Mrs Roy.

Slightly puzzled, I said nothing. There was a strange poignance in his claim. It was intended for me: the visitor from the metropolis. But I didn't realize this until much later.

It must have been as a young man full of promise that he travelled to Bombay. His years there, in the company of other big-thinking students, must have further enhanced his ambitions. And things might have seemed to be going his way when he came back to his father's flourishing business in Kottayam.

But then Rehmanika had arrived, and forced his shop into decline. It could not have been an easy thing to take for a man whose notions of success were formed in Bombay, and who probably always thought his proper place was there. It must have revived all his latent dislike for small-town efforts. And it must have revived his desire to reconnect himself with the larger world, a desire which, in the present circumstances, couldn't go beyond an attempt to distance himself from both Kottayam and the failure the upper floor spoke of.

Back at her office, Mrs Roy told me about her continuing harassment by fundamentalist elements within the Syrian Christian Church. It didn't seem likely that they would ever forgive her. Most recently, they had denounced as blasphemous the Lloyd-Webber play *Jesus Christ Superstar* which the children at her school had put up. On their prompting, the District Collector had raided the school twice to prevent the play from being staged. A close contact in the police department had warned her that drugs might be planted on the premises during the raid, and she had had to take anticipatory bail in order to avoid arrest.

She pointed out the anticipatory-bail order to me. It had been framed and hung just above her chair.

'Look carefully,' she said. 'Do you see something strange in it?'

I couldn't. it was too far from me to read.

'Look carefully,' she said, with a triumphant note in her voice. 'It is an order without any dates on it!'

She received a regular supply of hate-mail. Much of it concerned her daughter, Arundhati, who had outraged fundamentalist opinion by openly living in sin with a Hindu man in Delhi. She was alleged to be promiscuous, flitting from one man to another. Others thought her a prostitute. All concurred in thinking her a morally debased woman.

'All this small-town pettiness,' Mrs Roy said, 'I am so glad I sent my daughter out of Kottayam. I didn't want her growing up here.'

As we talked, a maidservant came in, wearing an immaculately clean apron, and holding a tray with two glasses of Thums Up. While I took an occasional sip from my glass, Mrs Roy never even touched hers. As the afternoon wore on, she grew more voluble, and I was called upon to say less and less. Her range of topics expanded; she turned out to be full of opinions on a variety of subjects.

A common strand ran through them: her desire to separate herself from Kottayam and its 'backwardness'. It wasn't easy to understand at first how she differed from Vasudevan in that. But then, unlike him, she had no cravings for metropolitan success. She was a well-established prominent citizen to Kottayam, the principal of a prestigious school. In however mixed ways, Kottayam offered her a stable existence; the place could even be, as I had seen, a source of pride. Her wish to be distinguished from it clearly had different roots. And it mostly seemed as if by repeatedly emphasizing the stultifying aspect of her surroundings, she was trying to throw into even sharper focus her own struggles for an independent modern identity. Kottayam and its backwardness were, in effect, merely the backdrop—albeit, an essential one—to a long and difficult process of self-creation.

The locals, who had witnessed it from close quarters, could take it for granted; it was the outsider, to whom it wasn't always apparent, who needed to be told about it. Thus, the manifold opinions, which were like cryptic assertions of her independence and modernity.

She talked about sex. She thought it a wonderful thing, and deplored the Christian attitude to it. 'I think Hinduism has a much more positive view on this. I mean, they even tell you how to have sex. And, look at Krishna! How sexual he is!' she said.

She talked about television. She liked the new satellite-TV serials. 'Serials like *Santa Barbara* and *The Bold and the Beautiful* are so much better than anything on Doordarshan. The story is all trash of course, but they are technically very good.'

Technically very good?!! *Santa Barbara* and *The Bold and the Beautiful*?!!

It seemed a strange thing to say, coming from the mother of a fairly accomplished filmmaker.

But just before I left, she said something even stranger. She said, apropos of nothing, with an unexpected passion in her voice, 'I think white people are a curse on mankind. Wherever you look, they are busy causing destruction to something or the other. And they think themselves so superior to everyone else! They are really awful!'

*

I was still pondering over that remark when I went to Kovalam Beach and found a good reason why white people, for admittedly no fault of theirs, could soon find themselves resented by more Indians.

On a previous visit to Kovalam with a friend I had noticed a hotel called 'Searock'. It was right on the beach, closer to the water than any other hotel. We were then staying at the Hotel Rockholm, a far more clean and pleasant place, but slightly expensive; and we had decided to ask at the Searock, which we knew to be cheaper, if there was anything there for us.

A tall broad-shouldered man with a gruff stentorian voice and absurd accent had met us at the reception. No, he had boomed out. There were no rooms available at his hotel. He had full bookings for the entire season.

It was then the month of October; the season hadn't even commenced. And, I knew that irrespective of which month of the year it was, the hotels in Kovalam were never quite full.

There was something else going on, and a British couple I met on a train had confirmed my suspicions. The Searock, they said, didn't admit Indians. They had come to know this from a French couple on the beach, who were also staying at the Searock and who fully approved of its policy of barring Indians. The British couple, to their credit, had been horrified by such blatant racism. They had left Searock the same day and moved into another hotel.

I had heard about similar hotels in the Caribbean, the playgrounds of rich white Americans, where local blacks, no matter how wealthy, were not welcome. And it had seemed a distinctive feature of the Caribbean's tourist economics: the self-abasement before foreigners, the frantic wish to please at any cost, the desire to be more white than the whites, the lust for dollars, the distrust and contempt for one's compatriots.

But India wasn't a tourist economy—at least, not yet. All the more disturbing, then, it was to know about places where the shoddy practices of poor parasitic nations had crept in. In India, they were an unpleasant reminder of old colonial hierarchies: whites at the top, Indians somewhere at the bottom, finding their own different levels of degradation. They spoke, at least in certain quarters, of the growing damage, after just forty-seven years of independence, to national self-esteem; and they were the unexplored darker side of globalization, the social consequence of joining the global market as a pavement beggar.

It was the same man at the Searock's reception when I went in. He had two friends with him this time: as tall and broad-shouldered as he was, and with the manner of bullies.

It was some time before he noticed me, standing there with my rucksack.

'Yes? What do you want?' he boomed out.

I said I was looking for a room.

'Single or double?' he asked.

'Single,' I said.

'Sorry,' he said, with an air of finality, 'we have no single rooms.'

I persisted. 'What about a double room?'

'We have them,' he intoned, 'but they are too expensive.'

'How much?'

'Two hundred rupees a night.'

'That's fine by me,' I said. I was expecting a much higher tariff.

But he wasn't listening to me. He had already turned to his friends and was conversing with them in rapid Malayalam.

I said in a louder voice, 'I'll take the room.'

He turned and looked at me, impatience writ large on his face. 'You take my advice and go to the main beach,' he said, in a commanding voice, 'you'll find much cheaper places there.'

'Thank you,' I said, 'but I like it here.'

For some reason, he didn't offer any more resistance. He did look vaguely regretful as I signed the register and paid out the advance, as if berating himself for not having told me that the entire hotel was booked for the season.

I was walked over by a servant to a small room at the end of the corridor facing the reception. The two beds left barely enough space to stand; in the bathroom was a torn towel with a scruffy surface, and a small bar of Hamam soap. I quickly undressed, and went in to bathe.

Two minutes later, the light went out. I finished my bath, dressed, and went out to the reception. The man smiled when he saw me, and exchanged a look with his friends.

'Yes? What do you want?' he asked.

'There is no power in my room.'

'Yes, I know,' he said. 'There is some fault in the fuse. It will come back after two hours.'

I walked back to my room and lay on the cool bed. It had been a long and tiring journey from Kottayam, and I was tired, I must have drifted off into sleep, for when I woke up it was fifteen minutes later, with the sounds of heavy pounding coming through the thin walls from the adjacent room. The noise was deafening; I must have woken up almost immediately after it started.

I got up and went out to the reception. He was still there, but without his friends, and there was a stern expression on his face.

'Yes? What do you want?' he asked.

I told him about the hammering sounds, and how they had disturbed my sleep.

'That will go on,' he said. 'My work cannot stop.'

'Do you have any other room?' I asked.

'No.'

I looked at him; he, at me.

And then without any warning, he took out two hundred rupee notes from his shirt pocket, and, handing them to me, said, 'I told you in the beginning. Take your advance back, and find another hotel. This is not the right hotel for you.'

*

I checked into another hotel, slept, wrote in my notebook and read an old collection of stories by Vaikkom Mohammed Basheer that I had picked up in Kottayam.

Later on the beach I ran into someone I knew from my last visit. He was a sixteen-year-old boy from a nearby Muslim fishing village. He had dropped out of school at an early age, and, while I was there, seemed to spend all his time soliciting beach-side tourists for business.

The business he offered was deep-sea scuba-diving. The vision he painted of it was exact in its details: the motor-boat drive before dawn, the lonely spot miles away from the shore, the Made-in-Germany scuba-diving equipment awaiting one in the boat, the army of expert swimmers ready to help in case something went wrong.

Moving from person to person on the packed beach, he retailed the same vision, making it all somehow sound like child's play. But I don't believe he ever got any customers. The reason was obvious at first glance. For such a glamorous-sounding sport as deep-sea scuba-diving, he was an extremely unconvincing salesman in his torn vest and lungi, all of whose talk about motor-boats and Made-in-Germany diving equipment could seem to be part of the idleness of the beach.

I met him everyday while I was there. He talked of different things to me after I had quickly discounted myself as a prospective scuba-diver. His ambition was to go to Saudi Arabia, and earn a lot of money there. Many people he knew had already done so, and he was determined to emulate them. As for now, he was content to earn a little money here and there, doing odd jobs.

I never asked him what those odd jobs were, but toward the end of my stay he gave me a truer idea of them. He asked me one day if I liked boys or girls.

I didn't at first understand the true import of his question.

'Both,' I said.

'Boys,' he said, 'you like boys?'

'Yes,' I said, still not understanding.

He said, 'You want to fuck boys?'

So great was the shock that I couldn't bring myself to say anything for some time. I saw him looking expectantly at me, without fear, without embarrassment. It was clearly not the first time he had asked someone that question. I finally managed to weakly blurt out, no. He appeared content with that, and did not offer me girls in place of boys. It was possible, of course, that there were no girls to offer, that there was only him and a few other boys who, struggling with desperate poverty, had fallen back on an ancient profession.

He was in the water, a few feet to my left, when I saw him. He was with a tall skinny girl in a fluorescent-green bikini, whose hand he held onto tightly as they dived headlong, shrieking with delight, into the base of a looming wave. He saw me, and his face broke into a smile of recognition, but he appeared unwilling to let go of the girl's hand and swim over to where I was.

He did so after the girl left. He had grown slightly since the last time I saw him. There were the wispy beginnings of a moustache above his upper lip; an Adam's apple bobbed in his throat; his shoulders looked broader. And he was wearing a skimpy Speedo swimsuit, a gift, no doubt, from one of his tourist-friends.

'See that girl,' he shouted above the roar of crashing waves, pointing to the figure wading back to the beach, 'she's from Israel. She's my girlfriend.'

'What about Saudi Arabia?' I shouted back.

But the sarcasm, in poor taste as it was, was lost on him. His blank face told me he had forgotten about Saudi Arabia, forgotten that he once wanted to go there. It was part of the now-discarded fantasy about motor-boats and scuba-diving; it had never meant anything.

We didn't talk much. He looked restless and distracted, eager to get away.

I commented on that. 'You look like a busy man,' I said.

'Yes, yes, very busy,' he said. 'Too much people wanting me these days.'

The imprecise English inadvertently expressed a kind of truth. Business had finally boomed. From being one who solicited, he had rapidly moved to being one who was solicited. He didn't have customers any more; he had girlfriends. And he was only seventeen, his body yet to achieve its full muscular development, yet to ripen into the bronzed glory which for many winters to come would keep finding new admirers, if not also bring old ones back to these shores.

The expanse of imagination

Jayanth Kodkani

Flirtations with persona

The other day I showed these lines to a colleague.

'What does your face look like?'

'Longish and fair. My hair is trimmed. I'm a little bald.'

'And eyes?'

'Rather small, elephant eyes.'

'Mine are large elephant eyes. Your chest?'

'Somewhat broad.'

'My chest is full too. And your waist?'

'It's trim.'

'My waist? Well, I wouldn't want to tell you!'

'It sure must be like a barrel! I could scratch and tear you to pieces.'

The colleague snickered like a schoolboy and said, 'So what have you been doing in chatrooms?' He deduced it was cyberspace dialogue. An activity that not only helps create a virtual persona but also allows flirtations with fabricated identities. Behind unseen walls. Where people play 'yours' and 'mine' with their own selves, inhabiting the realms of their creations.

My colleague didn't know those lines were from Vaikom Muhammad Basheer's 'The Walls' written in 1955.

*

An armchair near the wall

Many years ago, I chanced upon a Malayalam newspaper clipping featuring a write-up and photographs of Basheer working outdoors, perhaps in his frontyard. A particular photograph caught my eye; showing the old and frail writer settled in a cloth-backed armchair and penning down his thoughts. In front of him was a small table on which lay a sheaf of papers.

A similar armchair, although with shorter and narrower armrests, lay folded in the attic of my ancestral home. My cousin and I, then in our teens, took a fancy to it and egged on an uncle to pull it down for us. The chair was big enough for both of us to plop in its cloth-hammock and read comics on lazy afternoons under the mango tree in our backyard. Sometimes in the evenings, my uncle would occupy the chair with us perched on the armrests, and narrate ghost stories. Like all stories that elders tell youngsters, the tales got a twist depending on our mood and the elasticity of his imagination.

Around the same time, we were intrigued by little voices in the neighbourhood, separated by a high wall at the far end of the backyard. We could hear four distinct voices of children about our age but never got to see their faces, because the wall was covered with moss and the nearest view was from a coconut tree which we dared not climb. The children on the other side were lucky, though—a mango tree almost reached out to the wall. Sure enough, once we saw a small white hand groping for support on a branch to scale the tree. But as we waited in anticipation, a gruff adult voice roared and pulled down the boy. For some time after that we heard cries and sobs. We felt sorry for the children that their parents were so harsh.

In the evenings, we would hear them sing bhajans, the clang of the cymbals tearing the silence. The next day when we realized they were playing near the wall, my cousin mimicked them, 'Jai Jagadish Hare . . .' In response, we heard giggles and then slowly, the bhajan again.

Encouraged, my cousin yelled, 'What are you guys playing?'

There were chuckles again, followed by silence. And then a boy ventured to reply: 'Journey Around the World.'

We'd never heard of such a game.

'Don't you read comics?' my cousin enquired.

The laughter this time suggested we were talking of forbidden activity.

'Shall we read out a comic to you? It has a mystery solved by Inspector Azad.'

The chortling at the other end meant we should. But no sooner had my cousin finished reciting a page in his pealing voice than we sensed that our audience wasn't reacting.

'Are you there?' 'Are you listening?'

In a few seconds we heard a loud protesting voice and a wail in the distance. 'Inspector Azaaaaad!'—a young girl was crying.

For many days we didn't hear them. We tried to read out new books at the top of our voices, but there was dead silence. And then for almost three vacations in a row we didn't get to see them. We visualized their peculiar holidays—not climbing trees, not reading comics, not shouting . . .

Gradually, the armchair that we sat in moved farther away from the wall. We plumped down and set out on another imaginary foray into the world of stories. Armchair, adj., the Merriam-Webster's reminds me, also means 'sharing vicariously in another man's experiences'.

*

Lament on the loss of creation

In the years that followed, snuggled in the armchair and many other seats, I have envisioned and inhabited the worlds of many a writer and filmmaker. But whenever I think of Basheer's armchair, my mind returns to the mystery of those children and to 'Mathilukal'.

'Mathilukal' (Walls), Basheer writes in the opening lines, is a little love story, which he had thought of calling 'A Woman's Fragrance'. Thank the Muse that the writer's second thoughts prevailed, for the epiphanies and reflections that follow are rendered more illuminating through that metaphor. In the light-footed style of a diarist, the narrator begins the tale with his imprisonment on the charge of sedition during the last days of the British rule. Once inside, he is surrounded by men, virile or servile, and by high walls. Every essential commodity is rationed or difficult to get in this world of brute force and isolation. Yet, he finds ways of occupying himself—sometimes creative, sometimes ingenious; slitting matchsticks into four for future use, rearing a vegetable garden, chasing a squirrel or writing stories for the lifers. He also talks to plants and trees.

One day he hears the laughter of a woman from across the wall that separates women prisoners. He had heard it the first day when he was being brought to his cell but the warder mocked at him, believing it was the pangs of bachelorhood that made him pay attention to such sounds.

The woman of his imagination is there after all.

Narayani responds to his whistles and a friendship blossoms. She even knows he has tended a rose garden. How did you know, he asks, and she replies, 'This is prison. Everyone here knows everything. There are no secrets here.'

There are, well, no secrets except for their romantic exchanges from either side of the wall, their arrival signalled by a twig. Until, of course, they decide to meet and as if in an apogean moment, he is released from prison. Just as he is about to accept the most cheerful invitation of his life, he is shown out, only to wonder poignantly whether the free world is a bigger prison. Was it worthwhile then for the writer to endure the brush with romance?

It is here that Basheer hops past the mundane and lands in sublime territory. It is all clear now: the intrinsic value of freedom and the incidence of chance. When he gazes last, there is a twig reaching out from the other side of the wall. The heartbreaking inevitability of the brief relationship lingers all through, but it gets pronounced with the onset of freedom. Was the feeling a lie?

The woman is waiting, isn't she?

Is Basheer saying that when you dream, the cold vision of reality is as sure to follow as night follows day? Or is he hinting at the disengaging power of fortuitous relationships? Does happenstance necessarily end at the Lover's leap?

Something akin to the keening sense of lost ties when you end a railway journey. Once you hop off, the spirit of fellowship passes off in vapour. Or think of dull afternoons in strange towns, perhaps when looking vacuously out of windows from hotel rooms, when your imagination colours itself with fleeting sights and furtive glances at people down on the streets or in neighbouring blocks. Where the light catches a woman drumming her fingers on the parapet of her balcony. Or perhaps, beyond high walls where we can't see our neighbours. Whispers of stories lost across the frontiers of contemplation.

Our creations don't outlive the institutive process, my friend and namesake, the Kannada award-winning poet and writer Jayant Kaikini, once wrote. Once he writes a poem, the poet gets estranged from the creation. Basheer's narrator is fated to move on to a different space.

To us readers, of course, Basheer leaves myriad strands to pick up. How wide do we open the doors of perception, then? As much as you can, the writer seems to say. And like an expert raconteur, he leaves the story stranded at a dilemma, the soul journey at crossroads.

*

The crossing

But Adoor Gopalakrishnan had other ideas. He asked if Narayani existed in flesh and blood. In his film version of Basheer's story, he sees the love story as an exercise, albeit abidingly tragic, in creativity. Can a writer traversing the outbacks of imagination make a safe, and sane, return to the mainland, he asks.

In an earlier film, Adoor had tackled a protagonist who was ensconced in his own visions of an unchanging world. 'Elipathayam' (The Rat-trap) has Unni, the last surviving male descendant of a feudal family, not allowing any external force or system to penetrate his inner life. Regardless of the consequences, he lazes about in his imagined surroundings—the difference here from 'Walls' being that it is an atmosphere created for him over the generations. Snug in his armchair, he avoids meeting change face to face and drowns, literally, in his illusions. Eventually, the rat-trap springs shut and he falls prey . . .

The imagined space and circumstance in 'Mathilukal' is, however, constructed. Adoor concerns himself with the bond between the creator and the creation and thereby, goes beyond the love story. In his typical poetic and insightful manner, he combines the richness of Basheer's experience with metaphysical inquiry. Yet, on closer study, he isn't titivating Basheer's tale. Making no corrections in the narration, he sticks to the diarist's tone. How else can one get into the heart of the writer's thought process? If you tidied up a traveller's room, would you know what kind of a person he was?

Adoor's touch to the story attains a new dimension ahead of the conspicuous message about the limitations of freedom. And beyond Basheer's basic understanding of learning to accept the tragic. Basheer painted these ordinary pictures of life exhibiting his profound love for fellow beings. What made his story-telling more original was the vast treasure of experiences. Experience that constituted a three-course soul food. Having spent almost all of his youth wandering across the subcontinent and West Asia, he could tell stories in an intuitive sort of way and present emotional dilemmas with first-hand sincerity. He had been through it all—low life, political aspirations, prison life and asceticism. And when he rode the magic carpet, fundamental questions sprang up spontaneously.

Adoor, on the other hand, has been interested in the discrepancy between actions and imagined roles; of walls between people and places. He reads in 'Walls' the tale of an artist who transgresses physical imprisonment by weaving an object of fancy and gets ensnarled in the fantasy. Freedom in this context implies the mental space to create and boundaries are the purview of the artist's involvement with his creation.

Narayani here takes a life of her own. She is more than Basheer's cute little ploy. His sleight of hand not only gives her a vocal existence but also a purpose to crave for. And as the chain of anticipation keeps growing longer, the desire to flesh her out is acute.

The tragedy is that as Narayani leaps to freedom, the writer loses his liberty to create. He is humbled by the 'presence' of his creation. The moral: when we tremble excitedly over our inventive peregrinations, we must realize that the circling must end. It is one thing to scale imaginary heights and quite another to stay on that barrier, trying to straddle two worlds.

True, the strength of imagination and the strength of creation are equal. It is the freedom to imagine and thus create, that provides succour.

So, I often wonder, were the children behind the wall in my hometown better placed than us in their imaginative journeys?

Kerala Tourism

Karkitakam*

M.T. Vasudevan Nair

The rain in the months of Mithunam and Karkitakam is like a mother. It bursts out when you least expect it to, when you go close, thinking it is in a good mood. When the season of thunder and lightning sets in, it's not just going to school and coming back that is difficult, it's having to contend with hunger as well.

Once I had my kanji in the morning and went to school, I ate only after getting back home in the evening. For the first three or four days after Achan's moneyorder arrived, I was given two annas every day. After that, I starved at noon. When it struck one, a number of us would go to the back of Marar's restaurant to drink water. Marar used to fill the big idli vessel with water and place a large bell-metal glass next to it, for the children who had not brought lunch or snacks.

In the rainy season, it was always hunger that tormented me, never thirst.

By the time I walked the four miles to school, I would begin to feel hungry. By the fourth period, hunger would be raging inside me like a fire. And that was the moment when the fragrance of a dish being seasoned with mustard and chillies would waft in from the restaurant on the other side of the wall.

Most of the children jumped over the wall into Marar's restaurant when the bell rang. Some of them left their rice containers there in the morning. Others bought lunch there. Marar gave schoolchildren a concession. The villagers paid six annas for a meal but the schoolchildren paid only five. Rangan from Kalladathoor, Sivadasan from Kuttippalam, Vilakathra Govindan and I, we were the four who went there only to drink water. They said that O. Mohammed and P.

This story is taken from *The Demon Seed and Other Writings*, published by Penguin Books India.
* The lean monsoon month when food is scarce in the villages.

Mohammed had tea in the tea shop near the market.

By the afternoon, my hunger would have died down. I would no longer want to eat. It was not difficult to sit like a corpse until four o'clock. It was while going back that I would begin to feel hungry again. I would walk along wondering what curry there would be at home.

Govindan and I always went home together. During the monsoon, we would be wet by the time we came down the hill. No matter how we held our umbrellas, the water would steal in with the wind.

Rangan sometimes had a beedi with him. He would describe the delights of having a puff when it was cold, and I would feel greedy. But I did not have the guts to do anything wrong. For I was Thekkeppat Ammalu Amma's son. We were told that the villagers often said to one another, 'She's not rich, that woman, but her children have excellent character.' (It was Amma herself who told us they said this). After Rangan turned off, Govindan would be with me for the next two miles. Govindan was short and fat and wore a shirt and mundu. Only a few boys came to school in trousers. I was one of them.

Once Govindan turned off to his place, I would be alone. The thought of the bowl of kanji in the uri, the coir basket hanging in the kitchen, was enough for me to quicken my pace. What curry would there be? Jackfruit or plantain? If the jackfruit was from the tree behind the outhouse, it would be as soft as butter, and really delicious.

That day, the rain which started in the morning did not abate even when school gave over. I had to wring out the water from the hem of my trousers before I went into class. By noon, my shirt and trousers had more or less dried. My stomach ached.

It was easier to walk in the rain in the evening. We made our way home happily, splashing through the water.

I was completely drenched by the time I reached home. I placed my umbrella in the veranda, threw the packet of books held together by a black rubber band on the wooden ledge and went in, calling out as I usually did, 'Amme—'

Meenakshi Edathi's voice answered, 'Amma's gone next door.'

It was Amma who usually served my food. I did not like Meenakshi Edathi to serve me. She was a distant relative. She stayed with us and helped Amma with the housework. Cheriamma disapproved of her.

Amma would say, 'She's come to us because she doesn't have enough to live on, don't you see?'

'And we have enough paddy and money here, of course!' Cheriamma would say mockingly. 'That creature eats as much as four people eat,' she would add, taking care that Meenakshi Edathi did not hear her. Meenakshi Edathi's looks bore out Cheriamma's statement. She was a tall, stout woman with protruding teeth. She always left her breasts uncovered. When she went out, she would throw a small towel over her shoulders.

There was a little room in the house where the shakteya pooja was performed. Its doors were almost always kept closed. Meenakshi Edathi's body had the same odour which came out when the doors of this little room were opened.

Meenakshi Edathi would talk of this and that while she set out the plate for my kanji. I was always afraid that spittle would fall on me while she spoke. I would eat uneasily, reluctantly, when she served me.

I spread my shirt out on the bamboo pole hung up in the tekkini and heard Cheriamma reciting her prayers. This meant that she was back from her bath. Even during the monsoons, she bathed three times a day. And yet she would complain that her body smarted all the time. Cheriachan's nephew had laid a curse on her, that's why her body smarted.

Cheriamma took some vibhuti from the container hanging near the eastern window and made an obeisance to the household deity. As she went in to change into dry clothes I asked, 'Where's Amma, Cheriamma?'

'Who knows?'

Meenakshi Edathi was in the room next to the kitchen, chopping a plantain bulb. Had they had plantain bulb for lunch as well? It tasted best roasted, with powdered rice sprinkled over it before it was seasoned.

I pulled up a low stool, sat down and said, with a touch of annoyance, 'Serve the kanji, Meenakshi Edathi.'

Meenakshi Edathi continued to chop the plantain bulb and said, without looking up, 'The cat overturned the kanji today, child.'

I did not feel sad. I felt angry enough to kill her. How casually she had said that the cat had overturned the kanji.

Meenakshi Edathi said without looking at my face, 'Go and play, child. I'll give you some kanji before I drain the rice.'

This was something they usually did only during the harvest season, serving out a little kanji before the rice was drained for the evening meal. Amma considered it a despicable practice. Cheriamma had started it for Chandran and Kamalam. I would always refuse if I was asked whether I wanted some. How could I, a child with an exemplary character, do something so despicable?

And after all, Amma should be given an opportunity, should she not, to say, 'I've brought up two children as well. Let her learn from me.'

'Where's Amma?' I raised my voice. 'What a time to go wandering around.'

I could not scold Meenakshi Edathi. If Amma came, I could at least vent my temper on her.

'Amma will be back soon. Why don't you listen to me?'

As I waited with my hand on the half-wall of the kitchen, I caught sight of Muthassi. She was busy making a powder of little lumps of earth picked out of the fireplace, mixed with vibhuti and medicinal nuts. Whenever she had a cold, Muthassi would get one of us to rub this powder into her scalp.

The fire was not burning in any of the three hearths. Meenakshi Edathi must have realized this, for she said to me, 'Meenakshi Edathi will get everything ready for you in the wink of an eye.'

Muthassi caught sight of me and said, 'If there's palm jaggery, make him a glass of something to drink. He's not had anything after his kanji this morning.'

Meenakshi Edathi pretended that she had not heard.

I went to the front of the house. Cheriamma was seated near the pillar at the western end of the veranda with her legs stretched out, teasing out the knots in her hair.

'Where's Chandran?'

'They've both gone to Perassannoor.'

Chandran's and Kamalam's father's family house was in Perassannoor. He had died three years ago. He had given up his claims to his own family property in favour of his sisters and moved to our house. And he had died here.

'I asked them to go there for a visit. Let them have a break, even if it's only for three or four days.'

I heard Muthassi's racking cough from the northern room. She called out, 'Meenakshi—'

Meenakshi Edathi did not hear.

'If anyone is going to the bathing tank, tell them to take my towel and wash it.'

Cheriamma heard that.

'Couldn't the old woman have told us earlier? But no, she must wait till everyone has finished washing their clothes, bathing and all. Then she can start on her refrain to anyone who drops in : not a soul here to even wash a towel for me.'

Cheriamma said the last sentence in a voice that imitated Muthassi's hoarse one.

I sat on the front steps smouldering with anger against everyone. And saw Amma walking in from the southern courtyard. Which meant that she had not gone next door, to Thekkethu. She must have gone somewhere a little farther.

I did not look up. I kept doodling on the ground with a broomstick. I waited for her to say something so that I could explode.

'Couldn't you take off your wet trousers and wrap a towel around you?'

I did not say anything.

'Meenakshi—'

Amma sat in front of me, dangling her legs over the courtyard. When Meenakshi Edathi came in response to her call, she asked, 'Is there any coffee powder left?'

'I shook out the last of it to make coffee this afternoon.'

'Nothing will go right till we stop buying provisions from that Mappilla's shop,' Amma muttered.

It was just two days since Abdu had declared, when I went to his shop, that he could not give us any more credit until the accounts were settled.

'Has Achuthan come?'

Achuthan was my uncle, my mother's younger brother.

'I haven't seen him.'

'Um . . . so long as they get credit at the tea shop, men don't bother to find out how the house runs. Ask Kalyani from Vadakkethu to come here, Meenakshi.'

'What did Kunhathol of the illam say, Edathi?'

'She said she would try and give me something the day after tomorrow. I'm sure she will.'

'The woman is a miserly wretch.'

'Still, she's always been good to me. Imagine her not giving me a sack of rice when I ask for it. What an idea!'

Meenakshi Edathi prodded her, 'What about today? Shall I send someone to Gopalettan?'

'Phoo!' Amma waved her arms angrily, 'Gopalettan, indeed! It's better not to eat, then. When did people like him grow so big? Those women there think no end of themselves. After all, they were washing soiled clothes at Palakkal Menon's until yesterday, weren't they?'

Amma calmed down and repeated, 'Call Kalyani.'

Meenakshi Edathi left. I thought Amma would ask now if I had had my kanji. But she paid me no attention. Her eyes were fixed on Cheriamma, who was seated with her back to us on the western veranda. She was combing out the tangles in her hair and winding the broken strands around her fingers.

'Once women start to behave like her, only ruin will follow. Just look at her, every evening at dusk she sits in the front veranda to pull out the knots in her hair. And bits of hair fly all over the yard.'

As usual, Cheriamma did not seem to have heard.

I waited, ready for Amma to turn on me next.

'Haven't you had a bath?' Amma lowered her voice involuntarily. 'We didn't cook lunch today, child. It isn't that we forgot to keep something aside for you. The rice will be ready for dinner by the time you have your bath.'

When I did not move, Amma said, 'Run off now.'

The resentment and hunger that had been blazing inside me had already died down. I went in to look for a towel. Amma said, 'What's the use of his father struggling in some faraway place—'

The tank was in our neighbour's garden. It had filled completely in the Edavam rains and started to overflow into the fields. It had grown bigger because the earth at the sides had crumbled. The clump of thecchi that used to be on the bank was now in the water.

I came back from my bath and went to the kitchen on the pretext of finding out where to put away the worn bit of soap. A fire was burning in the hearth. Water was boiling in the big cooking pot. Meenakshi Edathi was cleaning the rice in the kitchen veranda, with Kalyanikutty next to her.

'This sack-rice has such a stench,' said Kalyanikutty. My heart filled with joy as Meenakshi Edathi washed the rice and transferred it to a small copper vessel.

'That's tonight's problem solved,' said Meenakshi Edathi. 'What about tomorrow?'

I stuck the morsel of soap in a crevice in the unplastered wall, from where it hung out like a dog's tongue, and went into the courtyard. Rain water had stagnated here and there. The calf lay in front of the cowshed, chewing cud. Flies hovered round a wound under its eyes. Its mother had fallen into a ditch during the rains last year and died. Meenakshi Edathi had gone to look for it first, then Achu Ammaman. Chakkan had been sent for in the morning. Chakkan plucked medicinal herbs for a living and there was no spot he did not know on the hillside. When he brought the news home that evening, everyone, including Muthassi, had wailed loudly. None of us at home had ever felt so sad, not even on the day that Cheriachan had died in the vadikkini.

I wandered around for quite some time, throwing stones into the banana grove behind the cowshed. Then I went to the veranda. Amma was still there. Kanakkrayi stood at the edge of the courtyard, his hand resting on the mouldy wall.

'We've lost this year's crop as well. If it continues to rain like this, we'll have nothing but chaff.'

'I've forgotten the time when we used to harvest enough paddy to last us for four full months.'

'That's how it is when times are bad.'

Kanakkrayi put on his umbrella-hat and was about to leave by the western gate when Cheriamma asked, 'Kanakkrayi, do you have betel leaves in your house? I couldn't get hold of anyone to send to the shop.'

I looked at Amma. It made Amma furious when Cheriamma asked someone from a lower caste for betel leaves or tobacco.

Kanakkrayi examined the bundle at his waist, took out a torn betel leaf and placed it on the edge of the veranda.

'I have only this withered piece.'

Cheriamma picked it up and went in. Cheriamma could manage without food but not without betel leaves. If there were no areca nuts, she managed with coconut palm roots. I had seen her give away paddy stealthily at harvest time, without telling Amma, in exchange for betel leaves and tobacco.

Kalyanikutty came out and sat down by Amma.

'How much did you get?'

'Three nazhis.'

'M . . . m . . . How will people who live off their daily rations have anything to spare?'

'Why don't you send someone to Kothalangatel, Malu Edathi? I heard they had bought four sacks of rice.'

'They'll give us some if we ask. And then proclaim it to the whole world the next day. Even if they starve, I want my children to be able to hold up their heads proudly before everyone.'

Amma started as usual on her figures.

Achan sent forty rupees a month. Most months, Ettan sent ten rupees.

'I get exactly fifty rupees on the first of every month. And I have to feed all these wretches on that.'

The wretches Amma spoke of included Achu Ammaman, Cheriamma, Cheriamma's children and Meenakshi Edathi.

'Didn't the children from across the river come this year?'

She meant Achu Ammaman's children, who lived on the other side of the river. In the month of Karkitakam, they made frequent visits to our house. They would stay for about a week each time, and when they left, Muthassi would invite them to come back soon, in a day or two.

Muthassi often talked about how difficult things were for Achu Ammaman's children. As soon as she began, Cheriamma would scold her, 'No one can be as partial as this old woman. She's always telling us about the problems those children have, the ones who live across the river. I have two children of my own, don't I? And Edathi has a twelve-year-old son. Does she ever call them to her, talk to them? But when those children are here, the old woman has no rheumatic aches or pains, no wheezing. She spends all her time giving them baths, washing their clothes, putting them to bed.'

What Cheriamma said was not completely true. Muthassi always called me to her if she heard me cough. She would rub the powder she stored in an earthenware pot into my scalp and ask me to hold my finger to my nose and breathe deeply.

Amma would rebuke Cheriamma, 'At least we harvest a nazhi of grain now and then. Don't you know that those people have to buy rice three hundred and fifty days a year?'

Chandran and Kamalam made frequent visits to Perassanur in Karkitakam. And Achu Ammaman's children came and stayed here often. Only I never went anywhere, because Achan's house was too far away, in Andathode. You had to go twenty-five miles by bus. And then by boat.

Kalyanikutty began to recount bits and pieces of village gossip. Amma ordered her to sweep the yard.

We went to Andathode only when Achan came home. Not that Amma liked to go even then. She did not like Achamma, my father's mother. Evidently, Achamma told people that Achan was so busy looking after his wife's family that he neglected his mother and sisters and their families.

Kalyanikutty looked very pretty when she tucked the end of her mundu into her waist and swept the yard. Her hair, tied in a knot at the end, would fall over her shoulder and almost trail on the ground, and her red glass bangles would tinkle.

It was only three years later, though, that I realized that Kalyanikutty was beautiful.

As I sat there, leaning against the pillar, trying to calculate how long it would take for the rice to be cooked, and listening to the tinkle of glass bangles, Kalyanikutty suddenly stopped sweeping, looked towards the gate and said, 'Who's that, Malu Edathi? I think he's coming here.'

I looked in that direction. Yes, he was coming here. It was someone wearing a shirt. Amma moved over to peer at him.

He came in though the gate and climbed the front steps to the veranda. I recognized him . . .

'Amme, it's Sankunni Ettan.'

'Which Sankunni Ettan?'

'Sankunni Ettan from Andathode.'

'Oh, God!' said Amma agitatedly to Kalyanikutty, 'run to the kitchen and ask them to drain whatever rice there is.'

Sankunni Ettan smiled, showing his big rotten teeth. He folded his umbrella and asked in his woman's voice, 'So, Ammayi, do you recognize me?'

'Sankunni? What a rare visitor! Come in. Unni, bring him some water.'

'I'll get it myself.'

Just as well, I thought, when Sankunni Ettan went to the end of the veranda and washed his feet with the water kept there. Imagine me, studying in the seventh class in school, bringing him water to wash his feet!

'Spread the fine grass mat for him, Unni.'

'I'll sit here, Ammayi.'

'No, you mustn't sit there.'

Sankunni Ettan hung his old umbrella with the bamboo handle on the rafter and sat down on the wooden ledge of the veranda.

'You're coming from Andathode?'

'Yes.'

'Anything the matter?'

'Oh, no. I've been wanting to come and see you and the children for a long time, Ammayi. I couldn't manage it earlier.'

'I'm glad you feel that way.'

Amma asked about Achamma and Achan's sisters. And about everyone in Sankunni Ettan's house.

'Which class is Unni in now?'

I said without looking at his face, 'The seventh.'

I had never liked looking him in the face. His face was pock-marked. He grinned all the time, for no reason, showing his rotten, disgusting teeth. He was a distant nephew of Achan's. We used to meet him when we went to Achan's house, that was all. He appeared there only when Achan or his younger brother were home on leave. Ammini Oppu and Lakshmi Oppu, Achan's sisters, used to remark in his hearing that he always hung around when Achan was there and was never seen afterwards.

He used to perform tasks like pounding rice, drawing water from the well and buying provisions from the bazaar.

I slipped into the house. Meenakshi Edathi was draining the rice. Kalyanikutty had left.

'Who's come, Unni?'

'Sankunni Ettan. You know, the one from Andathode.'

'I ran to hundreds of places to get three nazhis of rice. And then someone turns up to be fed!'

Meenakshi Edathi spoke loud enough for everyone to hear. Amma came in and said angrily, 'Shut your mouth, you wretch. We don't have to let everyone know how hard up we are.'

Meenakshi Edathi straightened the cooking pot and scraped the rice grains stuck to the lid back into it.

'What if it's only Sankunni, he's a man and he's come from Andathode. He'll go back and tell hundreds of people how he visited his aunt's house. You're a heartless creature. I tell you, so long as it's someone from Andathode, I don't care even if he's a low-caste Parayan, we have to show him courtesy. I have my own dignity to think of when I visit them.'

Meenakshi Edathi of the long tongue kept quiet.

Amma always scolded everyone, including Achu Ammaman. No one found fault with her, since it was Achan who had cleared all the debts after the family property was divided. It was because Achan sent money regularly that these wretches were able to survive.

'Unni, go and get an anna's worth of pappadam from the Chettichi's house. Tell them I'll send the money tomorrow. On your way, ask Kanakkrayi's boy to come here quickly. Meenakshi, tell him to pluck a good, mature coconut from the tree when he comes. We'll make a coconut chutney. How can we give someone from Andathode just a plantain bulb curry? Ask Kalyani to give us a drop of coconut oil.'

In the midst of all her commands and instructions, Amma remembered to say, 'Don't break the pappadams into bits. Fry them whole, otherwise it will look miserly.'

I stood there looking at the drained rice in the cooking pot and the vessel below it, full of pale yellow, steaming hot kanji from which rose an unpleasant odour.

Had Meenakshi Edathi forgotten that I had not had any kanji?

What if I told her I was thirsty? Pride would not allow me to say I was hungry.

I thought to myself as I walked to the Chettichi's house, it's good that Sankunni Ettan is here. There would be pappadams and coconut chutney for dinner. I imagined the flavour of rice mixed with a little salt and the oil in which the pappadams had been fried, and my mouth watered. I would have to coax Meenakshi Edathi to give me some of the oil secretly.

When I got back, Sankunni Ettan had taken off his shirt and folded it. Amma was talking to him.

She would have to wait until the rains were over to dismantle the thatched roof and lay tiles. Two jackfruit trees had been set apart for the wood for the frame. 'After all, the money we would use to thatch the house for four successive years will be enough to tile it. Govindankutty always writes and tells me that.'

Obviously Amma had Achan's house in mind. It was big and new and had a tiled roof.

'This house is not as small as it looks from outside. There's such a lot of space inside. It's like a palace, we need to employ someone just to sweep and mop the floors. That Meenakshi keeps it free of cobwebs and termites. How can I manage all this by myself?'

Sankunni Ettan grunted assent at regular intervals in his woman's voice.

Amma continued to talk about Ettan's job, Achan's monthly moneyorder, my great intelligence and how much she would spend on the feast on the day the roof was laid. Outside, the sky had darkened again. Dusk had fallen early.

'Don't you want a bath, Sankunni?'

'Yes.'

'Unni, ask Meenakshi to bring a towel and some vaka powder from that new earthen pot in the storeroom. And get Sankunni a little sesame-seed oil in a bowl . . . You'll find some in a jar in the southern room.'

Cheriamma was busy spreading a mattress on the floor of the vadikkini. She wanted to lie down all the time. She said her body smarted as if chillies had been ground and smeared over it. Every evening she would shake out her mattress and spread it afresh.

Muthassi's bedroom was very dark. The jar of oil was under her bed.

'What are you looking for?'

'The oil.'

'For whom?'

'Sankunni Ettan is here. From Andathode.'

'From Andathode?' Muthassi's voice was full of respect. It was no small event, someone coming from Andathode. Anyone even remotely related to Achan was described as belonging to Andathode.

The lid of the jar was covered with a cloth. Another piece of cloth dipped in kerosene had been wound around the neck of the jar to prevent ants from getting into it. I lifted the jar, took it to the door and opened it. There was very little oil in it.

We bought a nazhi of oil from the mappilla oil man who came every month. On Sundays, I was given a small spoonful to have an oil bath. I had to smear the oil over my body without spilling a single drop. Amma did not like to use coconut oil for her hair, that is why she bought sesame oil. The nazhi of oil she bought was meant to last a whole month.

I realized I had poured out too much. Only the lees remained in the jar.

When I came into the veranda with the oil, Amma's eyes were full of reproach.

Sankunni Ettan wrapped the towel Meenakshi Edathi had brought him around his waist, crumpled up his mundu and tucked it into the rafters. He began to smear the oil methodically over his body. Even after he had oiled his hair and body generously, half the oil was left over. Amma's silent anger was directed entirely at me.

I had not thought that Sankunni Ettan would sprinkle the vaka powder kept for him on a piece of paper into the remaining oil. He let the powder soak in the oil, rolled it into a ball and pressed it into his palm. Swinging his arms, he asked,

'Where's the tank, Unni?'

I'm not sure why, but Amma did not ask me to show him the way.

I went to the edge of the southern courtyard and pointed it out. 'You have to go that way.'

Meenakshi Edathi lit the lamp and showed it to everyone.

'Unni must be very hungry,' said Amma, speaking to me and

Meenakshi Edathi together.

I pretended not to hear.

'We'll eat as soon as it grows dark.'

Amma picked up the piece of paper in which the vaka powder had been wrapped, mopped up the oil that had dripped on the ground with it and threw it away, grumbling all the while to herself, 'The cost of oil now! But we can't let anyone say we were mean to visitors from Andathode.'

Why was she saying all this to me? All I was aware of was the flavour on my tongue of rice mixed with the oil in which pappadams had been fried. I waited, watching slivers of darkness gather like little dark-skinned Cheruman children amongst the banana trees.

Sankunni Ettan came back from his bath to the eastern veranda, took his mundu down from the rafters, put it on and patted his hair into place with his hands. He handed me his wet towel.

I heard Achu Ammaman coming. You could hear him coming from a great distance because he belched loudly. A digestive problem, too much acidity.

'Who is that?' asked Achu Ammaman hesitantly.

'From Andathode,' said Amma.

Achu Mama's voice suddenly grew soft. 'Who?'

'Sankunni.'

Sankunni Ettan washed his feet, came up and sat down on the wooden veranda seat.

'How come you found your way here?'

Sankunni Ettan stood up.

'Sit down, go on, sit down.'

So Achu Ammaman too had great respect for the visitor from Andathode.

And all this respect was for the Sankunni Ettan who usually hung around Achan's kitchen yard picking his gums, waiting hungrily for Ammini Oppu to call him in to eat.

Achu Ammaman belched loudly and lit a beedi. 'What's all the news from your side?'

Swinging his legs, Sankunni Ettan said, 'Nothing much. Just thought I'd come and find out how Ammayi and the children are doing.'

'I've been wanting to come that way for a long time. I'll do it when my brother-in-law is here. I wanted to worship at Guruvayoor as well.'

It grew dark early in Karkitakam. A kerosene lamp was lit and hung on the nail on the front veranda wall. The oil lamp in front of the puja room went out and the odour of the burnt wick hung in the air for a moment.

Amma called out as she went in, 'Haven't they got a chimney yet in Vappu's shop for the lamp in the big veranda, children?'

I had nothing to study today, since it was Friday. Usually, I sat with my books at this time every day. Except Friday, when I had all of Saturday and Sunday before me.

It had started to drizzle outside. I lay down against the wall of the western veranda. Achu Ammaman was describing a fish curry he had eaten at Andathode once, when he was on a visit there.

I could hardly hold my head up, I was so sleepy. The cool breeze made the hair on my body stand on end.

I heard Amma's voice again in the veranda.

'Achuthan, are you going to have a bath?'

'No. I've been having this persistent cold after the rains started. I'll just have a wash.'

'Come on then, Sankunni, and eat.'

The wooden ledge creaked when Sankunni Ettan got up.

'Where's Unni?'

'He'll eat later. He ate as soon as he came from school.' Sankunni Ettan followed the chimney lamp and Amma inside.

At that moment I really wanted to cry.

I could hardly stand up, but I managed to. I went to the front veranda. Insects fluttered around the kerosene lamp on the wall. An insect that had fallen accidentally into the lamp squirmed inside the glass. I crept into the dark tekkini and hovered at its northern door like a thief. Sankunni Ettan was seated in the kitchen on a grass mat with his legs crossed. There was a mound of steaming rice on the big banana leaf in front of him. Sankunni Ettan crumbled a pappadam for the stray cat standing next to him and started to eat with relish.

Amma said, 'There's been no fish in the sea after the rains set in. The curries are not very good, Sankunni.'

I went back to the front veranda. If only I could make myself think of something else, I would not feel so hungry. I thought of the Kalladathoor temple festival. And about Rangan's rubber wire hanging from the roof in class. And about the time I had escaped Veeraraghavan Master's needle-sharp pinches. Then everything went dark.

I opened my eyes to see Meenakshi Edathi standing in front of me with a lamp. 'Come on, are you already asleep?'

We went past Sankunni Ettan who was seated on the eastern veranda smoking a beedi. I heard him belch. It was not the kind of belch caused by indigestion. It was like the sound that emerged from Pandi the cow when someone filled her basket with karuka grass.

Amma was in the kitchen, seated by the chimney lamp. I took the small stool which was kept against the wall and sat down on it. Meenakshi Edathi brought me a bowl. It was filled with the water drained from the smelly rice.

I did not look up. Amma whispered, as if telling me a secret, 'There's no rice, child.'

Meenakshi Edathi's heels made a sharp sound against the floor as she walked.

'Tell her that she should have coaxed her nephew to eat some more. She kept forcing more on him, even when he said he had had enough. She could have at least kept a handful of rice aside after she drained it, to add to his kanji water now.'

I had never heard Meenakshi Edathi talk so arrogantly before. Amma bent her head and said quietly, 'Talk softly, Meenakshi. Don't you know I have to continue to face the Andathode people?'

I swallowed three or four mouthfuls of the kanji water and felt like throwing up. I took a bite of the salted plantain bulb. The kanji water refused to go down my throat. I got up and washed my hands.

I lay down as usual near Amma in the tekkini, but could not sleep. I could hear Sankunni Ettan snoring in the front veranda. Meenakshi Edathi, who lay on a mat near Amma's feet, tossed and turned. Hunger prowled inside me like a blazing torch, like steaming vapour, like a gentle ache. From time to time I thought I would lose consciousness, then I would suddenly open my eyes. I could hear Muthassi's racking cough and the sound of crickets in the distance. The croak of the frogs in the field grew so loud sometimes that it seemed next to my ears. Then it would drift away.

'Are you asleep, Meenakshi?' asked Amma.

'Um . . . m . . .'

'Ameena Umma will have money. Go and ask her for two rupees in the morning. Tell her I'll pay her back when Unni's father sends me money. I have to give Sankunni at least two rupees when he goes back tomorrow.'

Meenakshi Edathi did not respond.

'And I can't give him just the bus fare. Where can I get hold of some tea in the morning?'

Meenakshi Edathi did not answer.

'Whether he leaves or not, I have to give him a glass of tea in the morning, don't I? When people come from Andathode, we have to show them courtesy, don't we?'

Amma waited for a while, then said, 'How quickly you fall asleep, Meenakshi.'

Sankunni Ettan's snores glided around me like a snake in the cold darkness.

I closed my eyes and lay on my face. Pulling one half of her big shawl over me, Amma patted me and said, 'Poor boy, he's asleep. Guruvayoorappa, all I want is for him to sleep soundly.'

The sound of the raindrops on the banana leaves was like the thudding of drums. I heard thousands of musical notes flowing out of the secret lairs of the black Karkitakam night. But where could I find sleep lurking amongst them?

—*Translated from the Malayalam by Gita Krishnankutty*

The voice

Suresh Menon

There is football; there is Marxism; there is Onam, there is Vishu, Christmas and Ramzan. And like a golden thread running through all this, there is Yesudas. Malayalis who have nothing else in common share him with pride. When a CEO mocks his secretary with 'thamasamenthey varuvan . . .' (why are you so late in the coming?), he knows it sounds ludicrous, he is taking the song out of context, but both realize its import. Nothing further need be said, the CEO has made his point in a language the secretary identifies with. Thus it is wherever Malayalis live. Yesudas is the common currency. Malayali Samajams around the world measure their effectiveness by the number of times they are able to organize a Yesudas concert. Sometimes there are two or three in the same city (because, the legend goes, if you have two Malayalis you already have three opinions); they can't agree on anything except Yesudas. He is part of the collective consciousness of a people.

Malayalis have similar stories about how they first wooed their wives and girlfriends with his songs; they can remember their first rejections whenever they hear other songs; their eyes cloud over when they hear him singing songs about mothers or sisters (the scenes in the movies where these occur might be tacky beyond measure, but that hardly matters). And, naturally enough for a man who has sung over 40,000 songs (not all of them in Malayalam), there is one for every situation. Songs of innocence and songs of experience. When, approaching his sixtieth year, Yesudas made a foray into experimental, fusion music, and actually sang in English for a South American composer, newspaper columnists expressed strong views. If there is such a thing as a state treasure in Kerala, it is Yesudas. It could be a terrible burden to carry, but the singer himself carries it lightly. Early one morning at his Tiruvanmiyur residence in Chennai, he put it in perspective for me. 'Music brings people together,' he explained. 'And if mine does, then that is the force of the music. I am merely an instrument of a higher power.' Sincerity rescues the statements from being mere platitudes. Yesudas is aware of his power, of what it means to be the best-known Malayali from a region in the country that has produced scientists, writers, sportsmen and artists of international stature. Even a Head of State, K.R. Narayanan. Equally, he is humbled by the thought of being so many things to so many people. 'They bring me love everywhere,' he says of Malayalis of the Indian diaspora. 'It means that I feel at home wherever I am.' The reverse is equally true. Most Malayalis feel at home wherever they are in the world the moment a Yesudas song wafts through the music system.

It is said of great sportsmen that they are incapable of an ugly stroke; Yesudas is incapable of an ugly note. He is among the most-photographed of people. The thick hair, the beard, the soft mouth and sensitive eyes speak of a man who is at peace with himself. He has taught himself Sanskrit and a host of other languages in which he sings. In the seventies and eighties, much was made of his dodgy accent when he sang Hindi songs. Yet, he delivered some of the most memorable songs of that period, from Ni sa ga ma pa ni (for the movie 'Anand Mahal' which never saw the light of day) to Jub deep jale aana ('Chitchor'). When Amitabh Bachchan, reigning king of Hindi cinema, used his voice for 'Alaap', Rajesh Khanna, the deposed king used him for 'Majnoon'. The first movie flopped, the second was never released. It didn't bother Yesudas, whose constituency was in the south. When S.P. Balasubrahmaniam, one of the most talented singers the country has ever produced, performed with Yesudas, he thought it was 'a privilege to sing with this genius'. The two most successful singers in India have forged a relationship that goes beyond their profession. 'He is my brother,' says Yesudas of the younger man.

Through four decades of being the Voice, Yesudas stuck to what he is best at. He kept his feet and vocal chords above all turmoil, political or otherwise. Malayalis somehow find that reassuring; they like their icons to be apolitical, above the strife, as it were. When Prem Nazir, world record holder with over 800 films as hero, entered politics, he was roundly defeated in an election. Malayalis loved him for what he was, not for what he could be. So it is with Yesudas. His early struggles are now part of folklore. His attempts at breaking religious barriers have made it possible for Kerala to move towards true secularism. He is strongly identified with Sabarimala, and Lord Ayyappa. In mid-2001, when he gave his first concert at London's Royal Albert Hall, there was a request for a song: 'Guruvayoor ambala nadayil oru diwasam njan pogum . . .' ('I will pray at Guruvayoor temple some day . . .'). Born a Christian, he is denied entry to the holiest Krishna temple in Kerala. He accepts the situation with a mixture of humour and humility that is his hallmark. The humour comes from triumphing over the slings and arrows of outrageous fortune that might have destroyed a lesser man. The humility from a deep sense of understanding that he is not just the gifted one, but the chosen one.

'God chose me, and I am grateful for that,' he says, matter-of-factly.

This is a man who is aware of his talent, and its source. It is a lesson he hopes to pass on to his children, who live in the lap of luxury. 'I tell them of my past, of my struggles,' he says, 'All this (pointing to his house, his many awards) didn't spring from nowhere. I want them to have their feet firmly on the ground.' In the Yesudas book of virtues, level-headedness is high on the list, alongside love for parents and family, and the conviction that the fear of the Lord is the beginning of wisdom. These were the virtues that sustained him through his days of trial.

Born in Cochin on 10 January 1940, Yesudas, Slave of the Lord, had his first guru in his father Augustine Joseph, a popular singer and stage actor. Their house in Cochin was open to friends and relatives without discrimination. Then, as the actor fell on bad days, the visitors dried up. When Yesudas gives life to the philosophical lyrics of men like Vayalar, he doesn't have to dig too deep within himself for the emotion. His is a life lived hard. If method acting is an accepted technique in the actor's repertoire, Yesudas's 'method singing', bringing to the surface emotions from experiences few go through, probably places him at a level others cannot reach. It is not something the singer dwells on.

'I don't analyse my singing,' he says, adding, 'Perhaps I think about these things before or after a song, but when I sing I just get carried away by the moment.'

And yet it might have all been so different. Now, with nearly half a century of public performances behind him, it might be difficult to imagine a Yesudas being lost to the world. Talent will out, we will tell ourselves, and feel vindicated by Yesudas's career. But it could have gone wrong. For one, Yesudas nearly had to drop out of music college because he didn't have the money to pay his fees; for another, when a film director, K.S. Anthony, came seeking a fresh voice for his movie 'Kalpadukal' (Footprints), it was Yesudas's friend Vaikom Chandran he wanted to use. But Chandran suggested Yesudas's name, and that was how it began.

Yesudas sang in the movie about 'One caste, one religion, one god,' which considering his state then, dripped with irony. His Christianity made him unacceptable among Brahmins who dominated Carnatic music. And curiously, in 1961, when the song was recorded, those words from the Kerala reformer Sree Narayana Guru had already become his life's creed. Advaita, the philosophy, was born in Kerala; in Yesudas it found a modern evangelist. 'I keep in touch with Chandran,' says Yesudas. 'He has the run of my house; he visits me when I am in Kerala, or I visit him. To this day I don't know what made him suggest my name when the director came seeking him.' On such chance encounters are great careers built. When Yesudas decided to come to Madras to seek his fortune, his friend, a taxi driver, gave him a lift to the railway station and lent him a few rupees. In Madras, he often drank tap water to fill his stomach, and simply tightened his mundu when even that didn't help. 'Today I tease my wife about it, asking her if she would have married me had she met me in my tap-water-drinking days.' It is necessary to be able to laugh at such personal misfortune to come to terms with it, he says. Sitting in his room, surrounded by the photographs of his gurus, and his many awards and citations, it is hard to believe this man had to struggle at all. How could they not know once he opened his mouth to sing that they were in the presence of a blessed one?

Recalling those days, his eyes, soft and expressive at all times, can't keep the irony out. Semmangudi Srinivasa Iyer, the doyen of Carnatic music, allowed him to stay in his car shed. Yesudas repaid the kindness by cleaning the car everyday. There was no question of entering the house or being fed anything the great singer and his family might eat. Years later when Yesudas, now a star, visited Semmangudi, he was received with all the respect and excitement his status now deserved. He was fed and feted, and given a choice of drinks—tea, coffee or Horlicks. Years of privation having sharpened his sense of irony, Yesudas might have been forgiven for speculating on the difference a cup of tea or a glass of Horlicks might have made to his life some years earlier in the car shed.

'I was never alone, I had my dreams for company,' Yesudas recalls. Did the suffering test his faith, cause him to question the path he had chosen to follow, a path where music was his god? No, he says, adding gently, 'Just because you or I can't see the pattern does not mean that a pattern does not exist.' This is the Yesudas of today speaking, a man at the top of his profession, an area where spirituality is what matters. He breaks off at concerts on occasions to deliver a lecture on god, and on the many ways of realizing him. There is no rancour today. He sees the early suffering—Trivandrum All India Radio decided his voice was not good enough for radio—as part of the 'necessary pain' that man has to go through to make any achievement worthwhile.

It was only when Chembai Vaidyanatha Bhagawathar placed a ponnadai (shawl) on him at a concert that the more liberal among the classical singing community (read: Brahmins) began to accept Yesudas. The singer was determined to plough a lonely furrow. On the one hand he was a popular singer, on the other a serious Carnatic musician who put in hours of practice everyday. He gives two different types of concerts, therefore—as a popular musician and as a classical one. As a cricket fan, he cannot be unaware of the cricketing analogy— it is as if he is a leading player in both one-day cricket and Test cricket. 'Classical music is where all music begins, as well as what all music aspires to,' he says before going into a highly personalized (and picturesque) explanation of what the musical notes mean to him.

'Sometimes I am accused of making classical music too accessible by my style of singing. I take that as a compliment. If I can have the ordinary man humming pavanaguru or vatapiganapathim, then that is an achievement.' The two-way traffic initiated by Yesudas must rate as one of his most important contributions to music: on the one hand raising the tenor of popular music by using classical techniques, and on the other making classical music accessible by using popular techniques. It is useful to remember that in the Western classical tradition, the distinction didn't exist. Mozart's music was popular; it was played in bars and the marketplace during his lifetime.

'I try not to record any movie songs during the music festival season in Chennai,' says Yesudas. That is, December-January. He is a sought-after performer in all the sabhas. There is another reason too. 'I tend to get angry and a bit impatient when recording some of the modern songs, and I like to keep my mind clear during the period,' he says.

In recent years, the sabhas have been paying obeisance to mammon. Sponsors have made passes available to their near and dear ones, resulting in much noise off-stage. Often children run about in the auditorium, unmindful of the performance on stage. At a recent show, Yesudas hit a high note, kept it there, and chided these children (and their parents) in an aside. Point made, he went back to the note and continued where he had left off. It was sheer genius. So too was his performance at the Royal Albert Hall in London.

'I sensed the presence of the many gifted musicians who had performed there before me,' he recalled. 'I thought of my gurus, I thought of all the things that had to fall in place before I could get there. Once the concert started, my mind was clear of everything else.' And when he sang the hit from the movie *Nadi*, he threw a bridge across generations. Many who were children in the sixties when the song was first aired are now in positions of authority in the UK. The identification was complete. They had gone through school and college, early jobs and marriage and children, but the song hadn't changed. Neither had the singer. Like many Yesudas songs, it helped the listener find a mooring. In *Remembrance of Things Past*, Marcel Proust has his hero's memories flooding back to him on tasting a kind of cake with his coffee. The smell, the taste, brought it all back. For Malayalis the world over, a Yesudas song does the same thing. Memories come flooding back. It is impossible to listen to 'alliyambal . . .' Without being transported away from the present. This is incidentally one of Yesudas's own five favourite songs (the others are kannuneermuthumai, manikyaveenayumayen, parijatham and pramadavanam).

Curiously, these are some of the favourites of the modern generation too. Sons hearing their fathers sing (every Malayali is at least a bathroom singer) accept these songs as part of their own lives . . . and so it goes on.

'I am like a child playing with pebbles on the sand with the vast ocean of music in front of me,' says Yesudas, trying to put his achievements in perspective. Perhaps. But for the rest, he has provided a glimpse into divinity. To paraphrase Goethe, when the mind is at sea, an old song provides a raft.

Mattancheri in Manhattan

Ayyappa Panikker

The Yogi, who revised ever so little
the map drawn on the walls of the urinal
by the night-walkers of the mind,
picked his teeth with his imagination.
His armpit swallowed the tip of the dhoti
that wrapped his friend who scratched his bum;
the boy who watched the pendulum swing
was convinced it was twelve on the clock.
Looking for week-end fortunes,
the cat came today—not a mere tomcat;
stones and thorns are there: like greed
writhing in the flesh sticking to bones.
We thought it was just fiction that
once at an extreme moment of need
Sage Shankara turned into Amaruka,
sat down in suspense and held his breath.

The buses have all left. The wick of light
at the jetty has been put out. Kunjiraman's
bidi shop is shrunk and shut, the city smells
embrace and hug his nostrils never shut.
The piece of bread smeared with grease
and the shrivelled testes of the old bull
Mudaliar chews at length and swallows,
softened by beer in the dining hall.
The mongrel roams looking for company;
its feet pursue the paths it fancies.

This poem is taken from *Days and Nights*, published by National Educational Research Centre, Thiruvananthapuram.

School girls who have broken the hymen
lie around with their legs entangled.
Thanks to the devil, there is some link
with clothes around the shrinking waist.

Hair and breasts loose, with these scents
clutter on the road the flower children.
Dream within sleep or sleep within dream?
O do not tell me the truth, please; cover
the six-fold philosophical visions of
your breasts with a bark: mere humans are we.
Over the ebb tide flutters the sanitary napkin
thrown by the baby moon from the mansion.
The land tapers towards the backwaters;
partners in their sleep keep humming.
Although Wall Street maintains vigil,
the trade winds are hit by nightmare talk.
Standing on his head, the madman watches
the Empire State at his feet with scorn.

The girl slumbers at home, the wild snake
having tasted the street boy crosses over
freedom's altar aided by drugs in a lotus posture.
All ancient tales are stuck in the throat
of the snake whose eyes are ears too,
but if you dance a round on it, will vultures
sprout wrath in their beaks, talons and eyes?
See the scientist dancing across the waves
when the sea rages, with his forked tongue
shooting at the wind-swept festoon of water drops.

The moor's last sigh

Salman Rushdie

In August 1939 Aurora da Gama saw the cargo vessel *Marco Polo* still at anchor in Cochin harbour and flew into a rage at this sign that, in the interregnum between the deaths of her parents and her own arrival at full adulthood, her unbusinesslike uncle Aires was letting the reins of commerce slip through his indolent fingers. She directed her driver to 'go like clappers' to C-50 (Pvt) Ltd Godown No. 1 at Ernakulam dock, and stormed into that cavernous storehouse; where she momentarily stalled, unnerved by the cool serenity of its light-shafted darkness, and by its blasphemous atmosphere of a gunny-sack cathedral, in which the scents of patchouli oil and cloves, of turmeric and fenugreek, of cumin and cardamom hung like the memory of music, while the narrow passages vanishing into the gloom between the high stacks of export-ready produce could have been roads to hell and back, or even to salvation.

(Great family trees from little 'corns: it is appropriate, is it not, that my personal story, the story of the creation of Moraes Zogoiby, should have its origins in a delayed pepper shipment?)

There were clergy in this temple too: shipping clerks bent over clipboards who went worrying and scurrying between the coolies loading their carts and the fearsomely emaciated trinity of comptrollers—Mr Elaichipillai Kalonjee, Mr V.S. Mirchandalchini and Mr Karipattam Tejpattam—perching like an inquisition on high stools in pools of ominous lamplight and scratching with feathered nibs in gigantic ledgers which tilted towards them on desks with long, stork-stilty legs. Below these grand personages, at an everyday sort of desk with its own little lamp, sat the godown's duty manager, and it was upon him that Aurora descended, upon recovering her

This extract is taken from *The Moor's Last Sigh*, published by Jonathan Cape.

composure, to demand an explanation of the pepper shipment's delay.

'But what is Uncle thinking?' she cried, unreasonably, for how could so lowly a worm know the mind of the great Mr Aires himself? 'He wants family fortunes to drownofy or what?'

The sight at close quarters of the most beautiful of the da Gamas and the sole inheritrix of the family crores—it was common knowledge that while Mr Aires and Mrs Carmen were the incharges for the time being, the late Mr Camoens had left them no more than an allowance, albeit a generous one—struck the duty manager like a spear in the heart, rendering him temporarily dumb. The young heiress leaned closer towards him, grabbed his chin between her thumb and forefinger, transfixed him with her fiercest glare, and fell head over heels in love. By the time the man had conquered his lightning-struck shyness and stammered out the news of the declaration of war between England and Germany, and of the skipper of the *Marco Polo*'s refusal to sail for England—'Possibility of attacks on merchant fleet, see'—Aurora had realized, with some anger at the treachery of her emotions, that on account of the ridiculous and inappropriate advent of passion she would have to defy class and convention by marrying this inarticulately handsome family employee at once. 'It's like marrying the dratted driver,' she scolded herself in blissful misery, and for a moment was so preoccupied by the sweet horror of her condition that she did not take in the name painted on the little block of wood on his desk.

'My God,' she burst out when at last the white capitals insisted on being seen, 'it isn't disgraceful enough that you haven't got a bean in your pocket or a tongue in your head, you had to be a Jew as well.' And then, aside: 'Face facts, Aurora. Thinkofy. You've fallen for a bloody godown Moses.'

Pedantic white capitals corrected her (the object of her affections, thunderstruck, moon-struck, dry of mouth, thumping of heart, incipiently fiery of loin, was unable to do so, having been deprived anew of the power of speech by the burgeoning of feelings not usually encouraged in members of staff): Duty Manager Zogoiby's given name was not Moses but Abraham. If it is true that our names contain our fates, then seven capital letters confirmed that he was not to be a vanquisher of pharaohs, receiver of commandments or divider of waters; he would lead no people towards a promised land. Rather, he would offer up his son as a living sacrifice on the altar of a terrible love.

And 'Zogoiby'?

*

'Unlucky.' In Arabic, at least according to Cohen the chandler and Abraham's maternal family's lore. Not that anyone had even the most rudimentary knowledge of that faraway language. The very idea was alarming. 'Just look at their writing,' Abraham's mother Flory once remarked. 'Even that is so violent, like knife-slashes and stab-wounds. Still and all: we also have come down from martial Jews. Maybe that's why we kept on this wrong-tongue Andalusian name.'

(You ask: But if the name was his mother's, then how come the son . . .? I answer: Control, please, your horses.)

'You are old enough to be her father.' Abraham Zogoiby, born in the same year as deceased Mr Camoens, stood stiffly outside the blue-tiled Cochin synagogue—*Tiles from Canton & No Two Are Identical*, said the little sampler on the ante-room wall—and, smelling strongly of spices and something else, faced his mother's wrath. Old Flory Zogoiby in a faded green calico frock sucked her gums and heard her son's stumbling confession of forbidden love. With her walking-stick she drew a line in the dust. On one side, the synagogue, Flory and history; on the other, Abraham, his rich girl, the universe, the future— all things unclean. Closing her eyes, shutting out Abrahamic odour and stammerings, she summoned up the past, using memories to forestall the moment at which she would have to disown her only child, because it was unheard-of for a Cochin Jew to marry outside the community; yes, her memory and behind and beneath it the longer memory of the tribe . . . the White Jews of India, Sephardim from Palestine, arrived in numbers (ten thousand approx.) in Year 72 of the Christian Era, fleeing from Roman persecution. Settling in Cranganore, they hired themselves out as soldiers to local princes. Once upon a time a battle between Cochin's ruler and his enemy the Zamorin of Calicut, the Lord of the Sea, had to be postponed because the Jewish soldiers would not fight on the Sabbath day.

O prosperous community! Verily, it flourished. And, in the year 379 CE, King Bhaskara Ravi Varman I granted to Joseph Rabban the little kingdom of the village of Anjuvannam near Cranganore. The copper plates upon which the gift was inscribed ended up at the tiled synagogue, in Flory's charge; because for many years, and in defiance of gender prejudices, she had held the honoured position of caretaker. They lay concealed in a chest under the altar, and she polished them from time to time with much enthusiasm and elbow-grease.

'A Christy wasn't bad enough, you had to pick the very worst of the bunch,' Flory was muttering. But her gaze was still far away in the past, fixed upon Jewish cashews and areca-nuts and jack-fruit trees, upon the ancient waving fields of Jewish oilseed rape, the gathering of Jewish cardamoms, for had these not been the basis of the community's prosperity? 'Now these come-latelies steal our business,' she mumbled. 'And proud of being bastards and all. Fitz-Vasco-da-Gamas! No better than a bunch of Moors.'

If Abraham had not been knocked sideways by love, if the thunderbolt had been less recent, he would in all probability have held his tongue out of filial affection and the knowledge that Flory's prejudices could not be argued away. 'I gave you a too-modern brought-up,' she went on. 'Christies and Moors, boy. Just hope on they never come for you.'

But Abraham was in love, and hearing his beloved under attack he burst out with the observation that 'in the first place if you look at things without cock-eyes you'd see that you also are a come-lately Johnny', meaning that Black Jews had arrived in India long before the White, fleeing Jerusalem from Nebuchadnezzar's armies five hundred and eighty-seven years before the Christian Era, and even if you didn't care about them because they had intermarried with the locals and vanished long ago, there were, for example, the Jews who came from Babylon and Persia in 490–518 CE; and many centuries had passed since Jews started setting up shop in Cranganore and then in Cochin Town (a certain Joseph Azaar and his family moved there in 1344 as everybody knew), and even from Spain the Jews started arriving after their expulsion in 1492, including, in the first batch, the family of Solomon Castile . . .

Flory Zogoiby screamed at the mention of the name; screamed

and shook her head from side to side.

'Solomon Solomon Castile Castile,' thirty-six-year-old Abraham taunted his mother with childish vengefulness. 'From whom descends at least this one *infant* of Castile. You want I should begat? All the way from Señor Leon Castile the swordsmith of Toledo who lost his head over some Spaini Princess Elephant-and-Castle, to my Daddyji who also must have been crazy, but the point is the Castiles got to Cochin twenty-two years before any Zogoiby, so *quod erat demonstrandum* . . . And in the second place Jews with Arab names and hidden secrets ought to watch who they're calling Moors.'

Elderly men with rolled trouser-legs and women with greying buns emerged into the shady Jewish alley outside the Mattancherri synagogue and gave solemn witness to the quarrel. Above angry mother and retaliating son blue shutters flew open and there were heads at windows. In the adjoining cemetery Hebrew inscriptions waved on tombstones like half-mast flags at twilight. Fish and spices on the evening air. And Flory Zogoiby, at the mention of secrets of which she had never spoken, dissolved abruptly into stutters and jerks.

'A curse on all Moors,' she rallied. 'Who destroyed the Cranganore synagogue? Moors, who else. Local-manufacture made-in-India Othello-fellows. A plague on their houses and spouses.' In 1524, ten years after Zogoibys arrived from Spain, there had been a Muslim-Jewish war in these parts. It was an old quarrel to revive, and Flory did so in the hope of turning her son's thoughts away from hidden matters. But oaths should not be lightly uttered, especially before witnesses. Flory's curse flew into the air like a startled chicken and hovered there a long while, as if uncertain of its intended destination. Her grandson Moraes Zogoiby would not be born for eighteen years; at which time the chicken came home to roost.

(And what did Muslims and Jews fight over in the *cinquecento*?— What else? The pepper trade.)

'Jews and Moors were the ones who went to war,' old Flory grunted, goaded by misery into speaking a sentence too many, 'and now your Christian Fitz-Vascos have gone and pinched the market from us both.'

'You're a fine one to talk about bastards,' cried Abraham Zogoiby who bore his mother's name. 'Fitz she says,' he addressed the gathering crowd. 'I'll show her Fitz.' Whereupon with furious intent he strode into the synagogue with his mother scrambling after him, bursting into dry and shrieky tears.

*

About my grandmother Flory Zogoiby, Epifania da Gama's opposite number, her equal in years although closer to me by a generation: a decade before the century's turn Fearless Flory would haunt the boys' school playground, teasing adolescent males with swishings of skirts and sing-song sneers, and with a twig would scratch challenges into the earth—*step across this line*. (Line-drawing comes down to me from both sides of the family.) She would taunt them with nonsensical, terrifying incantations, 'making like a witch':

> *Obeah, jadoo, fo, fum,*
> *chicken entrails, kingdom come.*
> *Ju-ju, voodoo, fee, fi,*
> *piddle cocktails, time to die.*

When the boys came at her she attacked them with a ferocity that easily overcame their theoretical advantages of strength and size. Her gifts of war came down to her from some unknown ancestor; and though her adversaries grabbed her hair and called her jewess they never vanquished her. Sometimes she literally rubbed their noses in the dirt. On other occasions she stood back, scrawny arms folded in triumph across her chest, and allowed her stunned victims to back unsteadily away. 'Next time, pick on someone your own size,' Flory added insult to injury by inverting the meaning of the phrase: 'Us pint-size jewinas are too hot for you to handle.' Yes, she was rubbing it in, but even this attempt to make metaphors of her victories, to represent herself as the champion of the small, of the Minority, of *girls*, failed to make her popular. Fast Flory, Flory-the-Roary: she acquired a Reputation.

The time came when nobody would cross the lines she went on drawing, with fearsome precision, across the gullies and open spaces of her childhood years. She grew moody and inward and sat on behind her dust-lines, besieged within her own fortifications. By her eighteenth birthday she had stopped fighting, having learned something about winning battles and losing wars.

The point I'm leading up to is that Christians had in Flory's view stolen more from her than ancestral spice fields. What they took was even then getting to be in short supply, and for a girl with a Reputation the supply was even shorter . . . in her twenty-fourth year Solomon Castile the synagogue caretaker had stepped across Miss Flory's lines to ask for her hand in marriage. The act was generally thought to be one of great charity, or stupidity, or both. Even in those days the numbers of the community were decreasing. Maybe four thousand persons living in the Mattancherri Jewtown, and by the time you excluded family members and the very young and the very old and the crazy and infirm, the youngsters of marriageable age were not spoiled for choice of partners. Old bachelors fanned themselves by the clocktower and walked by the harbour's edge hand in hand; toothless spinsters sat in doorways sewing clothes for non-existent babies. Matrimony inspired as much spiteful envy as celebration, and Flory's marriage to the caretaker was attributed by gossip to the ugliness of both parties. 'As sin,' the sharp tongues said. 'Pity the kids, my *God*.'

(*Old enough to be her father*, Flory scolded Abraham; but Solomon Castile, born in the year of the Indian Uprising, had been twenty years her senior, *poor man probably wanted to get married while he was still capable*, the wagging tongues surmized . . . and there is one more fact about their wedding. It took place on the same day in 1900 as a much grander affair; no newspapers recorded the Castile-Zogoiby nuptials in their social-register columns, but there were many photographs of Mr Francisco da Gama and his smiling Mangalorean bride.)

The vengefulness of the spouseless was finally satisfied: because after seven years and seven days of explosive wedlock, during which Flory gave birth to one child, a boy who would perversely grow up to be the most handsome young man of his dwindling generation, caretaker Castile at nightfall on his fiftieth birthday walked over to the water's edge, hopped into a rowing-boat with half a dozen drunken Portuguese sailors, and ran away to sea. 'He should have known better'n to marry Roary Flory,' according to contented bachelor-spinster whispers, 'but wise man's brain don't come automatic along with wise man's name.' The broken marriage came to be known in Mattancherri as the Misjudgment of Solomon; but Flory blamed the Christian ships, the mercantile armada of the omnipotent west, for tempting her husband away in search of golden streets. And at the age of seven her son was obliged to give up his father's name; unlucky in fathers, he took his mother's unlucky Zogoiby for his own.

After Solomon's desertion, Flory took over as caretaker of blue ceramic tiles and Joseph Rabban's copper plates, claiming the post with a gleaming ferocity that silenced all rumbles of opposition to her appointment. Under her protection: not only little Abraham, but also the parchment Old Testament on whose ragged-edged leathery pages the Hebrew letters flowed, and the hollow golden crown presented (Christian Era 1805) by the Maharaja of Travancore. She instituted reforms. When the faithful came to worship she ordered them to remove their shoes. Objections were raised to this positively Moorish practice; Flory in response barked mirthless laughs.

'What devotion?' she snorted. 'Caretaking you want from me, better you take some care too. Boots off! Chop chop! Protectee Chinee tiles.'

No two are identical. The tiles from Canton, 12" X 12" approx., imported by Ezekiel Rabhi in the year 1100 CE, covered the floors, walls and ceiling of the little synagogue. Legends had begun to stick to them. Some said that if you explored for long enough you'd find your own story in one of the blue-and-white squares, because the pictures on the tiles could change, were changing, generation by generation, to tell the story of the Cochin Jews. Still others were convinced that the tiles were prophecies, the keys to whose meanings had been lost with the passing years.

Abraham as a boy crawled around the synagogue bum-in-air with his nose pressed against antique Chinese blue. He never told his mother that his father had reappeared in ceramic form on the synagogue floor a year after he decamped, in a little blue rowing-boat with blue-skinned foreign-looking types by his side, heading off towards an equally blue horizon. After this discovery, Abraham periodically received news of Solomon Castile through the good offices of the metamorphic tiles. He next saw his father in a cerulean scene of Dionysiac willow-pattern merrymaking amid slain dragons and grumbling volcanoes. Solomon was dancing in an open hexagonal pavilion with a carefree joy upon his blue-tile face which utterly transformed it from the dolorous countenance which Abraham remembered. If he is happy, the boy thought, then I'm glad he went. From his earliest days Abraham had instinctive knowledge of the paramountcy of happiness, and it was this same instinct which, years later, would allow the grown-up duty manager to seize the love offered with many blushes and sarcasms by Aurora da Gama in the chiaroscuro of the Ernakulam godown . . .

Over the years Abraham found his father wealthy and fat in one tile, seated upon cushions in the Position of Royal Ease and waited upon by eunuchs and dancing-girls; but only a few months later he was skinny and mendicant in another twelve-by-twelve scenario. Now Abraham understood that the former caretaker had left all restraints behind him, and was oscillating wildly through a life that had deliberately been allowed to go out of control. He was a Sindbad seeking his fortune in the oceanic happenstance of the earth. He was a heavenly body which had managed by an act of will to wrench itself free of its fixed orbit, and now wandered the galaxies accepting whatever destiny might provide. It seemed to Abraham that his father's breakaway from the gravity of the everyday had used up all his reserves of will-power, so that after that initial and radical act of transformation he was broken-ruddered, at the mercy of the winds and tides.

As Abraham Zogoiby neared adolescence, Solomon Castile began to appear in semi-pornographic tableaux whose appropriateness for a synagogue would have been the subject of much controversy had they come to anyone else's notice but Abraham's. These tiles cropped up in the dustiest and murkiest recesses of the building and Abraham preserved them by allowing mould to form and cobwebs to gather over their more reprehensible zones, in which his father disported himself with startling numbers of individuals of both sexes in a fashion which his wide-eyed son could only think of as educational. And yet in spite of the salacious gymnastics of these activities the ageing wanderer had regained his old lugubriousness of mien, so that, perhaps, all his journeys had done no more than wash him up at the last on the same shores of discontent whence he had first set forth. On the day Abraham Zogoiby's voice broke he was gripped by the notion that his father was about to return. He raced through the alleys of the Jewish quarter down to the waterfront where cantilevered Chinese fishing nets were spread out against the sky; but the fish he sought did not leap out of the waves. When he returned in despondency to the synagogue all the tiles depicting his father's odyssey had changed, and showed scenes both anonymous and banal. Abraham in a feverish rage spent hours crawling across the floor in search of magic. To no avail: for the second time in his life his unwise father Solomon Castile had vanished into the blue.

*

I no longer remember when I first heard the family story which provided me with my nickname and my mother with the theme of her most famous series of paintings, the 'Moor sequence' that reached its triumphant culmination in the unfinished, and subsequently stolen masterpiece, *The Moor's Last Sigh*. I seem to have known it all my life, this lurid saga from which, I should add, Mr Vasco Miranda derived an early work of his own; but in spite of long familiarity I have grave doubts about the literal truth of the story, with its somewhat overwrought Bombay-talkie *masala* narrative, its almost desperate reaching back for a kind of authentification, for *evidence* . . . I believe, and others have since confirmed, that simpler explanations can be offered for the transaction between Abraham Zogoiby and his mother, most particularly for what he did or did not find in an old trunk underneath the altar; I will offer one such alternative version by and by. For the moment, I present the approved, and polished, family yarn; which, being so profound a part of my parents' pictures of themselves—and so significant a part of contemporary Indian art history—has, for those reasons if no other, a power and importance I will not attempt to deny.

We have reached a key moment in the tale. Let us return briefly to young Abraham on hands and knees, frantically searching the synagogue for the father who had just abandoned him again, calling out to him in a cracked voice swooping from bulbul to crow; until at length, overcoming an unspoken taboo, he ventured for the first time in his life behind & beneath the pale blue drape with golden hem that graced the high altar . . . Solomon Castile wasn't there; the teenager's flashlight fell, instead, upon an old box marked with a Z and fastened with a cheap padlock, which was soon picked; for schoolboys have skills which adults forget as surely as lessons learned by rote. And so, despairing of his absconded father, he found his mother's secrets out instead.

What was in the box?—Why, the only treasure of any value: viz., the past, and the future. Also, however, emeralds.

*

And so to the day of crisis, when the adult Abraham Zogoiby charged into the synagogue—*I'll show her Fitz,* he cried—and dragged the trunk out from its hiding-place. His mother, pursuing him, saw her secrets coming out into the open and felt her legs give way. She sat down on the blue tiles with a thump, while Abraham opened the box and drew out a silver dagger, which he stuck in his trouser-belt; then, breathing in short gasps, Flory watched him remove, and place upon his head, an ancient, tattered crown.

Not the nineteenth-century circlet of gold donated by Maharaja Travancore, but something altogether more ancient was the way I heard it. A dark green turban wound in cloth rendered illusory by age, so delicate that even the orange evening light filtering into the synagogue seemed too fierce; so provisional that it might almost have disintegrated beneath Flory Zogoiby's burning gaze . . .

And upon this phantasm of a turban, the family legend went, hung age-dulled chains of solid gold, and dangling off these chains were emeralds so large and green that they looked like toys. *It was four and a half centuries old, the last crown to fall from the head of the last prince of al-Andalus; nothing less than the crown of Granada, as worn by Abu Abdallah, last of the Nasrids, known as 'Boabdil'.*

'But how did it get there?' I used to ask my father. How indeed? This priceless headgear—this royal Moorish hat—how did it emerge from a toothless woman's box to sit upon the head of Abraham, future father, renegade Jew?

'It was,' my father answered, 'the uneasy jewellery of shame.'

I continue, for the moment, without judging his version of events: When Abraham Zogoiby as a boy first discovered the hidden crown and dagger he replaced the treasures in their hiding-place, fastened the padlock tight and spent a night and a day fearing his mother's wrath. But once it became clear that his inquisitiveness had gone unnoticed his curiosity was reborn, and again he drew forth the little chest and again picked the lock. This time he found, wrapped in burlap in the turban-box, a small book made up of handwritten parchment pages crudely sewn together and bound in hide. It was written in Spanish, which the young Abraham did not understand, but he copied out a number of the names therein, and over the years that followed he unlocked their meanings, for instance by asking innocent questions of the crotchety and reclusive old chandler Moshe Cohen who was at that time the appointed head of the community and the keeper of its lore. Old Mr Cohen was so astonished that any member of the younger generation should care about the old days that he had talked freely, pointing towards distant horizons while the handsome young man sat wide-eyed at his feet.

Thus Abraham learned that, in January 1492, while Christopher Columbus watched in wonderment and contempt, the Sultan Boabdil of Granada had surrendered the keys to the fortress-palace of the Alhambra, last and greatest of all the Moors' fortifications, to the all-conquering Catholic Kings Fernando and Isabella, giving up his principality without so much as a battle. He departed into exile with his mother and retainers, bringing to a close the centuries of Moorish Spain; and reining in his horse upon the Hill of Tears he turned to look for one last time upon his loss, upon the palace and the fertile plains and all the concluded glory of al-Andalus . . . at which sight the Sultan sighed, and hotly wept—whereupon his mother, the terrifying Ayxa the Virtuous, sneered at his grief. Having been forced to genuflect before an omnipotent queen, Boabdil was now obliged to suffer a further humiliation at the hands of an important (but formidable) dowager. *Well may you weep like a woman for what you could not defend like a man,* she taunted him: meaning of course the opposite. Meaning that she despised this blubbing male, her son, for yielding up what she would have fought for to the death, given the chance. She was Queen Isabella's equal and opposite; it was *reina Isabel's* good fortune to have come up against the mere cry-baby, Boabdil . . .

Suddenly, as the chandler spoke, Abraham curled upon a coil of rope felt all the mournful weight of Boabdil's coming-to-an-end, felt it as his own. Breath left his body with a whine, and the next breath was a gasp. The onset of asthma (more asthma! It's a wonder I can breathe at all!) was like an omen, a joining of lives across the centuries, or so Abraham fancied as he grew into his manhood and the illness gained in strength. *These wheezing sighs are not only mine, but his. These eyes hot with his ancient grief. Boabdil, I too am thy mother's son.*

Was weeping such a weakness? he wondered. Was defending-to-the-death such a strength?

After Boabdil handed over the keys to the Alhambra, he diminished into the south. The Catholic Kings had allowed him an estate, but even this was sold out from under his feet by his most trusted courtier. Boabdil, the prince turned fool. He eventually died in battle, fighting under some other kingling's flag.

Jews, too, moved south in 1492. Ships bearing banished Jews into exile clogged the harbour at Cádiz, obliging the year's other voyager, Columbus, to sail from Palos de Morguer. Jews gave up the forging of Toledo steel; Castiles set sail for India. But not all Jews left at once. The Zogoibys, remember, were twenty-two years behind those old Castiles. What happened? Where did they hide?

'All will be told in good time, my son; all in own good time.'

Abraham in his twenties learned secrecy from his mother, and to the annoyance of the small band of eligible women of his generation kept himself to himself, burrowing into the heart of the city and avoiding the Jewish quarter as much as possible, the synagogue most of all. He worked first for Moshe Cohen and then as a junior clerk for the da Gamas, and although he was a diligent worker and gained promotion early he wore the air of a man in waiting for something, and on account of his abstraction and beauty it became commonplace to say of him that he was a genius in the making, perhaps even the great poet that the Jews of Cochin had always yearned for but never managed to produce. Moshe Cohen's slightly too hairy niece Sara, a large-bodied girl waiting like an undiscovered sub-continent for Abraham's vessel to sail into her harbour, was the source of much of this speculative adulation. But the truth was that Abraham utterly lacked the artistic spark; his was a world of numbers, especially of numbers in action—his literature a balance-sheet, his music the fragile harmonies of manufacture and sale, his temple a scented warehouse. Of the crown and dagger in the wooden box he never spoke, so nobody knew that that was why he wore the look of a king in exile, and privily, in those years, he learned the secrets of his lineage, by teaching himself Spanish from books, and so deciphering what a twine-bound notebook had to say; until at last he stood crown-on-head in an orange evening and confronted his mother with his family's hidden shame.

*

Outside in the Mattancherri alley the enlarging crowd grew murmurous. Moshe Cohen, as community leader, took it upon himself to enter the synagogue, to mediate between the warring mother and son, for a synagogue was no place for such a quarrel; his niece Sara followed him in, her heart slowly cracking beneath the weight of the knowledge that the great country of her love must remain virgin soil, that Abraham's treacherous infatuation with Aurora the infidel had condemned her for ever to the dreadful inferno of spinsterhood, the knitting of useless bootees and frockies, blue and pink, for the children who would never fill her womb.

'Going to run off with a Christian child, Abie,' she said, her voice loud and harsh in the blue-tiled air, 'and already you're dressing up like a Christmas tree.'

But Abraham was tormenting his mother with old papers bound up 'twixt twine and hide. 'Who is the author?' he asked, and, as she remained silent, answered himself: 'A woman.' And, continuing with this catechism: 'What was her name?—Not given.—What was she?— A Jew; who took shelter beneath the roof of the exiled Sultan; beneath his roof, and then between his sheets. Miscegenation,' Abraham baldly stated, 'occurred.' And though it would have been easy enough to feel compassion for this pair, the dispossessed Spanish Arab and the ejected

Spanish Jew—two powerless lovers making common cause against the power of the Catholic Kings—still it was the Moor alone for whom Abraham demanded pity. 'His courtiers sold his lands, and his lover stole his crown.' After years by his side, this anonymous ancestor crept away from crumbling Boabdil, and took ship for India, with a great treasure in her baggage, and a male child in her belly; from whom, after many begats, came Abraham himself. *My mother who insists on the purity of our race, what say you to your forefather the Moor?*

'The woman has no name,' Sara interrupted him. 'And yet you claim her tainted blood is yours. Have you no shame to make your mummy weep? And all for a rich girl's love, Abraham, I swear. It stinks, and by the way, so do you.'

From Flory Zogoiby came a thin assenting wail. But Abraham's argument was not complete. *Consider this stolen crown, wrapped in rags, locked in a box, for four hundred years and more. If it was stolen for simple gain, would it not have been sold off long ago?*

'Because of secret pride in the royal link, the crown was kept; because of secret shame, it was concealed. Mother, who is worse? My Aurora who does not hide the Vasco connection, but takes delight; or myself, born of the fat old Moor of Granada's last sighs in the arms of his thieving mistress—Boabdil's bastard Jew?'

'Evidence,' Flory whispered in reply, a mortally wounded adversary pleading for the death-blow. 'Only supposition has been given; where are hard-fast facts?' Inexorable Abraham asked his penultimate question.

'Mother, what is our family name?'

When she heard this, Flory knew the coup-de-grâce was near. Dumbly, she shook her head. To Moshe Cohen, whose old friendship he would, that day, forsake for ever, Abraham threw down a challenge. 'The Sultan Boabdil after his fall was known by one sobriquet, and she who took his crown and jewels in a dark irony took the nickname also. Boabdil the Misfortunate: that was it. Anyone here can say that in the Moor's own tongue?'

And the old chandler was obliged to complete the proof. '*El-zogoybi.*'

Gently, Abraham set down the crown beside defeated Flory; resting his case.

'At least he fell for a pushy girl,' Flory said emptily to the walls. 'I had that much influence while he was still my son.'

'Better you go now,' said Sara to pepper-odorous Abraham. 'Maybe when you marry you should take the girl's name, why not? Then we can forget you, and what difference between a bastard Moor and a bastard Portugee?'

'A bad mistake, Abie,' old Moshe Cohen commented. 'To make an enemy of your mother; for enemies are plentiful, but mothers are hard to find.'

R. Prasanna Venkatesh/Wilderfile

Sesame seeds, flowers, water

Lalithambika Antherjanam

Amme! I have come back. It is your second death anniversary today. The handful of sacrificial rice I hold in my hand was invoked from the heavens into the sacred tree and then into this darbha grass. I mix it with sesame seeds, flowers and water and offer it to you. I pick up some more sesame seeds and flowers, then water and sandalwood paste. Will you accept this offering? For we have nothing else to give you now.

Have we really nothing else to give? I have thought about this ever since the day you left us. What if I pour all my memories into this offering of sesame seeds and water . . .? Have you really left us, Amme . . .? I feel you are always with us now. When you were alive, I did many things of which you disapproved, certain that you would forgive me. But now I pause before I do or say anything and ask myself: Would you have condoned this, could you have borne it? And so, Amme, I have at last become the kind of daughter you wanted me to be.

I often wanted to write about you. Would you have liked me to? You had kept the article and the poem I had written about Achan with such care, I found them in the sheaf of papers you handed over to me at the end. My horoscope was there too, and a notebook that contained pieces I had written as a child. I hope you will forgive my temerity— among the papers that I have collected to hand over to my children and grandchildren, I want to include this article, in which I recall you with deep emotion.

Is it possible to write about you? No, not really. This is not because I consider it difficult to express the greatness of motherhood. I think that era is over, and motherhood is no longer held in high esteem.

This extract is taken from *Cast Me Out If You Can*, published by Stree.

There are mothers who behave as if their children were mistakes that they should not have made. Still, everyone has a mother, for the age of test-tube babies has not yet arrived. There are all kinds of mothers, from those who love and chastise their children to those who expect to be compensated for the agony of childbirth. Motherhood is an eternal truth, and also an ordinary occurrence. Why then should a sixty-four-year-old woman like me mourn a mother who was over eighty when she died? I do not merely mourn you, Amme. I think, and remember, and the memories go back over six decades. I put them down here, Amme, as they spill out of my mind—for your daughter has this unfortunate habit of wanting to record everything she thinks and feels, since she happens to be a writer. I know you cannot read this with your mortal eyes. But I am certain that you will understand why I have to do this. After all, you told me yourself once that death opens the doors to all realms of knowledge.

I know of the deep emotional bond that exists between a mother and a child, even while the child is in the womb, for I am myself a mother of eight. We look forward to our children with intense hope and longing, and communicate with them powerfully at many levels— through contemplation, sight, touch, and the processes of thought. They claim us totally. We live in a state of being dominated by prayer and hope, almost like penance. Even when a woman conceives after having decided to have no more children, the baby begins to enchant the mother once it quickens in the womb. I was not your eldest child, Amme. But since I was born after you had lost two babies, I became dearer to you than if I had been your first. You always told me that the sex of the baby you carried within you never troubled you and that you did not care whether it was a boy or a girl, even when you ate the butter blessed in the temple, or chanted the special prayers that would ensure you bore a son. You wanted a baby so that you could be a mother, that was all. You wanted the child to live, to be intelligent. That is all you asked for when you prostrated yourself before the Devi, half an hour before the baby was born.

And so you had a child, a girl. She was not as fair-skinned as you, nor was she pretty. But she tried very hard to be clean and presentable. Although I did not fulfill many of your prayers and hopes, I did give you satisfaction in one respect: I was intelligent, and you always said

I had a prodigious memory. If I was told to learn four verses from the *Manipravalam*, I learned and recited fifteen. I learned everything you taught me, Amme, and this is still the basis of all I know (none of the bits of useless knowledge I gathered stayed with me). When I was a child, we used to recite akshara slokams and samasyas to each other. Whenever you told me a story, you asked me to repeat it to you. But you never imagined, even in your dreams, that I would become a writer, nor did you think of making me one.

All your life, you were afraid of other people, of what they would think or say. It made you very sad when I said it did not matter what they said or thought. But you were never afraid of imparting knowledge to me. My childhood companions were the books you gave me, the newspapers and magazines you filed away for me: *Bhashaposhini, Lakshmi Bai, Rasikaranjani, Atmaposhini*. You arranged them in meticulous order, from the earliest issues. You even kept issues of *Swadeshabhimani* for me because it was the paper that sparked a revolution in your youth. Its courageous editor and his family were held in great respect because they had opposed the government fearlessly and been punished for it. Indeed, the matter was discussed so passionately at home that your three-year-old daughter was heard to exclaim, 'What a pity the editor was exiled!' You kept copies of prohibited books like *Parappuram* and *Udayabhanu* for me until I was old enough to read them. Was it because your daughter had access to such books that she later walked so easily on dangerous terrain and became a rebel?

You talked to me about Sita and Savitri, Yashoda and Shilavathi. We played in the forest with the little Krishna and the incidents of the *Manipravalam* filled my thoughts. Dreams, imagination and expression were my world. I did not even recognize the occasional assaults reality made on that enchanted world for what they were.

As I grew up, I also watched you tremble in fear. Your very nature was to be frightened of 'don'ts.' I had long, thick hair like yours. I remember how sad you were that you could not weave jasmines and roses into my braid. In those days, it was a great sin for an unmarried namboodiri girl even to think of wearing fragrant flowers in her hair. Only her husband could put flowers in her hair, on the fourth day of the wedding, when they were alone together for the first time.

Tradition dominated you and you were terrified of calumny. You were afraid of the disapproval of your elders and teachers. I wore a skirt and blouse at home, but you made me take them off when we visited my uncle's house and insisted that I wear only a palm-leaf *konam* and a fine *mundu*, because you feared the grandmothers. You longed to send me to school, but could not. When your grandfather's brother was alive, he had sent you to school. No one had ever dared oppose him, for he was a powerful person with the authority to function as a *smartan* or a *vaidikan*. However, the school you went to was reserved for upper-caste children, in the precincts of the temple. Life was very different for your daughter, who was born in this forest fortress and who had to spend her life within it.

Every day, when my lessons were over, I came to you. We had only each other for company: me for you and you for me. Do you remember one of the amusing games we used to play? You recited a stanza and I had to guess the poet from its style. Then I would recite something and you would guess who had written it. And so they all joined us in our room: Venmani, Sivolli, Oravankara, Naduvam, Kunhukuttan, Ulloor, Vallathol. I recognized most of the poets from the nature of the poem. You sometimes recited one of your own verses, or one of Achan's, and I did not guess correctly. So the days went by.

Then Muthassan died. Achan became the head of the household. When Muthassi died, you became the head of the household. When I think of it now, I want to laugh and cry at the same time—how could a timid, submissive, docile woman like you command a huge extended family like ours, with its innumerable servants, guests and relatives? It was an unbearably sad situation for you. You had to cook and serve two or three *paras* of rice at every meal. No one was allowed to enter the kitchen except you. And if you left it, you could only go as far as the room of the deities. And of course there were babies every year. Even with a child in the womb and another at your breast, you worked tirelessly.

Our ways separated eventually. You went to the kitchen and I to the reading room. My reading material changed. I read day and night, pondered, dreamed. For the first time, our opinions began to differ. Over the next few years, you did not understand me, nor I you. I had the courage to rebel against the customs you feared. Even if you broke with tradition without meaning to, you trembled for the consequences. Do you remember how you screamed and ran away, the day you almost collided with the priest?

You had to rush all the time from the kitchen to the *nalukettu* in the course of your housework, a distance of about a furlong. One day, Kittan Potti entered with the rice from the *naivedyam* and, in your hurry, you almost ran into him. Both of you were terrified. Hardly aware of what you did, you screamed, 'Ayyo—' and ran away. You were worried. Had a man other than your husband touched you? Had he seen your face? That agonized 'Ayyo' was part of you.

You liked me to write, but I was careful never to show you what I wrote because I was convinced that I was doing something wrong. And I was worried that you would not like the things I wrote about. Once, the teacher who coached me at home slapped me because my sums were wrong. He then discovered a heap of poems I had written. After Achan and his brothers laughed over them, they gave them to you. You kept them under your mattress, to read them later. I hunted them out and burned them. You said sadly to me, 'So many people read them, and you still wanted to hide them from me.' I thought the whole world was my enemy. Whenever my opinions differed from yours, I was careful to keep the fact secret from you. I could not help it, Amme! I wanted another sort of life, with more freedom. I longed to move from the shade of the *anterjanam's* umbrella into the bright sunlight. You must have grieved very deeply when I finally did so, you, who screamed because Kittan Potti almost touched you! What hurt you most of all must have been my insistence on doing what I wanted to do, regardless of what others thought.

I often think of what one of the well-known writers of the younger generation said: 'Whenever I see my mother look as bewildered as a doe that has given birth to a monkey, it makes me laugh.' I cannot help it, Amme, the laughter is part of the dilemma I find myself in.

I remember the blend of shyness and pain with which you posed for a photograph when Achan dragged you to attend a meeting of the anterjanam's association. When Achan broke your bell metal bangles to give you golden ones instead, you sobbed uncontrollably, as if he had broken your mangalyasutram. That day, you did not eat till he gave you permission to wear a bell metal bangle with each of your gold ones.

I remember how you went to Kollam with Achan when he was sick, in a closely curtained car, and how, when you arrived there, you jumped into a well to have a dip because you believed you had been polluted by the journey. Tanks or wells were all the same to you—you were called a water creature when you were a child.

The day I abandoned the system of seclusion, you beat your head and wept. You lamented as if your daughter had died, or been cast out
. . .

So many memories stab my heart. Slowly, you became used to it all, and you came to terms with the times you lived in. You did many things that you once thought were sins. Once you even said to me, 'I hurt you so much that day, I believed I was concerned about what was good for you. It doesn't matter, everyone is happy now.' It doesn't matter, Amme. I hurt you very much too, and both of us shared the pain. And I think I was not hurt as deeply as you were. What matters is that we have the satisfaction that we achieved Sree Narayana Guru's ideal: 'What you do for your own happiness should ultimately make everyone happy.'

After Achan died, you lived like an ascetic, and now your mind was entirely on your children. Eventually, all human beings became your children. Your affection flowed equally over animals and birds, trees, and creepers. You would often give the rice served on your plate to someone who you thought was hungrier than you, and starve. You would tell us that it was against the rules of a fast to cook and eat again. When I was a child, I saw you observe five consecutive days of fasting because they happened to fall in a row—Monday, Ekadashi, Pradosham, full moon and Sivaratri, in that order. On all those days, you cooked and served the usual three paras of rice. All sorts of people enjoyed your hospitality—fugitives, escaped convicts, high officials and representatives of the people, the rich and the poor. The local schoolchildren wept bitterly when they heard of your death, and someone remarked, 'Our "care centre" is gone.'

I wanted some of your poems to be published for my sashtiabdapurthi, or sixtieth birthday. By that time, many of the pieces you had composed as a child had disappeared. Poems were for you flowers for the prayers that blossomed everyday. Poems of praise occurred to you when you stood before the deity for your daily worship, with your eyes closed. You forgot some of these verses later, others stayed in your memory. Many were in praise of the deities—Kasi Vishwanathan, Annapurna, Rama; but they wee not only on devotional subjects. You wrote a hymn that extolled the value of principles that went beyond religion and caste in your eighty-second year, and even recorded it for us.

You were born in the month of Medam, when the star Rohini coincided with Akshaya Triteeya. We completed the last day of that year's Saptaham in time for your sathabhishekam. When we all sat together that day, four full generations—you, your children, your grandchildren and your great-grandchildren—I suddenly noticed a difference in you that made me want to weep. There was an expression I could not define, in those eyes that had seen a thousand full moons. You seemed to have gone away from this world, to be beyond joys and sorrows. You said to us: 'Enough. No more. Let's stop now.'

Yes, it was true, you were ready to die. There is for death, as for birth, a state of ripeness, of maturity of age and experience. I agree that it is best for oneself and for others to die at that stage of life, and that was what you wanted. Why, then, did you force yourself to survive a whole week on a few drops of *thirtham*, denying yourself all food, without letting any of us know? You had a problem with your heart, and you had already become so weak physically. You were certain that you would die without falling ill, because you had never sinned. You had often told us that disease was a consequence of sin! We tried to argue, to tell you that Sri Ramakrishna Paramahamsa, Ramana Maharshi and other holy men like them had fallen ill during their lives and submitted themselves to medical treatment. And you had often said that the body is the first entity to which one owes a duty.

In the end you allowed modern medicine and its needles to inject new life into your veins. Meanwhile, you meditated on the infinite, the great universal power and, oblivious to physical exigencies, you lay as light and weightless as a sliver of rust floating upon water. It was as if you slipped back into your childhood in the month that remained. You told us so many stories of that time, about your grandfather's brothers, who were all scholars and poets, one of whom had received the Veerashrinkhala from the Maharaja. About the poems that one of the most learned amongst them wanted to teach his disciples, which you learned and could recite before they did, and how you were given a gold-bordered saree as a prize. About how your father married your mother—he came to your sister's wedding as the bridegroom's companion, heard a young girl sing somewhere in the inner rooms of the house and was enchanted by her voice. So he found out who she was and married her. You told us about all the poems that you and your friends wrote and recited, and about your childhood friend, Lakshmikutty Varasyar, the mother of Madassery Madhava Variar.

It shocked the doctor when you told him that it was really best for him to administer drugs that would ensure quick death for bodies that were wasted with age and disease.

You told me that the tulasi branches you had collected over the years and stored in the attic should be used to make your funeral pyre. The old box that had once held palm-leaf manuscripts was filled with blocks of sandalwood for the same purpose. You had stored enough Ganga water too, for the last ritual bath. You wanted everything finished as quickly as possible. You told me I was the only person who would have to cope with the loss of a mother, referring perhaps to the commonly accepted notion that both daughter and daughter-in-law are equally related to a mother. After speaking to me of all these things, you said, 'Go now. We will meet again if we are destined to, when my time comes.' And you allowed me to leave.

What is this thing called destiny, Amme? How is it decided? Tell me! What power brought me the news, to a place nearly one hundred and twenty-five miles away from where you were, at one o'clock on the night of 16 October 1971? Someone told me later that you called out to me at the very moment when I knew. I started by car before daybreak, and rushed to you. When I arrived, you had had your bath and drunk your *kanji*. You looked very happy when I saw you, with your hand resting on your great-grandson's head in blessing. I said, 'Amme, I am here.'

'Good! I knew you would come. I have so much to tell you. But I am so tired. I have finished now with this life. I have promised the Devi that I will offer her *payasam* made with five measures of milk if she grants me a quick death. You must make her that offering. And you must give Kali a mundu.'

You looked at your son-in-law and said, 'I will die today or tomorrow. Let her stay with me till then.'

You died that day. I promise to be born as your daughter again in my next life, Amme, to listen to all that you have to tell me. But will I have the good fortune to be born again as your daughter, Amme? Will you have to be born again at all, Amme? I know that you are going to be one with the Great Mother, just as you wished. Give me the vision to look at that Mother as my own, through all my successive lives.

Your lips murmured Bhagavan's name and your fingers moved ceaselessly to count the number of times you said it. You were quite conscious. You were radiant with an inner light. Then you opened your eyes, at five in the evening, and asked what time it was. You told me to open all the doors, light the lamps, and lay you down on the floor. The light of the setting sun suffused the room. Even so, Amme, I did not understand. Someone had brought me an issue of the *Malayalanadu* magazine that carried Madhavikkutty's autobiography. It lay on my lap as I looked at you. Suddenly, the horizon rumbled and the earth pitched around me. I have a heart ailment, and I had travelled a long distance. What did you murmur, was it 'water' or 'Narayana?' You swallowed a mouthful of Ganga water, shuddered, and drew a deep breath. Then there was utter quiet.

People began to gather. Telegrams were dispatched, cars drove up to the house. What had to happen had happened. The children had one more responsibility—performing the funeral rites. When I sat at the feet of your still body, wrapped in an unbleached mundu, I felt nothing. I did not want to cry, or sigh, or even pray. I felt numbed, beyond joy and sorrow, caught in the kind of cosmic stillness that marks the end of a *yuga* or an era. At the height of deep emotion there is a feeling of utter emptiness.

Was it only my physical weakness that had led me to imagine the roaring of the air around me? Was it my blood pressure? Or was it what you used to tell me it was, Amme, did the chariots of the divine messengers come to take you? Who knows! We can only guess the truth. The moment when God becomes a human being and then becomes God once again, that is the moment of death. All human beings are a part of God. But can all human beings enter into God?

Can the human soul (or human reality), which has moved from life in the world to the life beyond, come back? I don't want to think about it any more, Amme! I will never be able to find an answer, so let this question, which has been asked from the beginning of time, remain a question.

Before I end this piece, however, I must describe a very worldly incident that took place that night. Kali was a poor harijan who still believed in old traditions. Although the laws of untouchability had been abolished, she hesitated to come anywhere near us. She would stand in the courtyard, you would be in the veranda, and you would both talk for hours at this distance from each other. You had a very special affection for her—perhaps because she was the same age as the first baby you lost. Shaken by the news of your death, she rushed into the nalukettu, crying loudly, 'My *thampuratti*, I've lost everything I had!' She beat her head, fell senseless at the feet of the body and began to roll on the ground. Her relatives came and carried her away. What was the nature of Kali's bond with us? Is it amongst people like her that you will be born again?

I gave the Devi the offering of milk payasam that you had promised her, to ensure a quick death for yourself, Amme! And I gave Kali her mundu too.

An era ended with you, Amme. I don't think that I can ever be its representative, for each generation has its own individual reality. And yet, I too am a link in the hereditary chain of universal motherhood, which was established from the beginning of time and which reached down to you, Amme. Its nature has permeated my blood vessels, my senses, my life. I know that motherhood is a universal truth. And so let me place this offering of sesame seeds, flowers and water here with the courage and conviction that I have understood this truth, for the souls of all the mothers that have died, on behalf of all the mothers who are alive. Come, in the form of my mother, and receive it!

Translated from the Malayalam by Gita Krishnankutty

The garden of the antlions

Paul Zacharia

On a piece of land overrun by wild growth, by the shore of a stream, I lived like a chameleon in a bower of leaves, hiding and prowling, camouflaged and contented. My house was like a mound of dead leaves heaped among the vines and green foliage. Along the edge of the courtyard, crowded with weeds and grass, flourished my medicinal plants, as if some unseen power had rescued them from the jungle outside. Only I knew the dividing line between them and the jungle— and once, a little girl thief too!

The old wood of my walls had turned black, white and green, under the growth of moss and lichen. In a corner of the kitchen were two hearths, a few earthen pots and pans and two plates. On one flame I prepared medicated oils and liniments, and on the other lunch and dinner. The veranda had not been surfaced and polished with cowdung for years and was filled with dusty holes in which antlions had made their little pit-like wells, at the bottom of which they lay in wait for their lunch and dinner. When a good many wandering insects had vanished without a trace into the fine dust of these traps, as if into a bottomless abyss, an occasional antlion would climb out and saunter around. Watching them promenade in their garden—my veranda—I would try to imagine the solitude at the bottom of their dusty wells.

My favourite seat was at the base of a pillar that stood on a length of wood running along the edge of the veranda. The wood had become very smooth at the place where I usually sat and so had the pillar I leaned against, which gleamed invitingly with oil and sweat. Lounging against the pillar with my legs stretched along the wood, stroking my long beard which hid a stray silver hair or two, exuding a fine aroma

This story is taken from *Bhaskara Pattelar and Other Stories*, published by East West Books.

of liniments, oils and salves, I would await my patients. I loved patients.

I could hear each patient and his party from a distance as they made their way through my jungle, whispering, parting the leaves and shaking the branches. I would then get up from the veranda, go inside and watch them through the slit of the closed window as they entered my courtyard.

'O, Vaidyare,' they call in a low, hesitant voice. I do not answer. They stand there, regarding my shut doors anxiously. They call again, but all is silence. They speak amongst themselves in disappointment and continue to stare at my shut house. I whisper to no one in particular: 'The broken limb is patient, it is the mind that is impatient. Calm your minds, my dear fellow human beings!' I resume my vigil. They squat for a while in the courtyard, stand up again, clear their throats and call out, 'O, Vaidyare!' There is only silence. After a while one of them says, 'I don't think Vaidyar is coming out today. We'd better go!' Some patients go away with their companions. But a few refuse to leave. 'No, I am going to wait. You can go.'

On one occasion, the companions had thus gone away leaving behind in the courtyard a young man with a sprained arm. He stood there, listening miserably to their voices moving farther and farther away. He waited, lost and fearful, gazing expectantly at the silent face of my house. Then I opened the door and came out. 'Quickly, clap your hands!' I said. 'Clap so that your companions can hear you! Clap and call them back! Tell them that Vaidyar is here!' For a moment he stood gaping at me. Then, his face registering agony, he tried to raise his sprained right arm to clap, but it fell back limply. I shouted, 'Clap! Clap your hands and call them! They have to come back!' Once again he raised his sprained arm a little, but lowered it, unable to bear the pain. I clapped my own hands and said, 'Like this! Louder and louder!' He tried painfully to mimic the motions of my hands. Looking at his face and roaring with laughter, I clapped again. My clapping hands lent sound to his agonized mime. I clapped, looking at the rising moon. I clapped so that the yakshis atop the palmyra could hear me. I clapped towards the other-worldly visitors who prowled behind the clouds. 'Come down to these green leaves, to this soil, to this dusk. This is our earth! Come! Here is pain, and here is relief!'

Walking up to the young man, and standing behind him, I held his arms in my hands and made him clap, lifting, dropping and pushing his arms around. Flocks of homing birds glided above. Winds bent towards the sunset, swirled around us. The face of the early moon floated through the clouds like a ritual mask. And I heard, like the grand percussion of many drums, the footfalls of the antlions strolling along the garden of my veranda. I felt the young man's pain-racked body regaining strength in my arms. Crushing him in a bear hug, I led him to the veranda and sat him down. I kissed him on the crown of his head with my beard spreading all over his face. I said, 'You are healed. You can go now.' Under the moonlight, his body slipped away like a shadow through my herbs. Then I heard a sound from the path beyond the honeysuckle thickets, a message that came darting through the green leaves—a handclap. Jumping down into the courtyard, I too clapped loudly. His hands replied from beyond the stream. Then, through the distant coconut groves, the farewell claps faded. And I had even forgotten to pose him a riddle! In wonderment, I squatted on the moonlit lawn and burst out laughing.

Except for patients, the only people who crossed the wilderness that was my piece of land were the village school children taking a short cut. The hushed whispers that rose from the foliage, the soft footfalls over the carpet of moist leaves and the hurriedly suppressed jingling of their tiffin carriers were the only hints of their passage through my dark empire. Sometimes they would suddenly forge a bond of fear amongst themselves, imagining that I was charging behind them with bloodshot eyes and flowing beard, and they would flee in unison, raising a commotion, crashing through the thickets.

One day, while grinding medicines for a liniment behind the shut doors of my house, I heard a footfall in the courtyard. I peeped through the slit of the window. In the dusk outside, among my medicinal plants, stood a little girl. Unawares, she was staring right into my hidden eyes. From my secret position, I looked at her and smiled. She slowly took a step into the courtyard and looked around her, not for a moment withdrawing her attention from the shut house. I joyfully nodded my head at her from my hiding place. I beckoned to her. I made faces at her from my secret place, showing all my teeth. In a

sudden burst of daring, she climbed onto the lower veranda and ran
her fingers over the shining smoothness of the place where I usually
sat, startling me. She also felt the gleaming pillar with her hands. As
I watched breathlessly, she moved back to the courtyard and approached
my well. Filled with a strange anxiety, I stood watching her. She
picked up a pebble and dropped it into the well. The sharp, distant
sound of the pebble hitting the water reached my ears. I was tempted
to rush out, but I continued to stand there, clasping the window bars,
even while I yielded to the thrill of the invitation that the clear, tiny
sound brought me. 'Hey, you,' I whispered, 'how dare you disturb the
peace of my home?' Suddenly, swift as a heifer, she bolted down the
courtyard and entered my patch of medicinal plants like a whirlwind.
Scooping up the leaves of the kacholam plant with both hands, she
went crashing through the thickets and was gone! I stood stupefied
for a moment, unable to contain my amazement. Then I jumped into
the courtyard, laughing and shouting. 'Come, one and all! A little girl
thief! A little girl thief stealing kacholam. Catch her!' I heard her
splash across the stream. I raised the tip of my beard towards the
moon which was climbing the sky beyond the trees and danced, roaring,
'O little girl thief, why did you steal the kacholam? To heal whom? Be
blessed with the greatest powers of healing, my little thief-doctor!
May God protect you.' Then, as I sat down in my usual spot, which
her soft hands had touched, and leaned against the pillar which her
tiny fingers had stroked, a tenderness and peace floated down the
waves of moonlight and embraced me.

The sky visited my dark house as raindrops and sunlight, filtering
through the holes in the mouldering palm leaf thatch. The raindrops
made craters on the floor, and the antlions dug still more wells in
them, spouting fountains of dust. The sun dived into the inner rooms
of my home through the holes, beamed down from the rafters and
danced on the floor in darting circles. My liniment bottles, the bundles
of herbs and roots, the torn mat, the blanket and pillow, all would
momentarily bear the stamp of sunlight's swift feet. For the rest, the
interior of my house was filled with a delicious darkness, and my land
with the lovely peace of branches and leaves. Seated on the veranda,
leaning against the old pillar, I would watch the somnambulist moon

in its candlelight procession, the trembling stars, and the waves of light amongst the clouds that reared their heads in the sky. Like a spider, the life of this solitary Vaidyar wove long webs, stretching from the base of the old pillar to the heights of the bunched stars.

I loved patients. I loved them through the melting tenderness of my liniments and the infinite patience of my fingers, understanding the screams of pain of the broken bone and the bruised nerve. Who is a masseur-physician? Even as he inflicts pain on the medicine-anointed body, he fondles it. In the consolation of his hands, as the patient re-embraces his own body, forgiving it and bearing with its bruises and pain, the crushed bone and fatigued muscles rejoice and grow whole again. The human being hides behind the skeleton and the skeleton behind the human being. Through the bone, vein and sinew, I seek the human being. Through the nerve, I listen to the laughter and lamentation of the soul.

How beautiful my solitude was! How wonderful were my disguises! What fine games of hide and seek I played with people, until they surrendered to themselves!

My crumbling house and cratered floors, my wifeless and childless home and the weed-covered land, and the sudden riddles I threw at people, terrified them. The riddle was my last resort. The jungles on my pathless land filtered people like a sieve. The silence of my home bent them like a liniment to my purpose. My riddles demolished their changeless minds. How many trips they had to make through my forest until they accepted against their will that the broken arm and crushed leg were themselves.

As my thumb probes deep into the bruised nerve, I shout at the patient, 'The one who makes it does not use it, the one who uses it does not know it, what is it? Answer quickly!' The patient's face, ready to register pain, stiffens as if it has been slapped. I ask again, 'Do you know what it is?' He answers, 'No, Vaidyare.' 'Think hard, think hard!' I say. By this time, my fingers have released the tangled nerve. And he gropes in vain in the cellars of his childhood for the answer, alarmed, unmindful of the pain. I shout, 'The answer is: a coffin. You owe me ten points.'

Everyone is afraid of the moment when the fractured bone is set.

Everyday, before the massage is begun, the patient asks, 'Vaidyare, are you going to set the bone today?' 'No,' I answer. Even on the day when I am going to set the bone I say, 'No.' When I feel in my fingers the broken parts preparing to unite again, I bellow at the patient, 'Does the pot know the taste of the curry?' The patient starts and stares at me in helplessness. 'Do you know the answer?' I roar again. 'No,' whispers the patient. I shout, 'You owe me ten points!' I ask again, 'Can you sit on the mortar and cry, oh, the pestle is descending?' In my hands, the broken bone comes together. 'You lose twenty points,' I roar. The patient, unable to answer, sits gaping at me, thinking of the inexplicable thirty points he owes me.

They feared me as they would a lone tusker. I was invincible. Ha! Ha! Ha! But no one knew that I was a lone tusker only in those gardens of the poor antlions.

So there I was, standing one day in the dazzling sunlight of the courtyard, combing my beard. A passing summer shower suddenly tattooed the dusty lawn. The air was filled with the fragrance of the heady mixture of earth, rain and sunlight. I stood happily in the courtyard, breathing in the smells, waiting, like my herbs and jungles, for the grand arrival of the rains, thinking of nothing, my mind flying free like a floating leaf. There was a sudden gust of wind. Behind it came a luminous drizzle from the rainclouds that rushed across the sunny sky. I wanted to leap into the joyous wind, the rain and the fleeing clouds. 'Here I come!' I jumped, my arms lifted, to touch the clouds. 'Aha! Aha!' I screamed. 'Take me too!'

Suddenly, through the corner of my eye, I saw someone at the far end of the courtyard. In great surprise I stopped. Without turning around, making up for my embarrassment with a gravity of tone, I asked, 'Who is there?' No answer. I turned slowly. A young woman stood regarding me with one hand on the circular parapet of the well, and the other pressed to a spot on her right thigh. The pain that she had perhaps forgotten as she watched my sky-leaps now returned to her face. She said, 'I fell down and something happened to my leg. I can't bear the pain. Could you take a look at it, Vaidyare?'

'Has anyone come with you?' I asked.

'No one,' she said.

'Go and bring someone. I don't usually treat women.'

'I can't walk, Vaidyare,' she said, 'and I don't have anyone to fetch. There's only my mother, she is old and can't walk.'

Uncertainly, I asked her, 'How did you fall?'

'When I climbed the stone wall to pluck the black mother shrub for my goat, a stone broke loose.'

I liked that. I whispered, 'Black mother, fair daughter. Daughter's daughter, fairest of the fair.' I muttered under my breath, 'You're a smart woman, you've answered a riddle[1] I did not ask.'

'Come here,' I said, 'let me see.'

She came limping across the rain-splattered courtyard, through the fresh scent of the rain, and sat down at my usual spot. She leaned back on my glistening pillar. Lifting her right leg with both hands, she placed it along the wood of the veranda, as I would have done. I wanted to shout, that's my place, it's I who sit there! Instead, I continued to stand in the courtyard and watch her anxiously. She began to sob. She sat there and wept in many soft notes which I had never heard before. Her hair, which had come undone, enveloped my shining pillar like a dark cascade. Her tears fell on the edge of my veranda, shattered, and flowed down into the wells of the hungry antlions, carrying the flavour of salt and sorrow. I stood silent in the courtyard, watching her forge a friendship with pain. At the same time, an intense desire possessed me to rush to my place and sit there. I controlled myself and whispered to the antlions, 'My friends, do not swoon in the salt of her tears. Escape to the waters of the springs beneath. Swim away like tortoises.' After a while, she stopped weeping and wiped away her tears. She gathered up her hair which had fallen loose on her face. Then she rolled her mundu up her thigh and showed me where it hurt.

The tumult of a world crashing filled my ears as I approached her and examined her thigh. There was a black and blue mark.

---

1. This riddle is based on the three-coloured appearance of the black mother shrub: the branches and leaves are green (black mother), two leaves just below the flower are white (fair daughter) and the flower itself is red (daughter's daughter). The answer to the riddle is: the black mother—which actually makes both the riddle and the answer redundant!

'Isn't your pain gone?' I asked. 'Didn't your pain drain away with your tears?'

'I don't know,' she said, 'I was crying for all of myself, not only for my pain.'

I said nothing. I took the softness of her thigh in both hands and pressed my fingers to it. The sunshine, the wind, the moving shadows, the dancing branches of my medicinal plants, all accompanied my fingers in their journey in quest of her pain. I did not look at her. I turned my face to the clouds in the sky, to the jungle and to the homes of the antlions. Her thigh, which was washed in pain and tears, lay pliant in my hands. O my antlions, I whispered, look at my condition! I saw they were out walking; they sauntered slowly through their gardens of dust like ancient creatures. Suddenly, I came back to myself; I knew I must act. I rolled my eyes. My beard flew up lethally. I stared at her with a hard and cruel look. The nerve that had gone astray beneath that black and blue mark trembled under my fingers. Keeping a tight hold, I roared, 'Would you like to die, woman?' The words, you lose a hundred points, waited on the tip of my tongue. My eyes awaited the bewilderment, dejection and defeat that would fill her face. At that moment, wiping the tear stains from her face with one hand, she asked me, 'Did you like to be born?'

I felt suffocated. It seemed to me that her errant vein was squirming out of my grasp. I held on to her thigh as if for support. Someone answering my riddles! My next roar faltered, 'Are you afraid to die?' And the words, you lose a thousand points, waited on the tip of my tongue. She asked me calmly, 'Were you afraid to be born, Vaidyare?' Her thigh, with its fine dark hairs, lay in my hands like a sleeping child. 'You owe me a hundred points,' she said. Then, covering my hands with her two palms and pressing them to the quietude of her thigh, she said, 'Heal me, Vaidyare, or else you lose a thousand points.'

Today, in my plot of land where jungles had been, a vegetable garden tosses in the wind and sunlight. My herbs flourish safely behind a bamboo fence. Those who come to consult me sit on benches on the veranda which was once the garden of my antlions. It is long since they fled from those dusty floors, now polished with cowdung mixture. They live on, under the awnings in my backyard. On the rolled-up end of a tiny thread dangled into the pit, I caught one of them and showed it to my year-old son. Then I returned it to the solitude of the dust and whispered to my child, 'My son, you'll never know their companionship. Nor will you know how the jungle can enfold and protect you. No girl thief will ever come prowling to steal your kacholam. My son, may God bless you and help you to invent riddles more difficult than those I invented.'

—*Translated from the Malayalam by A.J. Thomas*

Footballer

Ravi Menon

The passion that soccer triggers, and the number of people that fall prey to its hypnotic appeal, are all too staggering.

Citizens of Peringotupulam, a tiny hamlet in Malappuram district in north Kerala, would vouch for that. They had joined hands recently to build a 50m long bridge across the Kadalundi River just to watch the games going on in a seven-a-side football tournament at a nearby township.

'We had to travel over ten kilometres to reach the MSP ground in Malappuram town, where the tournament was being held. Now we trudge just a kilometre,' said a Panchayat member of Kodur, where the village is situated. 'Being a village of football-crazy men (and women), we just could not resist the temptation.'

The man was not joking. The words, coming straight from his heart, rightly sum up the soccer fever in Kerala. For the middle-class Malayali, football is a game like no other. From the sunny beaches of Kozhikode to the star-spangled 'sevens' fields of Malappuram, and from the dark and narrow lanes of Fort Kochi to the pastoral highlands of Munnar, it is an integral part of life itself. It is perhaps this profound involvement that has brought to bloom a galaxy of talented players from this state over the past few generations.

Some of them are real touch artists who have the delicate skills of ballet dancers, and the killer instinct of the merciless picadors of the bull rings. Footballers who play the game for the sheer joy of it, like that ebony antelope from Thrissur, Iyinivalappil Mani Vijayan.

Vijayan, undoubtedly the most popular footballer to have emerged from the state, has become a role model for every Malayali sportsman desiring to shrug off his inhibitions and march shoulder to shoulder with the rest of the country. Watching him on the move—sending those adroit passes which pack so much cunning and control, or making those fluent dribbles, in the manner of a master swordsman making his cuts and thrusts, or getting to striking range and rifling the ball home—is to know what football is all about.

Vijayan's humble beginnings and rags-to-riches story have attained folklore status in Kerala, where icons are seldom made or accepted. It's been a long journey for him, from playing with a *thunippanthu*— pieces of cloth tied together to form a ball—in the dried-up paddy fields of Thrissur. Born in 1970, to a family of agricultural labourers in Kolothumpadam, on the outskirts of Thrissur, Vijayan experienced the hardships of penury during his childhood.

Trapped neck-deep in poverty, the family of four (Vijayan has an elder brother named Biju), trudged along till the death of the father, when Vijayan was just eight. The mother, Kochchammu, worked as a daily wage-earner in the fields and took up small jobs here and there to feed her children. Vijayan gets a lump in his throat whenever he recalls those dark days when his mother used to go to bed on an empty stomach after feeding her kids. The pangs of hunger, however, failed to deter the carefree and spirited son whose only passion was football.

Like the Dutch football legend Johan Cruyff, Vijayan dedicates his goals to his mother. Cruyff's mother, a cleaning woman in Amsterdam, had her dreams cut out for her. She used to pause now and again in front of the massive Ajax football stadium to be transported to another world. A world where, in the scheme of things populating her dreams, her little son would be a soccer star. Before her son was ten years old, she would stubbornly ease him out of the cosy comfort of his bed and drag him along to the stadium. 'There my son, watch them practise. You can do it better than any of them,' she would tell the little Johan.

Kochchammu, on the other hand, was less ambitious. 'She did not even know what the game of soccer was all about. She just wanted us to grow up and make a decent living,' recalls the footballer. 'Her dreams ended there.'

But Vijayan's didn't. At twelve, he was selling soda and cigarettes to the crowds at Thrissur's Municipal Stadium, the venue of the Santosh Trophy National Football Championship in 1982. 'The money earned was too meagre. Still, I was happy, as I could watch the games without paying for the tickets.'

It was the youngster's soccer skills and his burning desire to excel that caught the attention of Prof M.C. Radhakrishnan, the then secretary of the District Sports Council who helped him get into a three-year coaching camp conducted by the council.

'Radhakrishnan sir was also generous enough to arrange food for me at the nearby Triveny Hotel,' recalls the player with gratitude.

At the camp, Vijayan was lucky to come under the tutelage of coach T.K. Chathunni, a former international defender who sensed class in the body language of the lean, hungry-looking lad. Chathunni later helped the boy land a job with the Kerala Police, where he found a godfather in the sports-loving Director General M.K. Joseph.

RISE TO STARDOM

'The realization that I could make a living out of soccer came the day I got my first pay packet from the police,' says Vijayan. 'Never before had I seen so much money. I still remember rushing home to share my joy with my mother and brother. It was the first day of celebration in our life.'

The celebrations, in fact, had just begun. Vijayan justified the DGP's high hopes in him by helping the Kerala Police to two triumphs in the prestigious Federation Cup inter-club championship. He ventured to Kolkata, to Mohun Bagan, and after that to Punjab's Jagjit Cotton Textile (JCT) Mills. Interestingly, from 1990 till 1996, he remained a member of the winning team in the Federation Cup, representing Kerala Police twice, Mohun Bagan for three years and JCT Mills for the next two years. Later he returned home to don the colours of FC Kochin, the country's first-ever professional club.

But the Kolkata maidan remained a passion somewhere deep within him, always beckoning him with its beguiling charm. He could not resist the temptation to return to the Mecca of Indian soccer when East Bengal came up with a tempting offer.

Vijayan believes that it was his stint in Kolkata that groomed him into a fearless professional footballer. He still regrets his decision to return to Kerala, after his maiden season with Mohun Bagan in 1991. 'I went back to Kerala on the assurance of Kerala Football Association that they would help me build a house of my own. But strangely enough, the monetary benefit was outrageously negligible, compared to the promises made,' he recalls.

Vijayan, who returned to the maidan a disgusted man the next year, was indebted to the Bagan management for extending him a helping hand when it mattered most—to build a house for him and his family in Thrissur.

Vijayan, addressed affectionately as 'Black Pearl' by his fans, made his debut for the Indian juniors in the Police Cup in Maldives (1990). Later he represented the senior team in the Super Soccer series against the PSV Eindhovan, and the Pre-Olympic tournament. For the next ten years he was a regular in the national squad, playing for the country in the qualifying rounds of the World Cup and the Olympics, the Jawaharlal Nehru Gold Cup, the Asian Games, the Asian Cup, the SAF Games, the SAFF Cup and the Sahara Cup.

BAPTISM BY FIRE

28 July 1993 was a red-letter day in Vijayan's career. 'It was a sort of baptism by fire for me,' recalls the player who scored Mohun Bagan's breathtaking match winner against East Bengal, when the traditional rivals met in the Centenary IFA Shield in Kolkata. The teams were locked 1-1, when Vijayan scored off a dead-ball. Having earlier blasted home Bagan's equalizer, he curved the ball around a seven-man East Bengal wall and beat the goalkeeper to give Bagan the game.

Vijayan was elevated to the status of a demigod when, a few days later, in the semifinal against Mohammedan Sporting, he converted a cross with a spectacular back volley from forty yards, a beautiful goal that revived memories of Shyam Thapa's brilliant reverse kick goal that stopped East Bengal in 1978.

Which was his favourite goal?

'Perhaps the one for JCT Mills against the Malaysian club Perlis in the final of the Scissors Cup in 1996,' says Vijayan. 'It was yet another back volley, this time off a well-angled cross from Tejinder Kumar. The goal was memorable because it gave us the match and the title.'

And his worst experience on the field?

'Certainly the penalty miss against Kerala in the 1992 Santosh

Trophy at Coimbatore. I was playing for Bengal then, and had been under severe psychological pressure, since the entire crowd was crying for my blood. A majority of them were Malayalis and they hated me for "deserting" my homestate to play for Bengal.'

One moment that Vijayan cherishes is the 12th-second strike against Bhutan in the South Asian Federation Games in 1999—a goal that has graced the soccer annals as one of the fastest goals ever scored in an international match. The scintillating effort by Vijayan eclipsed former England captain Bryan Robson's 29th-second goal against France in the 1982 World Cup. It also bettered another fast-scoring effort which came in the final of the 1974 World Cup, when Johan Neeskens slammed in a 78th second penalty, after Holland's Johan Cruyff was brought down in the box by West German Uli Hoeness.

Vijayan is so wonderfully versatile that it has always been impossible for him to play just one assigned role—upfront, midfield, or even defence. At his peak, he played everywhere, with the same kind of energy and skills. A man aware of his own gifts, Vijayan also understood the potential of other members of his team and helped them play to their peak.

A NEW CAREER

In the twilight years of his career, Vijayan has entered a new domain, a new passion that has been as challenging as the game of soccer. He made his debut as an actor, playing the lead role in director Jayaraj's National Award-winning film 'Shaantham'.

'It was at a function held in Thrissur that Jayaraj made the stunning announcement that he had plans to cast me in his next film,' recalls Vijayan. 'At first I laughed it off as a simple joke. Surprisingly, Jayaraj was quite serious. He wanted me to act, and he meant it too.'

After 'Shaantham' and 'Aakashathile Paravakal', the footballer is likely to don the greasepaint for a few more films. 'I really enjoy my film career. But that doesn't mean that I am fed up with soccer. Soccer is my first love and will remain so forever. It's the game that made me what I am today. How can ever I forget soccer?' asks Vijayan, who stays in Chembukaavu near Thrissur, with his wife Raji—a dancer— and his children Aaromal, Aarcha and Abhirami. 'After retirement I will get more time to spend with the budding talents at my soccer academy,' says the footballer who launched the I.M. Vijayan Sports Foundation in 2000, with the aim of imparting specialized training to aspiring footballers.

Vijayan is not merely a soccer maestro appealing to the romantics with his wizardry and inventiveness in the middle. He is also a go-getter, one who loves to set his goals and chase them all alone.

There is no shortcut to glory. It's a steep and gruelling climb with its share of dreams and nightmares. Vijayan is a man who has learnt it the hard way. 'I have no regrets. Soccer has given me more than what I deserve. Without soccer, perhaps I would have ended up as just another street kid in Thrissur, wondering where his next meal would come from,' Vijayan says with an innocent smile.

On the banks of the Mayyazhi

M. Mukundan

The rains had long been over and the month of Karkatakam had started.

Damu Writer was very ill, he could not perform the annual bali rituals for his dead ancestors on full moon day. He was ill all the time now. Apart from his chronic asthma, he had developed other ailments like a backache and swelling of the limbs.

Two more days to full moon. 'I can't do the bali rituals. May the dead forgive me,' said Damu.

'Let Dasan do them if you can't,' said Kurambi Amma. Dasan, the only other man in the house, had never performed these rituals before.

When everyone insisted, he consented to perform them.

The bustle in the kitchen started the day before full moon. Many kinds of payasams had to be prepared for the dead ancestors.

Girija got up at dawn and had a bath. Her hair still wet, she served the payasam on banana leaves, filled a vessel with water and went to the southern room, which was kept apart for the ancestors. Kelu Achan's bones were preserved there in an earthen pot, under the cowdung-smeared floor.

'Think of your grandfather, little one, keep his image in your mind,' said Kurambi Amma, coming up to the door. Girija invoked her grandfather, who had died of a snake bite long before she could remember, and placed the payasam and water on the floor.

She came out and closed the door. Then she served out some payasam on another leaf, lighted an oil-drenched leaf torch and went to the southern courtyard. The offerings meant for the spirits called Biran, Pena and Bhandaram were always placed outside the house, with a lighted cloth torch, because they were the spirits of people who had

This extract is taken from *On the Banks of the Mayyazhi*, published by East West Books.

died evil deaths. 'Those who drowned are called Biran,' Kurambi Amma had explained to Dasan when he was a child, 'those who hanged themselves are Pena and those who died of smallpox are Bhandaram.'

Kurumbi Amma and Dasan bathed, put on wet clothes and cooked turmeric rice over a fire in the courtyard. They then served the rice on banana leaves and sprinkled kuruka grass and sesame seeds over it. Kneeling by the side of the leaves, they clapped to the crows, inviting them to come and accept the offerings.

'Not a single crow, Achamma,' exclaimed Girija, who was watching from the verandah. What had happened to the crows that came every morning and perched in the yard and on the well parapets, cawing with hunger?

Kurumbi Amma knelt and clapped over and over again.

'They'll come,' said Dasan. 'It's a busy day for them today.' The same rituals were being performed in almost all the Hindu houses in Mayyazhi that day.

At last a crow flew towards them, but it suddenly changed direction because it heard someone else clap louder.

'Eight o'clock, oh God!' Kurambi Amma felt desperate. Where had all the ancestors gone? Why were they staying away? She clapped her thin hands repeatedly.

Dasan stopped his efforts to attract the crows and sat down on the steps. He felt chilly, in his wet mundu.

'Come, come,' Kurambi Amma called out again, looking up at the sky and clapping her tired hands. 'Come, come . . .'

Kurambi Amma's heart was heavy and she felt like crying. Her voice grew shriller.

The sun climbed higher. A crow flew up at last and landed near the banana leaf. It ate the turmeric rice and sesame seeds and gazed at Kurambi Amma with a drunken look. It was a miserable crow with bald patches on its scraggy neck.

'Come here,' Kurambi Amma called it nearer, affectionately. The crow cocked its head to one side and looked at her. It lifted a wing and scratched underneath with its beak. Then it flew down and perched on Kurambi Amma's banana leaf.

'So you've come at last, thank God!'

Kurambi Amma stared at the crow. It pecked at the side of the leaf and scattered rice and sesame seeds in all directions with its feet. Then it pecked at a few morsels again.

Kurambi Amma's eyes filled with tears as she watched it.

'What is it Achamma?'

'That's your grandfather.' Kurambi Amma burst into tears.

Was it really Kelu Achan, this scraggy crow with the bald neck?

*

The festival in the Church of the Virgin was as important in Mayyazhi as the Thira Festival in the Meethambalam temple.

As soon as the month of Kanni began, Kunhukutty Achan could be seen balanced on a wooden box suspended from the high steeple, whitewashing the walls of the church. This marked the start of the preparations for the festival.

The Padiri, the priest, came out and seated himself on a chair under the mango tree with his stole around his shoulders and his cap on his knees. The Kappiyar, the sexton, stood next to him with a sheet of paper in his hand. They would now auction the land for the stalls and booths for the festival.

'A booth near the lamp-post, ten by eight feet.' The Kappiyar read from his paper and looked around. Bangle sellers from Mangalore, halva makers from Kozhikode, hypnotists and gamblers from unknown places, they had all come to bid for a shop or a booth.

'Ten rupees.'

'Ten and a quarter.' That was the bangle seller.

'Ten and a half.' The hypnotist.

'A quarter rupee more.' The gambler.

And so it went on until the bangle seller bid for fourteen rupees.

'Fourteen rupees. Once. Twice. No one?' The bangle seller looked around anxiously. Everyone was silent. The Padiri moved in his chair.

The land near the lamp-post went to the bangle seller.

The festival started at noon on 5 October, with a single blast of dynamite. There were two blasts on the second day and three on the third. On the tenth and final day, there would be ten deafening blasts.

Stalls selling glass bangles, marigolds, crosses, candles, images of saints and angels had come up all around the church.

Pilgrims flocked to Mayyazhi. An endless stream of visitors flowed from the railway station and the bridge.

'Do you think all these people have really come out of devotion?' Pappan watched the crowd from the Vignanaposhini Library, which was right in front of the Church. You could watch the festival from start to finish from there. 'They've all come to drink liquor.'

'You mean this whole crowd is here to drink?' Dasan laughed. Bhakti can make people more intoxicated than liquor.

The library was full of people. Once the festival started, all sorts of people who normally never came to the library would flock in to watch the festival.

The Mother of Mayyazhi, as the Virgin was known, loved her devotees, just as the Thiya gods, Gulikan and Kuttichathan did. And exactly like them, she made short work of her enemies too.

One of the many legends Kurambi Amma had recounted to Dasan as a child was that of the origin of the Mother of Mayyazhi.

'Once upon a time,' she said, 'a ship that was going over the vast expanse of the Arabian Sea sailed into the shadow of the Velliyan Rock. Suddenly, it was grounded, as if the anchor had been dropped. The captain and the sailors were stunned, for there was no obstacle in sight. Three days and three nights passed. The ship refused to move.'

The sailors fell on their knees and prayed, their eyes raised to heaven.

'Install me in Mayyazhi.' The captain heard a voice. It came from the idol of the Virgin in the ship.

The captain obeyed the divine command. He went ashore with the idol and placed it at an isolated spot.

The ship moved.

'Our church is built at the spot where the captain placed the idol.' Kurambi Amma opened her ivory snuffbox, took a pinch of snuff and inhaled with her eyes half-closed.

Dusk. The sun dipped into the great calm sea. The cross on the steeple was etched clearly against the limpid sky.

The church bells pealed, gathering into themselves the grandeur of the sea and the sky. They resounded through Mayyazhi. The bells would ring continuously until the urukan, the procession bearing the holy image of the Virgin, came back to the church after circling the town.

'Look, there goes the urukan,' said Kurambi Amma as she sat in the verandah with her snuffbox open and her eyes closed, carried away by memories of bygone festivals.

The awesome bells swayed above the sexton, who lay suspended from the bell ropes. As he rang the huge bells, he swung between the earth and the sky, following the violent movement of the bells.

The procession wound its way through the Rue de l'Eglise with chariots, flags and coloured lamps. The scent of burning incense spread through Mayyazhi. Thousands of pilgrims moved with the procession, singing the praises of the Mother of Mayyazhi in many languages.

Even after dusk, the sun refused to set over Mayyazhi.

The procession came back to the church after four hours. The bells stopped ringing at last. As he let go of the ropes he had been pulling for hours, the exhausted Kappiyar fell down, losing consciousness. Blood dripped from his hands.

*

For two whole days, the people of Mayyazhi had not slept. Men wandered around the church, drunk.

Housewives were tired of cooking for guests. Only one house stayed dark and silent—Leslie Sayiv's. Missie, who had always made cakes for the festival for as long as people could remember, had not done so this year. Anyway, even if she had baked a cake, who would have eaten it? In the old days, people had come in carriages to her house and feasted and drunk the whole night long. Why would they come now, there was no one at home.

The man of the house, whose task it would have been to welcome guests, had shut himself away behind closed doors, doing penance, his hair and beard growing thicker with the years.

It was on the first day of the festivities that Missie lost the use of her right hand and leg. She fell down while mixing the batter for a cake and her head hit the floor.

Mambi, the maid, shouted for help. Gaston heard Mambi's cry as he drowsed with his guitar against his chest. He got up, opened the door a little and peered out.

He saw Mamma lying prone on the floor. His heart turned over. He opened the door a little wider and began to go down the steps. Just then the neighbours arrived, having heard Mambi's cry for help. Gaston withdrew at once.

It was twenty-five years since he had gone downstairs. Although he had been born and bred in Mayyazhi, its people had become strangers to him. Sometimes he peered out through the thick curtains at the window. He looked at the people walking along the Rue de la Résidence or seated on the pier, but did not recognize any of them.

Gaston felt only one emotion now—pain. Pain for his lost manhood. The pain of losing Teresa who had not stayed with him even a week. It was this pain that his guitar strings tried to express night after night, spreading its music over Mayyazhi. It haunted those who were asleep, disturbing them with bad dreams.

Pathrose and Policeman Chathu laid Missie on the cot. She was unconscious and her head was bleeding.

Someone ran to fetch a doctor.

Gaston longed to know what had happened but did not come down. He could hear voices downstairs. He was afraid of people. A conflict raged in his mind. His mother lay dying, the mother who had wept unceasingly for him over the last twenty-five years. But he could not move to go to her. The voices frightened him. How could he go amongst them?

No, I can't go. Gaston locked the door from inside. He paced up and down the room.

Missie regained consciousness next morning. She opened her eyes and looked around her. She saw Kurambi, Damu, Dasan, Pathrose and Policeman Chathu.

'Gaston . . .' Her lips moved. All eyes turned towards the staircase. The door upstairs remained closed.

The tears ran down Missie's cheeks. She lay in a faint, her eyes closed. Two small, pale feet could be seen outside her long black robe.

Damu could not bear it any longer. He looked at the stairs and cried out, 'Gaston, come down. Your mother is dying . . .'

Behind the closed doors, Gaston's footsteps quickened.

Missie's eyes stopped moving. Her body trembled from head to foot. 'Gaston . . .' Kurambi Amma wailed in despair.

Damu stood on the bottom step of the carpeted stairs and called as loudly as he could, 'Please come down, Gaston.'

Gaston did not answer.

Damu began to go up the stairs slowly, holding on to the banisters. Everyone's eyes were fixed on him. He came to the closed door and called out again. There was no answer. He knocked repeatedly. Gaston did not reply. There was only the sound of frenzied footsteps moving inside the closed room.

Damu came back, still leaning on the banisters for support.

That evening, Leslie Sayiv's Missie drew her last breath. Everyone except Gaston was at her bedside.

The beautiful Missie, who used to walk in her flowing white silk dress on the seashore, hand in hand with the charismatic Leslie Sayiv, lay still on the rosewood cot on a faded sheet.

With Missie's death, the curtain fell on the golden age of Mayyazhi's half-French citizens. An era ended with her passing away. She was the last link in the line of rich and generous half-French who had lived dignified and noble lives.

The half-French would continue to play a role in the life of Mayyazhi, but they were never to achieve the same measure of greatness and nobility. Poverty and its attendant evils were to force them to lead mean lives. Beggars and prostitutes were to be born amongst them. Missie's death marked the start of a tragic journey that was to destroy their very roots.

People crowded to Leslie Sayiv's house when they heard of Missie's death. Her closest friend, Kurambi, wept her heart out, seated next to the bier. Dasan and Girija, who had loved her delicious cakes, bit their lips to keep from crying.

Gaston still paced up and down his closed room.

Finally, the mourners went home, and the bungalow was empty.

It was past midnight. The sea was quiet under a clear sky spattered with stars.

After years, the door that had remained closed opened. Gaston's pale face appeared above the stairs. Golden hair streamed over his shoulders and a long, golden beard flowed under his chin. His blue eyes were as calm as the sky. Holding on to the banisters, he came down slowly.

Missie lay on a silken bier in Leslie Sayiv's empty living room, under the glittering crystal lamp, her hands crossed on her breast.

Gaston went up to the bier and looked at his mother's face. He knelt down beside her and said, 'I've no one now, Mamma, no one.'

He lay his head on his mother's breast and sobbed until the sun rose over the Mayyazhi river.

—Translated from the Malayalam by Gita Krishnankutty

The power of one

Bill Aitken

The power of one person to alter the course of history is best reflected in the career of Mahatma Gandhi, a briefless barrister whose inner strength overcame the might of the world's most vaunted empire. 11 September 2001 gave more evidence of how one individual, even one who is a religious fanatic, can humble the most powerful of opponents. As my train pulled out of New Delhi three days after the devastating terrorist attacks on New York, I pondered the ripple effect caused by the dedication of one determined individual who skims a stone across the smooth surface of events, little aware that awaiting me in Kerala was another example of how one man can create waves.

I had been invited by the Kerala tourism department to sample the state's scenic beauties in the off-season and unlike most tourists, jumped at the chance to experience the last fling of the receding south-west monsoon. The highlight of my three-week tour (of which five days were spent profitably on the train, boning up on the culture and history of Kerala) was an elemental interlude anchored in a houseboat. In the early hours of the morning, an electric storm hit the waterfront at Alappuzha and in the cataclysmic aftermath of wind and rain, our lumbering barge was tossed around as though on the high seas. JMW Turner paid sailors to tie him to the mast in North Sea gales in order to let him experience at first hand the raw power of nature he wished to capture on his canvases, while here was I, at no risk of getting sea sick, enjoying the full fury of the elements for free. It's true that with all the bamboo hatches battened down it was a bit claustrophobic, but on the other hand, the lake was only ten feet deep, a far cry from the fifty fathoms of Sir Patrick Spens at Aberdour where I had spent my childhood.

Kerala is a sea symphony attributed to Lord Parasurama who is said to have cleaved it from the ocean south of Gokarna. The real composer, in my opinion, is the goddess Saraswati whose garland of rivers from the high ranges of the Sahyadri define both the physiography and sociology of the state. Kerala's shelving coastline is the first step in the ascending uptwist of beauty so accurately termed 'South Western Ghats'. This range that runs from Gujarat to Kanyakumari encompasses a constantly changing profile. The Maharashtra movement of this symphony is both dreamy and heroic in the mesa formations where Shivaji performed his death-defying mission in honour of the goddess Bhavani. Karnataka introduces the dramatics of the Jog Falls where the goddess Sharada spills 800 feet in four booming cataracts. To Kerala falls the prize of Anai Mudi, the highest peak in India outside the Himalaya, and at its feet the backwaters of Kuttanad where my journey began.

I arrived at Ernakulam on a Sunday and was pleasantly surprised when accosted on the platform by a man I took to be my government host. Government servants even in a rationalist state like Kerala are religious in their observance of holidays. Though they may pooh-pooh the claims of Vedic astrology and ignore the inauspicious period of Rahu Kal, every one of them carries in his head the list of Second Saturdays for the next decade.

The gentleman, in fact, turned out to be a travel agent sent by an enterprising tour operator called Babu Verghese who had apparently got wind of my visit and by posting his man on the platform had beat the tourism department to the draw. By the time we reached the station exit where an official car awaited, I had been briefed most professionally on Babu Verghese and apprised of his revolutionary approach to tourism.

I have always felt that official tourism in India is an ongoing farce where pathos and bathos seem evenly matched. This was proved when my government host, having turned up late, showed me to the back seat of a beflagged Ambassador car, then got in alongside and bombarded me, without so much as by your leave, with official statistics. After two and a half days on a silent empty train (·11 September had halted all but the shameless in their tracks), I couldn't believe my ears at this grossly insensitive introduction to God's Own Country.

I just sat there and gaped as per capita income statistics were hurled at my head and male to female ratios were hammered home vociferously. Fortunately, on the outskirts of Kochi, my tormentor halted the taxi and abruptly got out. To my eternal credit, I had said no when asked if I needed an official guide.

*

As my tour unfolded, Babu Verghese assumed the role of Forster's Mrs Moore. Everywhere I went, people uttered his name in a hushed tone of respect (echoing 'Esmissess Mor'.) He sounded a bit like John Smith, the mysterious Cargo Cult figure of the South Sea islanders, a messiah who could deliver the goods. Significantly, Babu's name was bandied about by the working staff of the houseboats and jungle lodges where I stayed, but never by the officer class, who perhaps felt guilty for stealing his ideas and cashing in on them. There was sympathy for Babu Verghese amongst the lower-layer professionals in the tourist trade. I got the impression that here was a visionary and engineering genius like Trevithick the Cornishman who actually invented a working steam locomotive but was upstaged by the canny Scot, James Watt. (Watt improved on others' inventions to make them commercial successes and encouraged people to think he had invented them!)

Nowhere in official literature do you read of Babu Verghese's crucial role in the revival of the *kettuvallom*, the rice boat converted into a backwater cruise ship. These woven barges with stitched planks and bamboo canopy had almost gone out of business, thanks to faster transport options. The craftsmen who built and gave them an annual overhaul were pessimistic about the success of any conversion attempt and Babu Verghese's first job was to overcome their negativity. The barges had to be redesigned and this task Babu undertook personally, at his own expense, by trial and error, each model being an improvement on the last. As with India's fleet of steam locomotives which were saved from indiscriminate scrapping by the intervention of one man (Mike Satow), the *kettuvallom* (down to 200 survivors by the 1980s) was saved by Babu Verghese. He launched his first modified boat in 1991 which was powered *veils remisque*, but the traditional sails and oars were soon replaced by a Yamaha outboard engine that purrs along without too much of a wash. Run on kerosene, it is not as polluting as diesel-powered boats.

Very much alive to the sustainability of Kerala's eco-tourist appeal, Babu moved from the backwaters to apply his hands-on tourist doctrine to the threatened forests of the Sahyadri. Our Saraswati symphony starts here, especially south of the Palghat gap where the stepped rise of land from the ocean, combined with the warmer latitude, results in a riotous arboreal cover as well as spices and timber. With the steep fall of rivers slicing the Malabar coast, the Malayali has been forced to turn his attentions seawards. For millennia black pepper has been traded and this creeper of the middle hills can even claim to have been responsible for the accidental discovery of America by Europeans fed up of a starchy, salty diet.

The best place, I discovered, to understand the western-facing sea-stance of the Malayali over the centuries, is Top Station on the crest of the Sahyadri. Westwards, lush cash crops of tea, coffee, cardamom and a dozen other exotic plants descend gently with the altitude and the fall of the ghats. Steeply dropping eastwards from a formidable precipice, the South-West Ghats yield suddenly to the barren red plains of Tamilnadu.

Technically, Top Station is inside Tamilnadu and to prove the point, I bought a nip of brandy from the local *thekka*. Kerala at this time was convulsed with a change in liquor policy which meant that even if the tourist did manage to find an outlet he would be charged a fancy rate for his trouble.

In no other area is official thinking so disastrous for tourism as in the reluctance to sell liquor. Common sense dictates an application of first principles which would point out that Kerala is a hot country whose drinking water is not uniformly reliable and hence beer is a profitable alternative for both state revenue and tourist thirst. But what you get (at the government bungalow in Munnar) is a notice put up on the bar door, to greet a party of Americans returning from a trek—'Dry Day'. Amidst the expletives of these young tourists (who help create a market back home with their word-of-mouth recommendation) was the vow next time to visit China where pragmatism governs policy. At least in the privately run 'Coconut Lagoon', the management had the good sense to advertise the dry day well in advance and the rueful sympathy to add 'Please bear with us'.

For my nip I had to pay three rupees extra and when I queried this random surcharge, the shop owner pointed down the precipice where a goat track could be discerned. Then he wiped his brow to indicate the sweat involved in importing my grog. I accepted his reasoning and stored the nip away against the next dry day sprung upon unsuspecting tourists.

This brings us to the central doctrine of Babu Verghese's tourist philosophy, totally at odds with official 'couldn't care less' attitudes that have resulted in India's poor image abroad. In his company brochure he writes, 'We in Tourindia always give top priority to the demands of visitors and believe in the idea of welcoming a visitor and sending back a friend.'

What differentiates the south from other parts of India is the level of intelligence which, in Kerala, is tied to the impressive literacy rate, the highest in the country. This results in greater civic awareness and the very agreeable situation where things of better quality invariably come at a cheaper price. Added to the value-for-money scenario is the general air of self-respect the visitor finds. Even the poorly dressed are cleanly turned out. The only scruffiness I have found is in the plying of government buses where a free for all ensues amongst passengers, confirming Darwin's theory of the survival of the fittest. However, it is the sum of little excellences that flavours the memory of one's trips through Kerala. Good quality wood is not only tastefully carved but elegantly polished. Simple traditional fittings like sliding battens to close doors cannot be bettered for their functional beauty. Or, for that matter, the umbrella made in Alappuzha that I bought in the smartest showroom I have seen in India. Another elegant souvenir I acquired was a *kindi*, a water pot fashioned from sweet ringing bell-metal and distinguished by its superb design and graceful spout.

After Kuttanad I headed inland. The game sanctuary at Periyar was said to be noisy, with diesel boats shattering the sylvan quietude, but thanks to my privileged status as a government guest, I had the splendidly isolated Lake Palace bungalow all to myself. In the morning, looking across the lake, I could see the fawns splashing around in the water as the adults grazed. It was a scene from the first days of Creation, the calm expanse of water reflecting both the joy and wonder of Nature's pristine ordering.

The saddest thing I saw during my trip was the elephants at Guruvayur, two dozen temple beasts chafing at their chains and confined to the proximity of their steaming ordure. The most disturbing was to note the absence of birds on the backwaters. In 1986, when I made the ferry trip from Quilon to Alleppey (as they were know then), black shags dive-bombing to spear fish were a constant accompaniment to this most vivacious of voyages. But the toll of diesel outboard engines and the fallout of pesticide for increased rice yield have killed all the fish and in turn decimated the bird population. For all its acclaim as one of *National Geographic*'s 'must see before you die' destinations, Kerala's paradisiacal appearance is fragile and worms are visible at the core of Eden's apple.

'Coconut Lagoon', the sumptuous private resort done with superb concern for Kerala's architectural heritage sits on the bank of Vembanad, the shrinking lake alongside the Kumarakom resort recently visited by Prime Minister Vajpayee. Both resorts are shown in the advertisements as set amidst exotic, aquamarine, tropical beauty, but land there and you find the water soupy and the connecting canals choked by a deadly carpet of water hyacinth. Kerala's unique waterways are being reduced at an alarming rate and the government is in a dilemma whether to let in fresh water to clear them—and upset the farming lobby—or keep the level down and allow the state's most profitable tourist asset to die from the spread of weeds.

The horn of the dilemma can be witnessed at Eravikulam National Park where Tata Tea for years has provided a salt lick for the elusive Nilgiri tahr, native to the precipitous terrain around Anai Mudi. Sadly, I found these shy mountain goats begging outside parked tourist cars, the chief feature of this reclusive species having been lost in the successful bid to preserve them. They now behave just like the family billy-goat.

In Munnar's main street I dropped in on another of the characters who helped put the area on the map of foreign visitors. Joseph Iype is an unpretentious tour operator who stands in a nondescript office because there is hardly room to sit. Visitors from all over the world converge to meet him and pay fifty rupees for the privilege, which is extraordinary when you consider he only gives information similar to what the district tourist office provides free next door. The difference is that Iype is an enthusiast who is automatically interested in anything his client brings to his notice. Ask at the district office about vintage trains (for example), and the receptionist will look blank and press (figuratively) one of two buttons all government outlets are provided with—'I don't know' or 'Sorry, out of stock'. Iype, having pocketed your money, invites you to sit down (metaphorically) and share a cup of tea. He will tell you how to get to Ooty and on the way experience other fascinating railway lines. From Top Station you can hike down a precipice to Bodinayakkanur and take a branch line to Madurai, or go by a little used road through fine Ghat scenery to Pollachi on the line to Ooty. He will also provide a dozen other options that lie along the way because he likes his job and can earn a commission from his recommendations.

Throughout India, government tourist offices come in for scathing comment from most foreign guide books for their uselessness. Iype has been criticized for demanding a fee for providing information, but it is his commercial motivation that makes him popular with even budget travellers. People are ready to pay if they can get what they want. By adopting a more intelligent attitude to visitors, individuals like Babu Verghese and Joseph Iype have contributed to Kerala's appeal.

True to his innovative creed, Babu Verghese has sought to tackle the problem of eco-degradation by going to the root of the problem. In Periyar, he side-stepped the loud picnicking atmosphere and the clatter of diesel launches that disrupt the serene expanses of wood and water, by introducing wildlife walks led by a tribal who follows the spoor of animals for a silent and sometimes dangerous encounter. The aim here is to capitalize on the talents of the local villagers and give them employment that will blunt the urge to poach. Throughout India, wildlife parks tend to follow the colonial assumption that villagers are the problem, not the solution, to the conservation of wildlife.

Similar talents are harnessed in the mountains of Wayanad, where Babu has created the 'Green Magic Nature Resort'. Tribals have constructed tree houses in the canopy of the Sahyadri forest and Babu's engineering genius has worked out ways to reach them other than by a Tarzan of the Apes approach. Nowhere in India, nor probably in the world, will you find as glowing, almost mystical entries in the visitors' book. My houseboat kept two which were of high artistic and literary content, inspired by this lone ranger's skill in teasing out the poetry of Kerala's varied natural bounty.

Thanks to a handful of gifted and energetic individuals, tourism in India has flourished in spite of the government's unimaginative hand at the helm. Before Babu Verghese in Kerala, there was Mishra in Haryana, a bureaucrat who performed the miracle of putting this tiny adjunct to Delhi on the international map by the introduction of quality motels along Haryana's corridors to the capital. Thirty years later, few traces of Mishra's insistence on excellence remain, but his memory outlives that of the politicians. Another name to enter tourist folklore is that of the Poddar family in Khajuraho, who by the stubbornness of their belief in the sensational beauty of the temples, managed over the decades to convert this forgotten backwater into one of the world's most ravishing heritage sites.

Babu Verghese's role in Kerala has been to sow ideas and give traditional virtues modern expression. Perhaps his greatest (and unintended) achievement is to spur the Kerala government into taking tourism seriously as an industry. Investment in advertising has paid off, and today international guide book publishers issue a separate guide for the state.

Babu's pioneering instincts (now that some 200 *kettuvallom* ply the waterways) remain at the forefront of development. Now he has joined the struggle to contain the degradation of the Western Ghats whose biodiversity had till recently been one of Kerala's chief glories. I was unaware of this project when I was booked into a jungle resort at Vythiri in Wayanad, and set off with my magnificent Alappuzha umbrella in the pouring rain to explore the surrounding countryside. To my surprise, as I entered the really thick jungle I found a narrow but excellently surfaced tarmac road capable—but only just—of carrying a jeep. Having lived for the past forty years in the Himalaya and shouted myself hoarse over the wastefulness of building wide roads that see but one vehicle a day, I was astonished to find this intelligent solution in the jungles of Kerala. I walked for miles, blessing the road builder since it meant the single greatest curse of the Sahyadri in the rains—millions of tiny bloodsucking leeches—were kept at bay by the tarmac.

After three miles of a pleasantly undulating climb through the most sensational greenery, alive with bird song, the road ended and I turned back, puzzled at its sudden termination. When I reached my resort I asked who had built the road and why it stopped so abruptly. I should have guessed: 'Babu Verghese' was the reply. Apparently his 'Green Magic' tree houses lay just beyond the end of the tarmac. To preserve the integrity of the experience, visitors have to walk the last bit which puts them in the mood for the unnerving ascent to their lofty quarters. Strict control is exercised over the entry of non-biodegradable substances, which means humans are allowed in but without their television sets! Comforts, however, are in place once you get to your eyrie. Double beds with attached bathroom, flush toilet and shower are provided, albeit without windows or indeed walls, but at a height of a hundred feet the only voyeurs are birds, monkeys and flying squirrels. A phone, library and carpeted veranda testify to Babu's concern to get every detail right, but the first detail is how to get up that enormous fig tree on which the tribals have crafted the eco-friendly hut.

There are two models of ascent: 'Mark I' is the highly original and decidedly adventurous ascent by a bamboo chair that rises according to the amount of water poured into a canvas bag acting as a counter-weight to the rising body. (Fat people obviously take longer to arrive than thin ones!) One can have the extraordinary experience of being winched through different layers of jungle for fifteen minutes before reaching the platform. Meals are likewise winched up and must taste marvellous, especially to anyone suffering from a siege mentality.

'Mark II' is more conventional, but just as exciting. This involves approach by a swaying plank bridge, which means the visitor first climbs a hillside till level with the treetop, then commits himself to a rickety, sagging drawbridge, before it connects to the canopy residence.

Uncannily, as I was being briefed on these cunning devices, all derived from the mind and capable hands of Babu Verghese, a jeep emerged from the jungle to invite me to sample for myself his 'Green Magic'. Apparently I had been spotted from one of the tree huts during my walk.

The following day I went back in the jeep, but only after witnessing the shortcomings of official tourism. I was taken to the Edakkal caves, a fabulously numinous encounter with prehistoric petroglyphics, the like of which you can find nowhere else. However, the local authorities forbade me to take my camera in but allowed the local sons of the soil to use theirs—which they did by posing with their girlfriends to obscure the artwork! At a neighbouring museum of considerable charm, all visitors are required to doff their footwear which, while culturally ideal for purists, means that most parties of well-heeled visitors will simply give it a miss. (Narcissism is a wonderful feeling if you can afford it.)

In the evening, I repaired to Babu's den in the woods and found his 'Mark I' hydraulic chair (to my relief) under renovation. (The barefoot engineer was perhaps working on a faster model, with inputs from Otis?) So I was taken to the 'Mark II' swaying drawbridge. During my walk the previous day I had passed under, around and above this tree hut, but had been oblivious of its existence. I was not aware either that when we arrived unannounced, the person who opened the 'door' was any other than the chowkidar. In fact, he turned out to be a Bangalore infotec millionaire who, along with his wife and young daughters, was spending the weekend aloft in the Ghats. As it happened, they were glad to see us because they required extra blankets. Nesting with the birds means a severe drop in temperature.

All around was the living magic of a flying carpet of greens. The effect of being one with the foliage was hugely satisfying. If the Edakkal caves had failed to bring alive the hoary beginnings of human striving, Babu Verghese saw to it that his guests were reminded of the 130 million years invested by the life force to create the setting for his primeval treetop platform.

Alive to the polluting fallout of conventional tourist development, no generators were installed. Energy from the sun was tapped by solar panels and gobar gas, though in the monsoon this means an interrupted supply. The menu explores Malabar cuisine with acknowledgement to the Arabian inputs that came with the sea lanes. Vegetables and fruit are grown organically on site and Babu reminds visitors that the aroma of spices from the kitchen stimulate the intestines to secrete the right gastric juices.

Kerala's chief virtue lies in the awareness of nature's wizardry. The success of the state's tourism department has been the marketing of this virtue and straying from official policy which talks down to the tourist and tells us what we ought to like. To the rave reviews given by foreign and Indian visitors to the treetop residences, I add my own. I suggest that having single-handedly produced Kerala's best-selling tourist ideas, Babu Verghese should be consulted by the policy makers in New Delhi on how to turn around the embarrassing statistic that more tourists visit Madame Tussauds' waxworks in London than come to India. The problem is that the mandarins marketing the world's richest array of tourist destinations that India has to offer prefer preachiness to professionalism. But things are at last moving. Some years ago when the government's flagship hotel in the capital sought advice on how to shore up its sagging image, local professionals said, 'Sell it'. Instead, the tourism ministry paid a fancy fee to an American consultancy firm who recommended they paint it white! Now back in its post-socialist pink, the hotel is up for sale. As the Babu Verghese story shows, it only needs one man (or woman) of ideas to make a success of such things.

God's own country

Arundhati Roy

Years later, when Rahel returned to the river, it greeted her with a ghastly skull's smile, with holes where teeth had been, and a limp hand raised from a hospital bed.

Both things had happened.

It had shrunk. And she had grown.

Downriver, a saltwater barrage had been built, in exchange for votes from the influential paddy-farmer lobby. The barrage regulated the inflow of saltwater from the backwaters that opened into the Arabian Sea. So now they had two harvests a year instead of one. More rice, for the price of a river.

Despite the fact that it was June, and raining, the river was no more than a swollen drain now. A thin ribbon of thick water that lapped wearily at the mud banks of either side, sequinned with the occasional silver slant of a dead fish. It was choked with a succulent weed, whose furred brown roots waved like thin tentacles under water. Bronze-winged lily-trotters walked across it. Splay-footed, cautious.

Once it had had the power to evoke fear. To change lives. But now its teeth were drawn, its spirit spent. It was just a slow, sludging green ribbon lawn that ferried fetid garbage to the sea. Bright plastic bags blew across its viscous, weedy surface like subtropical flying-flowers.

The stone steps that had once led bathers right down to the water, and Fisher People to the fish, were entirely exposed and led from nowhere to nowhere, like an absurd corbelled monument that commemorated nothing. Ferns pushed through the cracks.

On the other side of the river, the steep mud banks changed abruptly into low mud walls of shanty hutments. Children hung their bottoms over the edge and defecated directly onto the squelchy, sucking mud

This extract is taken from *The God of Small Things*, published by Penguin Books India.

of the exposed river bed. The smaller ones left their dribbling mustard streaks to find their own way down. Eventually, by evening, the river would rouse itself to accept the day's offerings and sludge off to the sea, leaving wavy lines of thick white scum in its wake. Upstream, clean mothers washed clothes and pots in unadulterated factory effluents. People bathed. Severed torsos soaping themselves, arranged like dark busts on a thin, rocking, ribbon lawn.

On warm days the smell of shit lifted off the river and hovered over Ayemenem like a hat.

Further inland, and still across, a five-star hotel chain had bought the Heart of Darkness.

The History House (where map-breath'd ancestors with tough toe-nails once whispered) could no longer be approached from the river. It had turned its back on Ayemenem. The hotel guests were ferried across the backwaters, straight from Cochin. They arrived by speedboat, opening up a V of foam on the water, leaving behind a rainbow film of gasoline.

The view from the hotel was beautiful, but here too the water was thick and toxic. *No Swimming* signs had been put up in stylish calligraphy. They had built a tall wall to screen off the slum and prevent it from encroaching on Kari Saipu's estate. There wasn't much they could do about the smell.

But they had a swimming pool for swimming. And fresh tandoori pomfret and crêpe suzette on their menu.

The trees were still green, the sky still blue, which counted for something. So they went ahead and plugged their smelly paradise— 'God's Own Country' they called it in their brochures—because they knew, those clever Hotel People, that smelliness, like other people's poverty, was merely a matter of getting used to. A question of discipline. Of Rigour and Air-conditioning. Nothing more.

*

Kari Saipu's house had been renovated and painted. It had become the centrepiece of an elaborate complex, crisscrossed with artificial canals and connecting bridges. Small boats bobbed in the water. The old colonial bungalow with its deep verandah and Doric columns,

was surrounded by smaller, older, wooden houses—ancestral homes—
that the hotel chain had bought from old families and transplanted
in the Heart of Darkness. Toy Histories for rich tourists to play in.
Like the sheaves of rice in Joseph's dream, like a press of eager natives
petitioning an English magistrate, the old houses had been arranged
around the History House in attitudes of deference. 'Heritage', the
hotel was called.

The Hotel People liked to tell their guests that the oldest of the
wooden houses, with its air-tight, panelled storeroom which could
hold enough rice to feed an army for a year, had been the ancestral
home of Comrade E.M.S. Namboodiripad, 'Kerala's Mao Tse-tung',
they explained·to the uninitiated. The furniture and knick-knacks
that came with the house were on display. A reed umbrella, a wicker
couch. A wooden dowry box. They were labelled with edifying placards
which said *Traditional Kerala Umbrella* and *Traditional Bridal Dowry Box*.

So there it was then, History and Literature enlisted by commerce.
Kurtz and Karl Marx joining palms to greet rich guests as they stepped
off the boat.

Comrade Namboodiripad's house functioned as the hotel's dining
room, where semi-suntanned tourists in bathing suits sipped tender
coconut water (served in the shell), and old communists, who now
worked as fawning bearers in colourful ethnic clothes, stooped slightly
behind their trays of drinks.

In the evenings (for that Regional Flavour) the tourists were treated
to truncated kathakali performances ('Small attention spans,' the
Hotel People explained to the dancers). So ancient stories were
collapsed and amputated. Six-hour classics were slashed to twenty-
minute cameos.

The performances were staged by the swimming pool. While the
drummers drummed and the dancers danced, hotel guests frolicked
with their children in the water. While Kunti revealed her secret to
Karna on the river bank, courting couples rubbed suntan oil on each
other. While fathers played sublimated sexual games with their nubile
teenaged daughters, Poothana suckled young Krishna at her poisoned
breast. Bhima disembowelled Dushasana and bathed Draupadi's hair
in his blood.

The back verandah of the History House (where a posse of

Touchable policemen converged, where an inflatable goose was burst)
had been enclosed and converted into the airy hotel kitchen. Nothing
worse than kebabs and caramel custard happened there now. The
Terror was past. Overcome by the smell of food. Silenced by the
humming of cooks. The cheerful chop-chop-chopping of ginger and
garlic. The disembowelling of lesser mammals—pigs, goats. The
dicing of meat. The scaling of fish.

Something lay buried in the ground. Under grass. Under twenty-
three years of June rain.

A small forgotten thing.

Nothing that the world would miss.

A child's plastic wristwatch with the time painted on it.

Ten to two it said.

A band of children followed Rahel on her walk.

'Hello, hippie,' they said, twenty-five years too late.
'Whatisyourname?'

Then someone threw a small stone at her, and her childhood fled,
flailing its thin arms.

*

On her way back, looping around the Ayemenem House, Rahel
emerged onto the main road. Here too, houses had mushroomed, and
it was only the fact that they nestled under trees, and that the narrow
paths that branched off the main road and led to them were not
motorable, that gave Ayemenem the semblance of rural quietness. In
truth, its population had swelled to the size of a little town. Behind
the fragile facade of greenery lived a press of people who could gather
at a moment's notice. To beat to death a careless bus driver. To smash
the windscreen of a car that dared to venture out on the day of an
Opposition bandh. To steal Baby Kochamma's imported insulin and
her cream buns that came all the way from Bestbakery in Kottayam.

Outside Lucky Press, Comrade K.N.M. Pillai was standing at his
boundary wall talking to a man on the other side. Comrade Pillai's
arms were crossed over his chest, and he clasped his own armpits
possessively, as though someone had asked to borrow them and he
had just refused. The man across the wall shuffled through a bunch

of photographs in a plastic sachet, with an air of contrived interest. The photographs were mostly pictures of Comrade K.N.M. Pillai's son, Lenin, who lived and worked in Delhi—he took care of the painting, plumbing, and any electrical work—for the Dutch and German embassies. In order to allay any fears his clients might have about his political leanings, he had altered his name slightly. Levin he called himself now. P. Levin.

Rahel tried to walk past unnoticed. It was absurd of her to have imagined that she could.

'*Aiyyo*, Rahel Mol!' Comrade K.N.M. Pillai said, recognizing her instantly. '*Orkunnilley*? Comrade Uncle?'

'*Oower*,' Rahel said.

Did she remember him? She did indeed.

Neither question nor answer was meant as anything more than a polite preamble to conversation. Both she and he knew that there are things that can be forgotten. And things that cannot—that sit on dusty shelves like stuffed birds with baleful, sideways staring eyes.

'So!' Comrade Pillai said. 'I think so you are in Amayrica now?'

'No,' Rahel said. 'I'm here.'

'Yes yes,' he sounded a little impatient, 'but otherwise in Amayrica, I suppose?'

Comrade Pillai uncrossed his arms. His nipples peeped at Rahel over the top of the boundary wall like a sad St Bernard's eyes.

'Recognized?' Comrade Pillai asked the man with the photographs, indicating Rahel with his chin.

The man hadn't.

'The Old Paradise Pickle Kochamma's daughter's daughter,' Comrade Pillai said.

The man looked puzzled. He was clearly a stranger. And not a pickle-eater. Comrade Pillai tried a different tack.

'Punnyan Kunju?' he asked. The Patriarch of Antioch appeared briefly in the sky—and waved his withered hand.

Things began to fall into place for the man with the photographs. He nodded enthusiastically.

'Punnyan Kunju's son? Benaan John Ipe? Who used to be in Delhi?' Comrade Pillai said.

'*Oower, oower, oower*,' the man said.

'His daughter's daughter is this. In Amayrica now.'

The nodder nodded as Rahel's ancestral lineage fell into place for him.

'*Oower, oower, oower.* In Amayrica now, isn't it.' It wasn't a question. It was sheer admiration.

He remembered vaguely a whiff of scandal. He had forgotten the details, but remembered that it had involved sex and death. It had been in the papers. After a brief silence and another series of small nods, the man handed Comrade Pillai the sachet of photographs.

'Okaythen, comrade, I'll be off.'

He had a bus to catch.

*

'So!' Comrade Pillai's smile broadened as he turned all his attention like a searchlight on Rahel. His gums were startlingly pink, the reward for a lifetime's uncompromising vegetarianism. He was the kind of man whom it was hard to imagine had once been a boy. Or a baby. He looked as though he had been *born* middle-aged. With a receding hairline.

'Mol's husband?' he wanted to know.

'Hasn't come.'

'Any photos?'

'No.'

'Name?'

'Larry. Lawrence?'

'*Oower,* Lawrence,' Comrade Pillai nodded as though he agreed with it. As though given a choice, it was the very one he would have picked.

'Any issues?'

'No,' Rahel said.

'Still in planning stages, I suppose? Or expecting?'

'No.'

'One is must. Boy girl. Anyone,' Comrade Pillai said. 'Two is of course your choice.'

'We're divorced.' Rahel hoped to shock him into silence.

'Die-vorced?' His voice rose to such a high register that it cracked on the question mark. He even pronounced the word as though it were a form of death.

'That is most unfortunate,' he said, when he had recovered. For some reason resorting to uncharacteristic, bookish language. 'Mostunfortunate.'

It occurred to Comrade Pillai that this generation was perhaps paying for its forefathers' bourgeois decadence.

One was mad. The other die-vorced. Probably barren.

Perhaps *this* was the real revolution. The Christian bourgeoisie had begun to self-destruct.

Comrade Pillai lowered his voice as though there were people listening, though there was no one about.

'And Mon?' he whispered confidentially. 'How is he?'

'Fine,' Rahel said. 'He's fine.'

Fine. Flat and honey-coloured. He washes his clothes with crumbling soap.

'*Aiyyo paavam,*' Comrade Pillai whispered, and his nipples drooped in mock dismay. 'Poor fellow.'

Rahel wondered what he gained by questioning her so closely and then completely disregarding her answers. Clearly he didn't expect the truth from her, but why didn't he at least bother to pretend otherwise?

'Lenin is in Delhi now,' Comrade Pillai came out with it finally, unable to hide his pride. 'Working with foreign embassies. See!'

He handed Rahel the Cellophane sachet. They were mostly photographs of Lenin and his family. His wife, his child, his new Bajaj scooter. There was one of Lenin shaking hands with a very well-dressed, very pink man.

'German First Secretary,' Comrade Pillai said.

They looked cheerful in the photographs, Lenin and his wife. As though they had a new refrigerator in their drawing room, and a down payment on a DDA flat.

*

Rahel remembered the incident that made Lenin swim into focus as a Real Person for her and Estha, when they stopped regarding him as just another pleat in his mother's sari. She and Estha were five, Lenin perhaps three or four years old. They met in the clinic of Dr Verghese Verghese (Kottayam's leading Paediatrician and Feeler-up of Mothers).

Rahel was with Ammu and Estha (who had insisted that he go along). Lenin was with his mother, Kalyani. Both Rahel and Lenin had the same complaint—Foreign Objects Lodged up their Noses. It seemed an extraordinary coincidence now, but somehow hadn't then. It was curious how politics lurked even in what children chose to stuff up their noses. She, the granddaughter of an Imperial Entomologist, he the son of a grass-roots Marxist Party worker. So, she a glass bead, and he a green gram.

The waiting room was full.

From behind the doctor's curtain, sinister voices murmured, interrupted by howls from savaged children. There was a clink of glass on metal, and the whisper and bubble of boiling water. A boy played with the wooden *Doctor is IN Doctor is OUT* sign on the wall, sliding the brass panel up and down. A feverish baby hiccupped on its mother's breast. The slow ceiling fan sliced the thick, frightened air into an unending spiral that spun slowly to the floor like the peeled skin of an endless potato.

No one read the magazines.

From below the scanty curtain that was stretched across the doorway that led directly onto the street came the relentless slip-slap of disembodied feet in slippers. The noisy, carefree world of Those with Nothing Up Their Noses.

Ammu and Kalyani exchanged children. Noses were pushed up, heads bent back, and turned towards the light to see if one mother could see what the other had missed. When that didn't work, Lenin, dressed like a taxi—yellow shirt, black stretchlon shorts—regained his mother's nylon lap (*and* his packet of chiclets). He sat on sari flowers and from that unassailable position of strength surveyed the scene impassively. He inserted his left forefinger deep into his unoccupied nostril and breathed noisily through his mouth. He had a neat side-parting. His hair was slicked down with Ayurvedic oil. The chiclets were his to *hold* before the doctor saw him, and to consume after. All was well with the world. Perhaps he was a little too young to know that Atmosphere in Waiting Room, plus Screams from Behind Curtain, ought logically to add up to a Healthy Fear of Dr V.V.

A rat with bristly shoulders made several busy journeys between the doctor's room and the bottom of the cupboard in the waiting room.

A nurse appeared and disappeared through the tattered-curtained doctor's door. She wielded strange weapons. A tiny vial. A rectangle of glass with blood smeared on it. A test tube of sparkling, back-lit urine. A stainless-steel tray of boiled needles. The hairs on her leg were pressed like coiled wires against her translucent white stockings. The box heels of her scuffed white sandals were worn away on the insides, and caused her feet to slope in, towards each other. Shiny black hairpins, like straightened snakes, clamped her starched nurse's cap to her oily head.

She appeared to have rat-filters on her glasses. She didn't seem to notice the bristly shouldered rat even when it scuttled right past her feet. She called out names in a deep voice, like a man's: 'A. Ninan . . . S. Kusumalatha . . . B.V. Roshini . . . N. Ambady.' She ignored the alarmed, spiralling air.

Estha's eyes were frightened saucers. He was mesmerized by the *Doctor is IN Doctor is OUT* sign.

A tide of panic rose in Rahel.

'Ammu, once again let's try.'

Ammu held the back of Rahel's head with one hand. With her thumb in her handkerchief she blocked the beadless nostril. All eyes in the waiting room were on Rahel. It was to be the performance of her life. Estha's expression prepared to blow its nose. Furrows gathered on his forehead and he took a deep breath.

Rahel summoned all her strength. *Please God, please make it come out.* From the soles of her feet, from the bottom of her heart, she blew into her mother's handkerchief.

And in a rush of snot and relief, it emerged. A little mauve bead in a glistening bed of slime. As proud as a pearl in an oyster. Children gathered around to admire it. The boy that was playing with the sign was scornful.

'I could easily do that!' he announced.

'Try it and see what a slap you'll get,' his mother said.

'Miss Rahel!' the nurse shouted and looked around.

'It's out!' Ammu said to the nurse. 'It's come out.' She held up her crumpled handkerchief.

The nurse had no idea what she meant.

'It's all right. We're leaving,' Ammu said. 'The bead's out.'

'Next,' the nurse said, and closed her eyes behind her rat-filters. ('It takes all kinds,' she told herself.) 'S.V.S. Kurup!'

The scornful boy set up a howl as his mother pushed him into the doctor's room.

Rahel and Estha left the clinic triumphantly. Little Lenin remained behind to have his nostril probed by Dr Verghese Verghese's cold steel implements, and his mother probed by other, softer ones.

That was Lenin then.

Now he had a house and a Bajaj scooter. A wife and an *issue*.

*

Rahel handed Comrade Pillai back the sachet of photographs and tried to leave.

'One mint,' Comrade Pillai said. He was like a flasher in a hedge. Enticing people with his nipples and then forcing pictures of his son on them. He flipped through the pack of photographs (a pictorial guide to Lenin's Life-in-a-Minute) to the last one. '*Orkunnundo?*'

It was an old black and white picture. One that Chacko took with the Rolleiflex camera that Margaret Kochamma had brought him as a Christmas present. All four of them were in it. Lenin, Estha, Sophie Mol and herself, standing in the front verandah of the Ayemenem House. Behind them Baby Kochamma's Christmas trimmings hung in loops from the ceiling. A cardboard star was tied to a bulb. Lenin, Rahel and Estha looked like frightened animals that had been caught in the headlights of a car. Knees pressed together, smiles frozen on their faces, arms pinned to their sides, chests swivelled to face the photograph. As though standing sideways was a sin.

Only Sophie Mol, with First World panache, had prepared herself, for her biological father's photo, a face. She had turned her eyelids inside out so that her eyes looked like pink-veined flesh petals (grey in a black and white photograph). She wore a set of protruding false teeth cut from the yellow rind of a sweetlime. Her tongue pushed through the trap of teeth and had Mammachi's silver thimble fitted on the end of it. (She had hijacked it the day she arrived, and vowed to spend her holidays drinking only from a thimble.) She held out a lit candle in each hand. One leg of her denim bellbottoms was rolled up to expose a white, bony knee on which a face had been drawn. Minutes before that picture was taken, she had finished explaining patiently to Estha and Rahel (arguing away any evidence to the contrary, photographs, memories) how there was a pretty good chance that they were bastards, and what bastard really meant. This had entailed an involved, though somewhat inaccurate description of sex. 'See what they do is . . .'

That was only days before she died.

Sophie Mol.

Thimble-drinker.

Coffin-cartwheeler.

She arrived on the Bombay-Cochin flight. Hatted, bell-bottomed and Loved from the Beginning.

Hangman's journal

Shashi Warrier

'Tell me about your family,' the writer asked. 'What do your brothers do now?'

'Raman is gone . . . His children don't write, we don't have the habit. But we meet once in a while, at festivals or weddings or funerals. Paraman lives near by. He never married, and he lives alone. He's the caretaker of a small house here.'

'In those days large families were common . . . It's strange that you had only two brothers.'

'Yes,' I said. 'Mother was ill sometimes, I suppose that must be why. I never thought of it.'

'Write about it, then. I'd like to know.'

He told me a bit about how to recall an image, to concentrate on it and write it out. Then he finished his coffee, and as he got up to leave, something popped into my mind. A small memory of someone challenging my father. A friend who said, 'Guess my weight. If you get it right, to within a kilogram, I'll admit you're a better judge of weight than I am.'

Father won his bet that day. That was, after all, part of his job, guessing a man's weight. I, too, learnt it. 'Guess what,' I told the writer. 'I just remembered something.'

He stopped, then sat back down on the concrete. 'What?' he asked.

'You weigh eighty-six kilos.'

'A little more, actually,' the writer replied. 'But you're only a kilo away.'

'Right. And you're . . . Ummm . . .' I stopped. I can no longer calculate as fast as I used to. 'Shall I say how tall you are, in feet and inches?'

This extract is taken from *Hangman's Journal*, published by Penguin Books India.

'Of course,' he smiled.

'Five feet nine inches. A little more, maybe, but less than five ten.'

His jaw dropped. 'That's pretty exact,' he said. 'How did you get that close?'

'Practice,' I replied. I had done it over a hundred times, after all. These judgments were the heart of the hangman's art.

The drop. The drop was everything. I wrote about it. I wrote what I could about it, and was happy with what I wrote. So I copied it out separately, and when the writer came next I gave him the clean copy I had made. 'This is for you to keep,' I told him. 'This is the best of what I've done so far.' He read it carefully, not struggling too much with the Tamil script, I could see. He finished it and said nothing. He folded the sheet and put it in his shirt pocket. He kept that piece. I knew it was good.

*

After I wrote about the drop I found that I could not think of anything to write.

I told the writer about this. He came regularly, and we went for longer and longer walks as the days grew longer. There was no sign yet of the rains: memories came, of long scorching summers, but they were only memories. Few starved these days. On these walks we kept quiet most of the time, talking rarely of writing, but mostly of other matters that he thought might help me find something in my mind worth writing about.

'Next time I come,' the writer said one day, 'will you show me where you met your teacher? Show me your favourite places. Would you like that?'

'Yes. We'll do that. I might remember things . . . But why wait for next time? Let's go now, for a bus ride.'

'Where?' he asked, a little surprised by my enthusiasm.

'To a temple. To meet a friend.'

'Which temple?'

'A Bhadrakali temple. The one where we used to go before a hanging. We'll meet the ringmaster in one of the little sideshows.'

We walked back along the canal to Parvathipuram. The packed earth road beside the canal joined the main road near a bridge, which is only a couple of hundred yards from the bus stand. At the bus stand we found the bus we would take, Number 31, which takes a circular route, starting here, going on to the bus stand at Vadassery, and returning here for a fifteen-minute break before starting off again. At this point the bus is usually empty: further on it fills up.

The bus started with a jerk, and all the seats filled up at the first stop, near the bridge. It proceeded jerkily on, getting more and more crowded, and when the conductor came along to give us tickets he had to push his way through a thick crowd. We shoved our way out of the bus at Vadassery, and from the junction near the bus stand we took the road that curves downwards towards SMRV school, one of the oldest schools in the district. About a quarter-mile down the road we took a lane to the right, a narrow, crooked, cramped lane, down which we could see rows of cramped old houses. All the buildings in this area seemed ancient—whitewashed squat buildings with tiled roofs blackened by the sun and the rain, and tiny windows fitted with wooden bars.

When I passed through here I went back twenty years in time, it had changed so little. We went past the school, which was built in the nineteenth century, and the bunch of old houses, then round a corner where there were fields to the west and a tiny temple to the right.

The temple door was shut, and a man in a small shop—a new one, less than five years old—at the corner told us to come back next morning. But this was familiar territory for me. I had been visiting this place off and on for the past nearly seventy years, and the older people knew me. We went around to the side of the temple compound, and I opened the small rusty gate at the side.

The *gurukkal* wasn't there but his wife was. This wasn't my *gurukkal*, of course—Ramayyan Gurukkal, who had been the priest here during my father's day. Ramayyan was gone now. When I replaced my father as the *aratchar*, he was the one I could visit any time. Ramayyan's son Kuppan runs the show these days, but he doesn't have the depth or the devotion of his father. I introduced the two, the writer and Kuppan, and the writer asked the *gurukkal* to do a small puja in his name. I saw a fifty-rupee-note change hands, and Kuppan bent to put it away. In the moment he bent over he looked exactly like his father.

I miss Ramayyan. He was one of those, like Maash, who made the silence bearable. I still remember the first time I saw him. I was a child then.

The temple is dedicated to our deity, Bhadrakali, the angry face of Parvati, wife of Shiva. This is my first visit to the temple. I am with my father, and he is going there to sacrifice a rooster to the goddess before going to a hanging, as is the hangman's custom of the day.

I don't understand why he is taking us along, me and my elder brother Raman. But we go without protest, because he takes us out so rarely that any outing with him is a pleasure. We are usually in bed by nine in the evening and up by six, but on this chill morning Father has woken us at four, when the starlight is still bright and the moon long gone. He has woken mother, too, and she has coffee ready, coffee to wake us up, coffee so hot that it scalds my mouth.

We bathe in the pond, finding our way by the bright starlight. As we wash we disturb the moorhens that nest at the far end of the pond, and they in turn wake the crows roosting in a tree nearby. I start when the cacophony shatters the stillness of the morning, and drop the slippery soap in the dark, cool water. Father puts his hand in the water and finds the soap, handing it to me without a word.

We finish our bath and leave home before dawn, clothed in fresh clothes, new off-white *mundus* for both Raman and me. We walk half-blind in the deepening mist of December, through the paddy fields to the broad tarred road which leads to town and to my school. Father carries a large white rooster by its legs—its wings and legs are tied together—and we can hear it cluck in bewilderment.

The road is deserted at this time, but as we walk we see the dim lights of faraway kerosene lamps in huts by the fields: people are coming awake. In the mist the dark is menacing, and I hold on to Father's thick and callused thumb for fear of losing sight of him. From this point, where we reach the tarred road, it is six kilometres to the temple, which lies by the fields near SMRV school, which is older than the prison at Poojapura, Father's workplace.

We reach the temple just after first light, the mist beginning to lighten in the faint sunshine. A slice of golden sun above the fields lights up the moment of excitement: I look forward to sharing something—anything—with my father, for it is a sign of growing up.

The temple door is closed but Ramayyan Gurukkal lives right next to the temple, in a two-room house with a low-roofed veranda in front and basil growing by the gate. Father coughs as he swings the small cane gate open, and Ramayyan comes to the door to see who it is. I hesitate at the gate. Father takes my hand to lead me in. The touch of his hand, hard and square and at that moment incredibly gentle, is reassuring, and I follow him in without fear.

The six *adiyaans* are already here, some of them are members of the original *aratchar* line. Father said last night that they had already done a puja at their own temple in Bimaneri, where the family's ceremonial sword is kept. They are aloof, their manner a strange mixture of respect and contempt that I don't understand. They don't seem to respect Father much and that I can't understand at all. I wonder why Father tolerates them. In his place, I would not speak to them. I wouldn't even let them into the temple to watch.

The flames in the brass lamps in the shrine flicker in the breeze as Father smears ash on his forehead before bowing to the fearsome icon of the goddess. Ramayyan Gurukkal, young and recently married, speaks to him briefly. He goes into his house and brings out a little cloth-wrapped bundle of flowers, and Father hands him a bottle of liquor and the rooster.

Ramayyan is short and stocky, with his stiff hair cropped short. He has sandal and ash on his chest and upper arms and on his forehead. He wears a thin cloth towel wrapped firmly about his waist, it is so thin that one can make out the outline of the loincloth that he wears under it. His chest is bare and hairless, and he has a few days' stubble on his face. He holds the bottle and the rooster before him in his square, strong hands and mutters some mantras in Sanskrit. When he stoops to put the bottle down he bends smoothly at the waist. Over the rooster he says some more words in Sanskrit before handing it back to Father.

I have seen a rooster being killed before—on feast days, a cousin or even my father would wring its neck in the backyard. One moment the creature would be alive, and dead the next. But what I see at the Bhadrakali temple is strange. Father holds the rooster between his legs, with its feet under his own and its head in his left hand. Then, suddenly, he beheads the rooster cleanly with a single diagonal stroke of a large knife that the *gurukkal* has given him. The head comes away in his hand.

I had always thought that a rooster would lie still after having its head cut off. But it doesn't: in the dim light the blood spurts blackly from its neck, and its wings flap, strongly at first, then weakly as its lifeblood ebbs away. I step back in fear: here is a dead creature showing all the signs of life.

Father still has the rooster's feet firmly under his own. If he were to let go, I'm sure the headless rooster will run blindly away. Even with him holding on, it struggles for several minutes while the *gurukkal* chants his violent mantras, the like of which I have not heard at any other temple. His breath comes in brief explosions as he speaks the first syllables of the invocation of Bhadrakali. I can see the strange wildness in his eyes and I shrink from it.

The puja takes an hour. When I have got over my fear, the chanting and the fresh blood on the ground seem inconsequential: the sun is up, and the herons feeding in the fields outside seem more important. After the puja Father rises from his seat on the floor. Ramayyan stands up before him and blesses him, and then the rope that Father had put in his bag, with the bottle, as we left home. By this time it is broad daylight and when we go out, to Ramayyan's house, I can feel the warmth of the sun on my back bringing out sweat. Ramayyan's wife offers my brother Raman a banana for the two of us to share, and we sit on a cot in the long verandah outside the house to eat it.

Father puts the rope back in the little bundle that he carries with him to hangings. The bundle contains what little he will need for a night at the guest house in Trivandrum, including a fresh shirt. He never carries a toothbrush because he prefers a *veppu* twig instead, or a fistful of charred rice husk which is commonly used in these parts.

He picks up the rooster, too. Later in the day it will be cooked. Father will have a share of it, and of the contents of the bottle.

Father leads us back home to where Mother waits nervously. 'Give them coffee,' he tells her. 'They watched it quietly. They'll learn.'

After he leaves I think of what he did to the rooster. I have got over my fear, and wish that I could behead a rooster the way Father did it, with a single clean stroke of the knife. I decide that I will do it one day, no matter what I do for a living.

*

After I became a hangman I performed this ceremony with the rooster a hundred and seventeen times. As a boy I had wanted to behead a rooster as expertly as my father did. But thinking of the times when I went to the temple before the hangings, I remember looking at my *adiyaans* standing lined up with me, and the people from the original *aratchar* family, and wishing I didn't have to do it. But it was part of the ritual, and I went through with it for form's sake.

For form's sake? I'm not so sure.

Rakesh Haridas

Those were the daze

Shreekumar Varma

I was ten when I was introduced to a broken legacy.

Schooling in Chennai was a no-nonsense affair, riotous and ordinary. During one of my vacations, I was taken to Attingal, some twenty miles from Thiruvananthapuram. There we were welcomed into the old family temple with traditional honours, mind-boggling for a schoolboy. For the first time I was confronted with the trappings of royalty. Shirtless and sweating, wearing a brand-new gold-bordered dhoti, I was horrified to find the probing gaze of a couple of hundred locals focused upon me. My mother, aunt and sister bore the limelight far more gracefully.

There were pipes blowing, and drums. Our grand procession made its way from the palace buildings to the temple. I was in the forefront, a most uneasy exhibit. My eyes were rooted to the ground. My hands clutched a rebellious dhoti. Each step was torture. This was almost twenty years after Independence, and the crowd followed with more curiosity than reverence.

We were almost there when I gazed up and spied a large cow surveying me coldly. She had broken through the crowd and was blocking our path. My terror was complete. I was sure the temple authorities had deliberately thought this up to crown their inflictions. We stared at each other for a tense moment. Her horns looked magnificent and devilish. I vowed I'd never again baulk at going to a temple. My prayers hit home. The cow's eyes seemed to melt. A cool breeze sailed in, bringing relief from the heat. As I thanked the deity with all my heart, she lifted her head and trotted forward. I retreated with a shrill cry, right into the temple officials bearing their paraphernalia. We collided painfully, upsetting a couple of ritualistic vessels. That was the first time I remember being involved in a royal do.

I was out of the palace in Thiruvananthapuram before I turned four. During vacation trips from Chennai, I wandered about its large airy rooms, the vast grounds. I would then wonder about the complications of a ceremonial life. You couldn't step out of the building without an attendant retinue of liveried servants. My mother mentioned the embarrassment of parading down the grounds on festive days, attendants in tow, heralded by piped music, as she and her sister proceeded to the tank for a ritual bath. If this was royalty, I thought, give me a quick shower any day.

And yet there were state dinners where the guest-list included magical names like Tagore and Nehru. Where, despite the teeth-crunching formality of etiquette, it was fun to be pampered and fed. Marriages went on for full seven days, replete with religious ceremonies, entertainments, processions and feasts. Being a member of the royal family was like being a favourite bird in a golden cage. You were watched and humoured and spoilt and loved. It was only when you were alone with yourself that you remembered the cage.

*

My grandmother ruled the State of Travancore as the Regent Maharani. She began as a reluctant little Rani, plucked out from her family in the innocence of childhood. Soft-spoken and considerate, she initiated several far-reaching measures during her rule. After meeting her, Mahatma Gandhi wrote that he felt he'd seen the Goddess Lakshmi herself. He also remarked that he was struck by her utter simplicity. Later came Independence, Communism and a rescheduling of social priorities. Her daughters left for other cities. She found it difficult to continue living in Thiruvananthapuram and moved to Bangalore.

I remember the small rectangular room where she spent her last days, lonely and occasionally visited, watching the dusk slip in and out of a series of windows. She read the newspaper and listened to songs by Yesudas. She kept toffees and carefully clipped-out comic strips ready for her grandchildren. She spent her days waiting for festivals like Onam and Vishu when she would get streams of visitors. One day towards the end, she confessed she was in danger of 'forgetting how to talk'. But an inherent optimism kept her going.

Kerala society is at best a precarious balance of the assured and the perilous. There is much political awareness, and this has generally led to a sense of frustration, the problem of helpless knowledge. There exists in the state a wide spectrum of experience, from the rigidly traditional to the wildly experimental. Imagine the plight of the unprotected, the unprepared, trying to eke out a living in this robust scenario. Imagine a bird from the gilded cage suddenly let out into bellicose skies.

After my first novel, *Lament of Mohini*, was published, most interviewers and reviewers dwelt incessantly on my 'royal past'. They seemed reluctant to accept the fact that there was hardly anything autobiographical in the book. One reviewer said I was being cruel to my family by revealing such colourful details. On the whole, this past had become a bit of a bugbear. I was considered with raised eyebrows as if I walked around with the paraphernalia of royalty draped about my shoulders. 'Tell me how it was,' was the refrain.

How it was, is a good question. How it is, is even better.

There are hundreds of tiny to big-time aristocratic families scattered all over Kerala. Their situation is far from glamorous. In fact, many of their members eke out a hand-to-mouth existence. Gone are the times when people shut their eyes and gave their girls in marriage to such families. Now the first question asked is: 'Is the boy employed? How much does he earn?' And that's where quite a few of the boys take a beating.

At any given moment, each of these families has a case or two pending with the Government, appealing for an increase in their allowance or trying desperately to hold on to their land. Some of the palaces are sooty, crumbling buildings that house nothing more than cobwebs, bandicoots and the occasional snake. Their owners have made an exodus to more livable surroundings or locations closer to their jobs. The few who remain wander about like ghosts, sticking stubbornly to tradition, discussing endlessly the past and the present, grabbing eagerly at morsels of life. Pictures of by-gone grandeur adorn their peeling walls.

It wouldn't be an exaggeration to say these people are frozen in a time capsule neither here nor there. They are stunned witnesses to history more than fifty years after Independence. These are the real-life counterparts of the lead characters in Satyajit Ray's 'Jalsaghar' and Adoor Gopalakrishnan's 'Elipatthayam'.

A relative told me of the time he had lunch with such a family. They were thrilled to have him over. They were lavish as they served him. After a delicious meal, he got up to wash his hands. Standing in the veranda, the hostess poured water from a spouted vessel. He then wiped his hands on a towel hanging nearby. As he was replacing the towel, my relative noticed something colourful on the wall. On a closer look he discovered it was a painting. A soft hole had appeared on the canvas where the wet towel regularly caressed it. He was horrified to notice the signature of the artist Raja Ravi Varma at the bottom.

The aristocratic family, who was even related in some way to the famed artist, was living in a time warp. The painting was a faceless part of their house, as faded and useless as anything else. The fact that priceless Ravi Varmas had passed through Sotheby's had nothing to do with this wall decoration that had merged with the wall at some point or the other. This is the bewilderment that allows enterprising antique-hunters to make a beeline for such houses, quoting dismally low prices for 'useless household items' like spittoons, carved chests and doors, old furniture and works of art, and then display them in fancy shops with indecent price-tags.

The palace where Ravi Varma was born is now almost deserted. Family members have moved to cities, leaving behind a remembrance of withering history. The Government recently woke up to the fact that a heritage was being ignored. The studio where the artist worked would be turned into an exhibition hall and a 'tourist attraction'. The proud artistic past of the state would be redeemed in some measure. But then the Government changed hands and the new incumbents discovered they had little money left for routine administration let alone to keep a tradition alive.

*

There are also those who survived. Resisting their family riches, they sought jobs to assure themselves of a regular income. The lucky ones did this while they still had their share of the family wealth. These are the only ones who retained their cake while routinely consuming it. Others were forced into employment when riches ran out. There are numerous aristocrats who do well as peons, clerks, and even sweepers—as long as it is a Government job.

And a countable few invested wisely and became successful in business. A countable few. I know of several entrepreneurs with a 'past' who stepped out into the world, armed with money and a 'name'. They felt they were equipped to take on the big bad world of business. By the time they realized they were no longer protected by a joint family, and that running a successful business required more than benevolent overall supervision, it was too late. I know of hotels, theatres, hospitals and factories that have collapsed under the weight of disillusionment.

However, a new generation is fortunately finding its feet. They are breaking away from rigid rules and are open to all kinds of experience. They are marrying into other castes and even religions. They are willing to travel far and work hard to maintain a good living.

*

The head of the Travancore royal family, the Maharaja, is also called Sri Padmanabha Dasa. He is a servant of the deity Sri Padmanabha, and used to rule in His name. As a child I was taken to the massive temple in Thiruvananthapuram and placed at the feet of the Lord. Every member of the family is thus handed over to Him. Thereafter, they are permitted to prostrate only on the single-stone mandapam once they enter the Lord's presence.

The temple is run by a Trust administered by the Maharaja. It employs a large number of people. I remember a tea-time conversation with the late Maharaja Sri Chitra Tirunal Rama Varma. The subject of the temple came up. He folded his hands and shook his head in a characteristic gesture of humility. 'It is not in our hands any more,' he smiled. Some decades ago these words would have meant that everything was in the Lord's hands. But now it meant everything was in the hands of labour unions.

However, in the first land of Indian Communism, there is still quite a bit of respect left for the erstwhile royal family. I was surprised at the passion 'the good old days' still evoked in some people.

One stormy afternoon in Thiruvananthapuram, I was in a shop opposite the Secretariat, watching the elderly shop assistant fold and pack a dhoti for me. It was pouring outside. I overheard the conversation of two men who'd come in to take shelter. They were discussing the rulers of 'those days'. I was overwhelmed to learn that they still remembered civic and welfare projects undertaken during my grandmother's rule, quoting figures and dates accurately. Finally, one of them pointed to the grand white Secretariat building before them and said, 'And now see what we have!' It was an eye-opener to me. That the cynicism of our local Thiruvananthapuram Malayali should hide a soft spot for a pre-democratic dynasty!

But there was more to come. The very next day, I was to visit the temple and then have lunch at the Kowdiar Palace. The Maharaja's personal car was sent to pick me up. The vehicle and the chauffeur's cap were easily recognizable because of the royal insignia on them. We entered the Fort area. The streets were narrow and crowded with people starting their day. Little bright shops. Flower-sellers and other vendors. School-going children ambling along. Suddenly I noticed pockets where people stood with folded hands, looking reverent as the car passed. I realized they were paying obeisance to the regular occupant of the car. I could do nothing but slink back in my seat, concealing myself till the car reached its destination.

This may not have been unusual in a North Indian context. Former royals are venerated even today. But in good old Thiruvananthapuram?

*

My mother was the first woman graduate from the royal family. Education was traditionally imparted at home, and there were tutors who were institutionalized by successive generations. Miss Watts was one such tutor. She handled her little wards with discipline and affection. Some of them were regular brats, playing truant, playing practical jokes, playing when they should be at their books. But Watts carried on, undimmed.

My grandmother and her cousin, the Maharaja's mother, read so much that they became storehouses of information, impressing every kind of visitor who conversed with them. They were exposed to western as well as traditional Indian literature. They were proficient in English and Sanskrit.

My mother was also the first person from the royal family who went out and studied in college. For her it was a rare freedom. For the first time in her life, she was moving about with people outside the palace. It was thrilling to learn about the warp and weft of real life. 'For some reason I went about barefoot,' she recollects. The other students stared and commented about this.

She also noticed with awe that her classmates and teachers wore silk saris and a great deal of jewellery. Barring ceremonial occasions, the family lived an unostentatious life, dressed and ate simply. Compared to other royal families in the country, Travancore's must have appeared singularly devoid of glamour.

Life in the gilded cage was pathetic in several ways. My mother wasn't allowed to communicate like ordinary children even with relatives of her own age. A vast collection of toys and books testifies to the solitary hours of her childhood. And when old uncles and aunts came to visit, they regarded her with reverence and she had to act like an adult, making wise observations and asking after their health.

She relates one such incident when a scholarly old uncle turned up. Her father asked her to meet the visitor in the audience hall and do the honours. She panicked. 'What will I say to him?' My grandfather thought for a moment and said, 'Begin by asking him if he's had his bath.' And that is what she went and asked him. After that the words just dried up. It must have seemed bizarre to the old man when the little chit of a girl confronted him with this strange and single question. She was barely ten at the time.

*

I feel a writer is a part of his environment, his times. Some of his influences will surely rub off on his work. Though I was born nearly a decade after Independence and my upbringing was ordinary and only as exciting as the next-door boy's, I share a heritage that is unique. I have real-time recourse to rare reminiscences. Every experience I've been through has been filtered by a past that is different, enriching my writing in one way or the other.

It is, in fact, a highly rewarding activity, watching and writing about the inmates of a gilded cage. Especially now that the door is open.

Ancient promises

Jaishree Misra

The rain continued unabated through the rest of the afternoon, adding chaos upon chaos. It even seemed to doggedly follow the convoy of cars that later took me to my new home on that long road to Valapadu. They were waiting, the whole convoy of them, at about six o'clock when all the ceremonies were done and it was time to leave Guruvayur. I hurriedly gave a quick round of hugs to my family who had crowded into the lobby of Elite Hotel to say goodbye. Dad was looking suddenly bereft . . . Ma, always practical, whispered a cheerful, 'We'll see you soon at the reception, moley . . .' Both my Ammummas were either crying or laughing, I couldn't tell . . . Appuppa smiled toothlessly from his wicker chair . . . But I couldn't be long. The Maraars were waiting, smiling. Pretending not to mind waiting. 'We have a long journey now, you know . . . Five hours from here, it'll be midnight when we get there . . . Let's hope it stops raining soon . . . Is she ready to leave now?' Someone had already put my suitcase into a Maraar car. Ma patted me firmly on the back, a pat that firmly told me (and her) that it was now *really* time to go. I turned and, without daring to look anyone in the eye, made a quick dash for the car, careful not to spoil the cream and gold mundu-sari I had been changed into. The car smelt brand new . . . ('They change them every year, my dear . . .' Maheswari Aunty had whispered unnecessarily to a by-then terribly impressed Ammumma.) From the deep depths of the middle of the back seat, I watched my family crane their necks to see me better and to smile reassuringly. I smiled reassuringly back at them. They and the Maraars were exchanging nods and looks that indicated that the matter at hand now was one too serious for small talk. I found myself suddenly squashed as new husband and new mother-in-law got into

This extract is taken from *Ancient Promises*, published by Penguin Books India.

the back seat on either side of me . . .

Nobody talked much during the journey, weddings are exhausting affairs and these were a few precious hours to be able to catch up on sleep. Every so often one head or the other would nod off, jerking awake a little later with a start. The car screamed noisily towards Valapadu, overtaking obdurate lorries and cars less new. The neck of the driver poured sweat in copious quantities that were wiped away at fifteen-minute intervals with a towel draped across his shoulder. I tried very hard not to drop off myself, terrified of putting an unaware head on an unfamiliar shoulder. But, in the drifting memories I now have of that long journey, I know that at some point I must have slept too. Closing my eyes and closing away knowledge of things too frightening to contemplate for any length of time . . .

When my eyes flew open again, it was to find that the convoy had stopped. Tall iron gates were being pushed open, revealing a garden and house. We must have overtaken the rain somewhere on the national highway. It was now dark and hot. The car started up again, moving slowly up a concrete drive, carefully making room for the other cars. The house loomed out of the still night. Large and white, with all the parapets painted in pink emulsion. Some enthusiastic architect had created a large plaster rose-shaped design on the front of the house, just under the roof, making me think of a huge birthday cake. Birthday! It had been my birthday too today. Even my parents had barely been able to remember that in the day's excitements. This new family didn't know it at all. Happy Birthday, Janu, I said to myself, trying to be cheerful. Just imagine, a *wedding* for a birthday present, a big expensive wedding for a growing-up and going-away present. Eighteen now, everyone has to grow up at some time or the other . . .

*

The morning after the wedding was as full of watchful eyes as the night before. I'd found myself suddenly wide awake at break of day and slipped out of bed as silently as I could. The windows had heavy wrought-iron grills, painted black and red. The garden outside was sodden from the rains that pelted down late at night, every little leaf looked like it carried a burden too sorrowful to bear.

I remembered Ma's careful instructions from the day before. *Don't go wandering out in your nightie! Have your bath as soon as you get up! Remember to wash your hair* (in Kerala you haven't had a bath even if you'd scrubbed yourself mercilessly but omitted to pour at least a mug of water over your head). I opened my suitcase, holding the clasps down with my thumbs so that they wouldn't snap open making a noise. Gathering the set of clothes that Mini's mother had carefully chosen and placed in a bag right on top, I crept into the adjoining bathroom. I'd been told to take everything I'd need for the first few days, and there they all were in dear Ammini Kunyamma's neatly arranged pack . . . soap, soap powder, talcum powder, toothbrush . . . oh dear, no toothpaste! I rummaged frantically around the plastic sari-shop bag that had been carrying everything. No, certainly no toothpaste. I crept back to my suitcase in the bedroom, gingerly opening it up again. I knew I had to be quiet because I was terrified of awakening my new . . . the word refused to form itself in my mind . . . *husband* . . . In my head I was using the same tone of voice that Mini reserved for 'bloodydamn' and 'boyfriend'.

Still no toothpaste. I sat back on my heels and contemplated my first foray out into the gracious, well-dressed world of the Maraars, in my crushed clothes from the night before, unwashed body and, worse, unwashed hair, strange vagabond from Delhi, begging for toothpaste. ('Don't they brush their teeth where you come from?') I could picture the look of horror on my mother's face and knew I just couldn't let the family honour down. Creeping back into the bathroom, I slid the bolt silently shut again. I picked up the pasteless toothbrush and rubbed its bristles vigorously against my small pink bar of Luxury Lux soap. Taking a deep breath, I brushed the resultant pink gloop against my teeth. I'd never tasted anything so awful, but, twenty minutes later, I was scrubbed and clean, the ends of my hair bearing tiny drops of water like so many tremulous, glittering trophies. I got into the carefully chosen brand-new sari (yellow nylon 'Garden Hakoba' very-nice-madam-very-well-draping) that had been hotly debated back at home, Ma favouring a more formal silk and Kunyamma going for the more casual, about-the-house look for 'The first day at the Maraars'. Remembering the kohl in my eyes and a little red bindi on my forehead, I was ready for them.

The house was dark and no one seemed to be up yet. I could see, even in the half darkness, that everything was in its place and the cushions on the divan were eerily upright, like soldiers on parade. I wandered through a seemingly endless dining room with a polished table big enough to waltz on and then found myself in a small verandah. From there I could see some movements in the kitchen . . . a Maraar! Gingerly I pushed the door open, startling a bent little Ammumma who was pouring oil from a large urn into two little bottles.

'Oh, it's you, Janu, you frightened me. Why are you up so early?'

I spoke my first words to a member of the In-Laws, 'I usually wake up early' . . . oh dear, my first words and they'd turned out to be a lie. Getting up early was something I only *ever* did to get to school on time and when I couldn't block out my father's shouts any more with warm blankets.

'Would you like some coffee? There's some in that percolator over there. I'd make it for you but my hands are oily.'

I went over to the percolator and contemplated the small steel contraption. Yes, I would like some coffee, please, but I was familiar only with the stuff that came out of bottles in a spoon. My second lie was on its way.

'No, I don't drink coffee, thanks.'

There was a busy sound at the door and my new mother-in-law entered the kitchen. She'd been the subject of most of our speculation in all conversations that had taken place about the Maraars back at home. The two families had met on a few occasions to discuss the planned 'alliance' and my uncle, amongst others, had developed a strong 'Janu's-mother-in-law phobia'. Mini's father, normally an easy-going sort of individual with a wicked sense of humour, had found his laughs drying up uncharacteristically in the presence of that forbidding figure. On one of his early attempts at breaking the ice, he'd informed the Maraars that my father's official designation of Director of Signals in the Indian Air Force really only meant that he was the man who stood on the airport tarmac waving cardboard lollipops at taxiing aircraft. This brought the usual round of affectionate sniggers that gradually bubbled away as my family realized, one by one, that they were the only ones laughing. The Maraars appeared to be taking their cue from the matriarch leading their delegation. She had fixed a cold gaze on Kunyachen, clearly signalling that no jokes demeaning The Alliance in any way would be harboured. Her son was marrying the daughter of a Highly Placed Official, and *nothing*, especially not the buffoonery of lowly uncles, was going to detract from that.

I unfroze myself and tried to sidle along the wall as she approached the percolator.

'Have you had coffee?' she asked, without seeming to address anyone in particular. I shot a look at the Ammumma still pouring out her oils and decided the question must be aimed at me. Before I could reply, however, the Ammumma said, 'Janu doesn't drink coffee.'

My chances of getting some sustenance seemed to be slipping away. The taste of bath soap still lurked horribly in my mouth.

'Tea, then?' Still no eye contact.

I decided to take the plunge. Boldly, I replied, 'Yes, please.'

'Look, you're not in Delhi any more. Like it or not, you now live in Kerala, so I suggest you drop all these fashionable Pleases and Thank Yous. Here we don't believe in unnecessary style.' She accompanied this with a short laugh, perhaps attempting to take the edge off it. But the edge was clearly there. It tore a tiny little scratch inside me somewhere, and suddenly the many times that I'd been told off for forgetting a little kindness or gratitude seemed so falsely, so pretentiously *Delhi*.

Deeply ashamed, I pushed my back as far as it would go into the wall behind me and watched her briskly make the tea. Was her displeasure because I'd spoken in *English*? I cast about frantically for the Malayalam to use when she gave me the tea she was making, remembering vaguely that there were no equivalent words for a casual Please and Thank You. I couldn't very well have used the only option I knew, unless I wished to express the deepest, most flowery gratitude more suited to a court than a kitchen. Non-Kerala families like mine tended to mix up English and Malayalam into an easy, casual city-speech that had worked reasonably well on my holidays here. Now that I was here for ever, it looked like that brand of Malayalam was going to be woefully inadequate. Even worse, seen as *stylish*. Thankfully it didn't look like I was expected to join the rest of the conversation between the two women. It was about the food that would be cooked for the large extended family staying till the reception, and the old

Ammumma appeared to be taking orders from her daughter. 'You can cut two kilos of beans for the thoran, and six carrots. Make sure you do it yourself, that Thanga will make a complete mess if you leave it to her. Last week the pieces were so big, I could not even chew them. You don't watch her closely enough, sleeping instead of supervising.' Nary a please nor a thank you, I noticed, and delivered in a tone of voice that was deeply frowned upon in my family, but we'd evidently got a lot of things wrong. 'Here's your tea.'

I walked to the kitchen counter to pick it up, 'Thank . . .' I remembered just in time to swallow my unbidden English gratitude with a hot gulp of tea.

As I was sipping my sugary tea, different members of the clan started to drift in. First Sathi (the older sister-in-law I had already met when I was first seen by the Maraars) followed by her brood of cheeping chicks (Vinnu, Annu and Joji), then Latha (the Kerala-brought-up-daughter-in-law . . . *washed, bathed* and not in a *nightie*), followed by various other aunts and cousins. The men were probably congregating elsewhere, in some distant and privileged verandah or living room, to which large trays of tea were being regularly despatched.

Perhaps out of kindness, I was not spoken to very much, which was a relief. It didn't sound as if anyone in this family had grown up outside Kerala, the Malayalam flying around me was fast, fluent and elegant. My years of growing up in Delhi and having to struggle with Hindi in school, had relegated Malayalam to a very low priority. It was getting clearer by the minute that my holiday-Malayalam, so comical it sometimes even made my grandparents giggle, was unlikely to endear me to this family. I hoped I could get away with looking sufficiently interested in everything going on around me *without* having to make verbal contributions. Don't appear *overly* agog though, I warned myself, that might be misconstrued as well . . . as being idiocy or something.

As the morning outside brightened, I noticed that the younger set had started to drift around and were getting ready to play some board games in the dining room next door. Most of them looked about my age, and I hoped I would be asked to join them when I saw Gauri, my new younger sister-in-law, carry out a large carrom board. She had not been a part of the Maraar group that had first come to see me, but had not shown any interest so far in getting to know me. She was Mother-in-Law's pet we'd been told, still a schoolgirl and the one that I had marked out to befriend in this household. She had looked busy all morning, chatting and giggling with the cousins who were visiting, now organizing them efficiently into teams to play carroms. That looked like much more fun than the kitchen activities and conversation that was all about people and relatives I did not know yet. I continued to play with my teacup, listening enviously to the gales of laughter emanating from the room next door. I don't suppose it would have done for me to be included in that happy set. They were the *daughters* of the family, and *unmarried*. It was okay for them to be unwashed at ten o'clock and wearing nighties, unlike me. I missed home dreadfully and hoped that the expression on my face did not give it away. A small frock-clad battalion of new nieces had assembled itself in front of me and was now observing my every movement with eyes that moved in perfect military unison.

'Hello,' I ventured softly. Annu, about four, slid hastily behind her mother. Two-year-old Joji showed me a furry bear and then hid it behind her back. Vinnu, who was probably about the same age as Mini, maintained an unbroken gaze. Occasionally her eyes would wander up and down my person, carefully examining an ear-ring or a toe. I wondered what to make of this careful inspection. She was looking at the chain around my neck when she suddenly piped up, 'Is it gold?'

No one else appeared to have noticed I was attempting my first full-fledged (Malayalam) conversation with a Maraar. 'It is,' I replied.

'Is *that* gold?' She was now looking at my ear-rings. I nodded.

Her gaze wandered to my hands, she wasn't going to give up easily. 'Diamond?' She looked like a suspicious jeweller.

I shook my head. It was only an ordinary Rangoon white stone that Ammumma had set in gold for me on my last holiday in Kerala. The little girl nodded in satisfaction, she'd finally caught me out. I thought our conversation had petered out, but a few minutes later she startled me by reaching out a small finger to stroke the yellow nylon of my sari. 'Imported?' she asked.

I didn't see my new husband until it was time for breakfast. The wizened old Ammumma, who had not stopped to rest once, had warmed two dosa griddles and was now turning out crisp, golden dosas at great speed. The Maraar clan seemed enormous and the meal-time routine seemed to be men first in the dining room, children alongside at the kitchen table, then the women, the drivers and servants and finally, after she'd fed everybody else, the old Ammumma. I thought of the fuss my grandmother would have made if anyone had ever attempted to relegate her to that position in our house.

Suresh came in with his father. Both of them smiled briefly at me as they sat down and were served their dosas with sambar and chutney.

'Do you eat dosas for breakfast in Delhi?' Hopefully a kindly, and not sarcastic, inquiry from Father-in-Law.

'Not often,' I replied, 'my mother doesn't get the time on working days, but we do have them at the weekends sometimes.'

'Well, you can't expect any better when women go out to work, can you?' This was another barbed shaft from Mother-in-Law. It wasn't taking me long to work out that my choice as bride had not been a universally popular one in this household. Had Suresh defied his parents' wishes to choose me? Perhaps from among the thousand hopefuls who, we'd been told, had been vying madly to become his wife?

I looked at the back of his head. He seemed to have had a bath as well. I was glad I had remembered to remove my washed underwear from the bathroom after finishing my bath, carefully spreading them out to dry on top of my suitcase. They would be nearly dry now, discreet and untempting on their perch under the bed. I was grateful that he had not forced himself on me last night and now strangely touched at the possibility that he'd perhaps defied his mother's wishes to marry me. I also knew by now that I was going to need an ally to fend off the many shafts that were undoubtedly going to be heading my way. He was the obvious choice to be that ally.

I couldn't remember the details of his face from that first awkward meeting, and hadn't needed to look at it during the marriage ceremonies yesterday. While walking around the flickering vilakku at the temple with my head bowed, I'd had plenty of time to observe his feet as he walked ahead of me. I'd felt a sudden lurching realization that I was getting more time to familiarize myself with the feet of the man I was marrying than his face! They looked about size eight, with slightly blotchy skin, the big toe was shorter than the one next to it, the nails were pale with jagged edges. That was when the shivering had started. I had quickly struck up an inner dialogue with myself to stop the shaking, which seemed to work briefly. 'Surely you must be able to remember *some* other details about him from that first meeting?' 'Nope, it's all a complete blur.' 'You're not *trying*. Remember a largish nose?' 'Hmm . . . maybe . . .' 'Now try again, he's not very tall?' 'Yes, I sort of remember that . . .' 'Good. And there's lots of other things you know. That he runs a verrry successful motel business, my dear. Developed (from scratch!) by his father. Verrry good family he belongs to also.' 'Yes! And now I also know the shape of his feet!' At that point my thoughts had been completely drowned out by the thumping of the temple drums and lowing of conch shells. The smoke from the oil lamps and the heavy perfume of the joss sticks had been threatening to throw me over in a dead faint. Maybe it was safer, I told myself hastily, not to think too much.

Here in the kitchen, I couldn't stare for too long, of course, but I could see in brief darting glances that he had a small bald patch developing at the back of his head. His back looked narrow, he was quite slim and wiry. Dark skinned. I knew he was twenty-six and a half years old. A fair bit older than me, but Ma had said that would probably make him protective and kind. Leaning on the kitchen wall, watching him talk to aunts and cousins, I felt weary at the thought of how much I still had to find out.

I was also beginning to get a sense of having a lot of reassuring to do. That hadn't occurred to me before, that this new family of mine might have developed a pre-conceived notion of me! Somehow I had to let these strangers know that I was kind-hearted and affectionate. That children and animals usually liked me. And that, despite Delhi, I was really not *too* stylish and had come into their lives very eager to love them. *Despite* having lost my heart once as a sixteen-year-old, which of course had to be carefully hidden from them. How on earth was I going to convey so much and soon? And in broken Malayalam! It felt like there was an awful lot of catching up to do, as there were obviously certain things about me that had already failed to make the grade. Beginning with an account in debit was *not* the best way to set out on a new life. Suddenly I was terribly homesick again and very close to tears.

*

Over the first few days with the Maraars, I progressed into little more than monosyllabic replies. This, I was sure would be considered a good thing, as brides were expected to be bashful. And a bashful bride from *Delhi* (who could have turned out to be God-only-knows-what) would, I thought, endear me to them greatly. It certainly wasn't coming very naturally to me as there were times when I longed to break out into animated chatter, joining in the general conversation. But speaking in English would be misconstrued as attempting to be stylish and speaking in Malayalam had on occasion been greeted with sarcastic laughter. I was better off pretending to be a bashful bride.

I now knew where the rice was kept, at what time lunch was served, what everyone's names and relationships were. I had even been taken by my mother-in-law to Dr Gomathy's clinic to have a 'Copper-T' fitted. The thing that was going to prevent inconvenient babies from arriving and interfering with the BA my parents had been promised I'd complete. It nestled snugly now deep inside me somewhere, having been pushed in by Dr Gomathy's efficient rubber-gloved hand, after which she patted my bare bottom announcing sagely that I was now 'ready' . . . Ready for Lurve, I thought anxiously.

The reprieve I had been granted on my wedding night hadn't lasted, of course. It seemed to be quite late at night that people began to retire to their separate rooms in the Maraar household and I'd hung around the following night until I was actually told to go to bed. Suresh was already in the room, stretched out on the bed, reading a magazine. Hoping that minimal eye-contact would somehow have him fail to notice that I was in the room too, I tip-toed about getting ready for bed. When I could put it off no longer, I finally perched myself delicately on the edge of the bed, swinging my legs demurely over, quickly tucking them under the sheet. I could hear sounds of a magazine being put away and of an arm reaching out for me and knew I couldn't put it off any more. When it finally came, with an ungraceful conjoining of arms and legs, and clothes and sheets, with buttons and hooks adding to the chaos, I greeted it with the stoic sense of one of those things that had to be done. Like a visit to the dentist, where things went on in intimate parts of you that you could neither see nor control. Love didn't seem to play much of a part. And laughter, that might have been more comforting under the circumstances, didn't come into it at all. It felt awkward to be kissed by a mouth that had not had very much to *say* to me up to that point. I tried to quell the feeling of revulsion that rose in my chest. And decided I was no nearer either to feeling loved or to wanting to love. Even my few tentative explorations with Arjun had not prepared me for this sudden invasion. Later, looking up at the ceiling fan, feeling sore, mentally and physically, I wondered why Leena had advocated chasing after this thing with such fervent enthusiasm? Perhaps it was one of those things that would *grow* on me, I hoped, watching my figure whirling slowly around in the steel cap of the fan above. Next to me, the eerie night-call had started up . . . coo-wee . . . coo-wee . . .

But there was at least a kind of rationale to the nights that my days in the Maraar household still seemed completely devoid of. It was getting clearer that it was the *Maraars* I had married, not Suresh. He had not been unkind, but had not seemed to want to spend much time alone with me. The couple of hours before breakfast he spent discussing business with his father on the verandah. After breakfast, they would leave for one of the motels. I, left with the women folk, attempted to look useful, which wasn't very easy because between school and Arjun, I'd never found the time to learn to cook. In the evenings, if Suresh was not touring and did get back early enough, we sometimes went for a drive or to the cinema where rats as big as small cats ran down the aisles. Gauri, my schoolgirl sister-in-law always accompanied us because, as Suresh's mother said, she only had her brother to take her out, poor thing.

'Suresh chettan had promised me he would only marry someone who would agree to my being taken everywhere too,' Gauri informed me archly one evening as we waited for Suresh to pick us up for the six o'clock show of *padayottam*.

'I don't mind,' I said quickly, not very sure of whether I ought to mind or not. At fourteen, Gauri was closer in age to me than Suresh was, and there seemed to be potential to make a friend. She had already shown me how to stamp my feet every three minutes in the cinema to prevent the rats from coming scampering over our feet, reducing us to hysterical titters. 'I really do like it when you come as well,' I said with more conviction.

'You realize, of course, how lucky you are,' she continued, 'to have in-laws like my parents. My older sister, Sathi chechi, really has a hard time with hers. Always interfering with everything, useless people.'

I'd met Sathi's in-laws at the wedding. They had seemed to be a timorous old couple, as much in awe of the Maraars as we were. 'But they live quite far from here, don't they? Pathanamthitta or somewhere?' I was genuinely curious.

'Yes but they visit her and us about once every six months and they want to poke their noses into everything. I never speak to them politely if I can help it.'

I wondered how she got away with it. My parents expected me to be polite to everyone, even children. She was still talking, now getting quite animated. 'Do you know, I refer to your father as "Air Commode". Only air comes out on the lavatory. It always makes everyone laugh.' She giggled loudly and looked slyly at me to gauge my reaction.

My father had worked hard to acquire the rank of Air Commodore and it hurt me deeply now to hear him referred to so rudely. I shot a look at my mother-in-law who was stringing flowers near by. She was laughing too, proud of her daughter's clever wit. I looked down at my feet and wished I could be less sensitive.

Mother-in-Law, who I'd been told to address as Amma, was showing little sign of thawing towards me, although I did notice that she certainly wasn't universally icy. She absolutely adored Gauri and was full of smiles whenever Sathi visited, which was frequently as she and her family lived just down the road. Amma was also a dedicated grandmother, full of treats for Sathi's three little girls. The Ammumma was Amma's widowed mother who lived with them and seemed to earn her keep by slaving all day to keep the kitchen gleaming, despite churning out vast quantities of food. I hoped that she got more of a holiday when she went to live with her son in Calicut once a year. Latha, the older daughter-in-law, was quite obviously not a part of the charmed inner circle, but, efficient and brisk, seemed to have gained some hard-earned respect. She and Suresh's older brother, a college professor, did not live in the family home but in distant Madras. I was sorry to see them being driven off to the station the day after the reception and would see them again only about once a year.

The reception had been a confusing affair. I'd woken up that morning with an overwhelming feeling of excitement at the thought of seeing my family again . . . after four long days! I jumped out of bed to brush my teeth and prepare for the day, bumping into Suresh who was just emerging after his shower. In my joy I gave him an impetuous hug, startling him. Suddenly unsure of his reaction, I looked at his face and thought he looked pleased. He did not, however, ask me what it was infecting me so. He didn't seem to notice at all—as I didn't then—that there were hundreds of opportunities like that one, missed carelessly and without thought for the price we would have to pay later. Tiny little chances to ask each other how we were feeling. To talk and share our thoughts and learn to become friends. That morning, however, the thought of seeing my parents again was obliterating everything else. I hugged myself in glee, sitting down again on the edge of the bed to look out of the window, wondering how like sad fat babies the dumpy jackfruits looked, clinging helplessly to matronly tree trunks. Suresh carried on humming to himself, brushing his hair and carefully choosing a shirt from the wardrobe.

'You'd better go with Amma to the bank locker to get out your jewellery and things for the reception,' he said vaguely.

I nodded, 'Shall I wear the necklace you had put on me at the wedding?'

'I don't know, you'd better check . . . there might be some traditional piece or something you'll have to wear . . .'

'Are you going to the motel today too?'

'Of course. Business is not like an Air Force job where you can take leave. Always things to worry about.' He was ready and about to leave the room. I was being a nuisance now, prolonging the conversation.

'What? What sort of things to worry about?'

'Oh you won't understand, unions, accounts, tax matters . . .'

I could understand, I thought. I knew all those words and *wanted* to understand. But Suresh was now half out of the door, swinging his briefcase impatiently. Holding the curtain open he said, more kindly, 'You'd better get ready soon, Amma and all the others would have had their baths by now. Married girls don't create a good impression if they stay in their rooms till late.'

I was more keen on creating that good impression with the Maraars than with attempting to impress Suresh with my business acumen and hastily scrambled up to get ready for my bath. But baths before dawn, making sure I washed my *hair* each time and being first past the post in the kitchen wasn't going to be quite enough. I could tell, fairly early on, that some of the things I needed to create that good impression were completely out of my control. Later that morning, I returned with Amma from the bank locker, carrying my small sandalwood jewellery box. She was staggering under the weight of numerous large maroon boxes stuffed full, no doubt, with beautiful Maraar jewellery. It felt safer not to offer help in carrying them, as it might have been seen as an eagerness to get my hands on Maraar jewels. I let the driver do the honours instead. In the house, my little box was opened up and the women of the house gathered around to decide what pieces I should wear at the reception. I could feel that familiar feeling of discomfort creeping in as it was clearly an exercise in 'Let's see what these Highly Placed Delhi Officials give their daughters'. I had heard that Sathi had been weighed down with gold when she'd got married some years ago and was fairly sure my parents' scraped-together savings had not bought me enough in Maraar terms. I was right.

'Oh look, Sathi, have you ever seen such tiny ear-rings? They're like your jumikis, only ten times smaller.'

'Well they'll match the sari she'll be wearing, but we can't have such tiny ones. What'll people think!'

Oh no, what *were* people going to think of me? That my father loved me less because he hadn't been able to afford elephantine jumikis?

'I . . . I've always liked small pieces of jewellery . . . I feel they suit me better . . .' I stuttered, lying.

Amma was holding up a beautiful old layered gold chain. My father's gift to my mother at their wedding. 'Now, *this* is a nice one, is it new?'

Rare words of praise! I struggled briefly with a desire to lie again and, hopefully, look good. but this was something it was going to be difficult to lie about. 'No it's not new, it was the swarnamala put on my mother at her wedding.'

The chain was flung aside. 'Can't have her wearing something *old* at the reception. Sathi, go and get something out of your jewellery. Just make sure it's something people in Valapadu haven't seen before.'

The happy feeling I'd woken up with was dissipating at a rapid rate and got no better as, later in the afternoon, I had to start dressing for the reception. I was helped by Sathi and an aunt who did a 'tip-top' job, as they put it, in making me look like someone else. A plait of hair had been bought from the local Ladies' Store and was firmly attached to my shoulder-length Delhi tresses with a multitude of pins that now dug into my scalp. A thick layer of black eye-liner was painted around my lashes, quite unlike the tiny smudge of kohl I was more accustomed to. A pair of pretend lips were outlined around my own smaller ones with a deep maroon pencil and then painted in, giving them a sultry Tamil heroine pout. By the time I'd worn Sathi's jewellery and the brand-new Kanjeevaram sari that had been bought for me, I *was* somebody else!

When my parents arrived at the house, I was trotted out to show them how easy it had been to make me look like a Maraar. In a Maraar sari and make-up and jewellery. Maraar lips and Maraar eyes. Even a hip-length plait of hair to match the graceful Maraar tresses.

I stood in front of them, a counterfeit Maraar, hiding Delhi insides and a very heavy heart.

The thief of memories

Vijay Nambisan

At lamp-lighting time, when the elders had had enough of our running about and the noise we made, all of us children would be made to sit in a row along the narrow strip of veranda which extended towards the main gate. There we were urged to say our prayers, or as the Malayalam phrase literally has it, 'recite names'. 'Rama-Rama-Rama-Rama' becomes quite monotonous, and for variety and from the wickedness of our minds we would, like Valmiki, often say 'Mara-Mara-Mara . . .'

The electric supply was fitful and unreliable then. I think only one or two rooms in the old house had electric fittings, and the light would wane and wax like that of an oil lamp. There was, of course, no TV; there was a vacuum-tube radio set. The house was older than my father, having been built about the beginning of the century, though generations of his fathers had been born in houses which had stood on the same site and one after the other been torn down and replaced. There was a sense of the continuity of the clan, especially when the house was full of cousins, which I was too young to understand then and only appreciate in retrospect.

As we sat there for as long as we could sit still, the darkness fell, such a darkness as city-dwellers are now unaccustomed to. The air was full of night-birds and night-insects, and frogs at the appropriate season. I was town-bred myself, and with the darkness a gloom would settle on me. There was nothing to do: I couldn't read, couldn't play, and night in an old house is always full of devils. I vastly preferred my eldest uncle's town house in Trichur (now Thrissur), where there were lots of books and the sounds of traffic and electric lights. I could also speak English there and be understood by everybody.

My Malayalam is much better now—I never studied it formally, though my parents taught me to read and write—and my sensibilities are better educated. I go back to the old house in the village with a sense of passionate expectation, though nothing ever happens there. Both the uncle who lived there and his older brother in Trichur are dead, the town house was sold long ago and, as in most of Kerala, the city has come to the village. The roads are good; I have driven the 18 kilometres from Trichur in under 40 minutes, and there is no reminder of the two-kilometre walks we had to take across the paddy fields from the State highway. We had to walk on the narrow, often crumbling earth boundaries between the tiny fields, and in the rains it was always difficult for me to keep my footing. Once, when I was eight, I slipped and fell off the path into two feet of muddy water, and I vividly remember my consternation as I sat there and looked up at my smiling parents and hooting sisters.

The old house is very quiet now. My aunt is there, and her son and his wife; their daughter is in college. Not more than once or twice a year is it full of people, and there are no crowds of children to swell the corridor and the veranda with their riot. The last wedding there was my sister's, almost ten years ago.

A couple of days after that wedding I sat with another cousin on the steps of the two-storied 'gate-house' across the yard from the main house and talked about such things. We both hearkened back to the old days, an impossibly romantic Gandhian dream which always overcomes me when I go back. Later I retailed the conversation, in a self-congratulatory manner, to my mother, who said, 'It's all very well for you men to talk like that. Just think what our life was like then, it was work all the time with hardly any time to rest. You may sneer at mixies and washing-machines, but they've made our life easier.'

I realized how far my sentimentality had carried me into folly. For me the ancestral house was a museum of memories (not only mine) which I wanted to remain just so. But for my cousin and his family, it was the house they were living in. How should I object to the fluorescent light in the 'drawing-room' (plain *thekkini* or 'south room' in Malayalam), or to the TV-watching for two hours after dinner? I, who spend no more than a week there in a year and am writing this by fluorescent light in my 'study' which is, coincidentally, also south-facing? In many ways, as we grow up and look out at the world, the only romance left to us is in childhood memories; and Kerala is a very skilled thief of those.

All Kerala is divided into three parts: the Church, the Party, and the Gulf. Going to the Gulf is, of course, escapism, not escape, as return is mandatory. But temporary escapee or returnee—or one of that irredeemable majority who'll never have the chance—the Gulf is very much with the Malayali. Two generations of it have transformed the very architecture of the state, and most definitely its culture. Such gewgaws as rechargeable torches, emergency lamps and walking talking dolls are found in homes whence no one has been to 'Saudi' to work. Even the villages have 'Duty Paid' shops.

Our toys were very simple. We played, indoors, a game like Ludo, with certain shapely seeds for dice; outdoors we ran and shouted, played rude games with bat and ball, racquet and shuttlecock. Or we climbed trees or raided the mango orchard, and the feel of the viscous yellow juice of those country mangoes running down my chin is still with me. I remember Narayanan, my uncle's factotum (he's still there, much greyer on top, and has smoked my cigarettes) making me a beautifully pliant bow with steel wire for a cord. The arrow went simply miles. I still regret the loss of that bow—it was probably confiscated.

Malayalis used to be good at football, I think because of something in the genes. Now, however, as you pass the village maidans in the train you see only cricket everywhere. That's where the money might be, and it's certainly where TV is. Hardly anyone is seen playing ball-badminton, and I wonder how many kids play our old favourite, 'Seven Tiles'. Certainly my nieces and nephews don't. A little badminton occasionally (though not ball-badminton!) and even tennis, when living in the city. They may swim, but never in a river; they may hike, but for fun and not because there are no buses and indeed no roads.

Of course, the Gulf is not responsible for such wholesale changes in a way of life. Kerala's prosperity—although the state is said to be in the red, and the government is being dunned by Indian Airlines—is in great part due to the redistribution of land which began in the '50s. The equality of man (not quite, yet, of woman) and the assertion of equality, carried off with an assurance that would be fatal in a state like Bihar, is a creation of the Left. Though trade unionism has

its abuses—such as the extortion practised by the 'headload workers'—
it is surely preferable to the crimes of caste. My father remembers a
time when the shadow of a Dalit was pollution, and his mother was
very sore at Gandhi for advocating what Arjuna called *varna-sa kara*,
the evils of which she deplored.

The Naxalite movement must have been swelling when I was a
child. However, we only went 'home' in the school vacations, and in
any case it was not a subject to discuss in the presence of children. I
don't recollect hearing anything about it. I know now that many of
my rural cousins were (and some still are) ardent Communists.
Communism in power, in practice in a democratic system, has proved
deserving of Gandhi's comment on Western civilization: 'I think it
would be a good idea.' I can see that for myself, and stay away from
any organization that would take me; but my sympathies tend my
cousins' way.

Perhaps one reason for this is a legend in our family concerning
my mother and Mrs Gandhi. While on her campaign to bring down
Namboodiripad's government in the late '50s, that stern daughter of
the Voice of God passed through my mother's village, near Sankara's
birthplace Kaladi. A sudden downpour drove her and her chamchas
into the veranda of the village school, where my mother, home for a
visit, was also sheltering. She had an umbrella but was in no hurry.
Mrs Gandhi was. One of her aides drew her attention to the umbrella;
she snatched it from my mother's grasp; my mother very properly
snatched it back. The glare she got!—luckily, however (for Mrs
Gandhi), another umbrella had been procured, and the lady swept
out.

So appealing is this story that I've never bothered to have it
confirmed. Even in 1972, when the whole country applauded Mrs
Gandhi as Shakti, as Durga, the remembrance of this story leavened
our homage. And in times when the Congress is the party to get
behind, we—or at least I—recall what they did to Namboodiripad,
and get as far behind them as possible. Kerala is such a small state
that many voters possibly have such personal reasons to vote against,
or for, a party or a candidate.

As for the Church, I never studied in Kerala and so was fortunate
enough not to have to attend a convent school. I have known some

very fine nuns, but in the mass—like any other mass—the sorority has a depressing effect. That goes for the fraternity too. I never knew how pernicious their influence could be until I lived in Kerala as a citizen. Those six months in Idukki district—the most backward region of the State—showed me how much in the Church's interest it was to keep people backward. It was no longer possible to keep them illiterate; but I saw how distinct are literacy and education, news-consciousness and awareness.

Yet someone I know, who teaches English in a college run by the 'Fathers', speaks his mind on these and other subjects, and the Fathers are content so long as he does his job well. It is certain that the Church's stranglehold on education has not been to the detriment of several very fine minds Kerala has produced. It is also certain that it's dangerous to generalize.

All Kerala is divided into three parts, the Church, the Party and the Gulf; and thus divided also are the minds of most Malayalis who are not active participants in any of the three processes.

*

These were matters I never thought about when a child. Very naturally. The old house was simply a fact, immutable, and causes and effects left it unmoved. It always required an outside stimulus to make me think about them. Not studying in Kerala was a handicap. I don't know why it is that the history of Kerala was always passed over in the NCERT textbooks. There was a mention of the Cheras, then nothing until da Gama's landing. There were references to high literacy (ho-hum) and social justice (ho-ho). But when I was in school there was nothing about the matrilineal system, or such great men as Marthanda Varma and Kunchan Nambiar.

I remember being amused in my boyhood by an essay of Aubrey Menen's, 'My Grandmother and the Dirty English'. Menen's mother was Irish, his father from a proud old Malabar family. On a visit to his paternal grandmother, Menen found all his notions of the superiority of the white race shaken by her calm, unassumed authority. His portrait of her is delightful, and one line has remained with me: 'My grandmother thought any married woman who covered her breasts was aiming at nothing short of adultery.' Of course that was the custom then, that married women wear only a cloth tied at the waist. I wondered until I remembered that my own paternal grandmother— old and stooped when I knew her—had only worn two cloths, one about her waist and one over her shoulders.

Now it would be shocking. A Hindu Civil Code, applied equally all over the country, has been unfair to Kerala in that even the vestiges of matrilineal power have disappeared. Where will the matriarchs be in a generation? Those cylindrical white-clad ladies who strode on the front verandas like colossi? Younger women all over Kerala now seem to favour the shapeless pastel-coloured night-dress (horridly called a maxi) which makes such a blot on the landscape. The blouse and long skirt were much more sightly. Even a burkha would be an improvement.

Modernity has come too rapidly, as it has all over India, before we have had time to adjust. In a generation, I dare say, there will be practically no one who cannot read and write; and I also dare say we will have little need of those skills. The folklore of Kerala is fortunately well preserved, and so are the performing arts, though few Malayalis can afford any more to see a really first-rate Kathakali performance. The problem remains how to reconcile those arts and skills with the demands of daily living—with, if you like, the Gulf, the Party, and the Church.

*

An hour or so before dawn every morning my cousin rises, bathes in the *kulam* or water tank some hundred metres from the house, and plucks fresh flowers in the garden. He then sits in the veranda— really a commodious room open on three sides, with long wood-topped benches along two of them, worn smooth and shiny by the years—and weaves them into garlands. A deft twist of the fingers and another flower, or a small bunch, or a leaf, is held firm.

He has been doing this unaided for some ten years, since his father fell ill. Sometimes, if my father is on a visit, he has help. There was a time when there would be six or seven men making the garlands, my uncle leading them and firing off his sharp jokes. The flowers are for the little temple to Bhagavati just beyond the gate-house. After my cousin there will be no one left to gather the flowers and weave them into garlands, but the temple will carry on without my family's help as it has for centuries with it.

Sitting at dusk on the old-fashioned wooden stile of the gate-house, which keeps out cows and village dogs, I can look at the temple and give way to sentimentality. Right opposite there is a huge old banyan rising from a four-feet-high plinth. Looking the opposite way from the temple, there is a long uninterrupted vista of fields running past the village tank to lose themselves at the feet of the hills. The hills, in Kerala, are never far away. The view used to be a soothing one; but three years or so ago, a returnee from the Gulf built a spanking new house just next to the tank, and it doesn't quite fit in. Neither do the loudspeakers in the branches of the banyan, put there in about 1990 to compete with the muezzin's call. The bhajans' blare at 5.30 a.m. is hideous.

Three times a week the local RSS shakha drills beneath the banyan. The pramukh barks out his commands in Hindi, and the devotees turn and bend and swing their arms smartly. Excellent training for the fifteenth century. However, it is quite late by the time they begin, and perhaps the boys—they are scarcely more than that—have just come back from their training for the twenty-first century at a computer institute in the rather bigger village on the state highway two kilometres away.

And again I ask myself, What right have I to comment? I don't even live here. I don't even know who the local representative is in the Panchayat, the Zilla Parishad, the Assembly, the Lok Sabha. I don't even know what a day-labourer is paid. My cousin knows all that and much more, he is influential—though he doesn't mix in politics—and he is, if not contented (I have no means of knowing), at any rate accepting.

My sentiment and folly lead me to think it would be an evil if a tradition of weaving garlands for Bhagavati were to die, and an evil if the shakha were to become part of village life. But thinking the first an evil is itself backed by a long history of evil. Such is the confusion that Party, Church and Gulf—and Bhagavati—make in my mind. Besides, these boys may be pioneering a tradition too. A century from now some local stripling might say with pride, and just pride, 'My great-grandfather was the first shakha pramukh in this village.' And the old house may no longer stand; a Gulf returnee may have purchased the land, cleared it of all that rubbish and built a virtual reality park there, or a cyber stadium, or a rocket-taxi rank.

My stake in Kerala is made up of ephemeral what-nots, not solid quids and quos. That is why I wish I was sitting again in my shorts on the cool earth floor, with dusk deepening about me, mortally afraid of the night and chanting 'Narayana-Narayana' with increasing conviction. And with a mind to comprehend the loss soon to be mine. At least, I don't wish it, but I wish that I could wish it.

The mountain that was as flat as a football field on top

Anita Nair

From behind the Pulmooth mountain, the sun peeped out surreptitiously. The trees were wreathed in cobwebs of gossamer mist; the paddy fields shivered in the chill of the dawn breeze and the cocks waited anxiously in their coops. One by one the cocks raised their heads and searched the air for the warmth of the sun's lips. Unable to contain their impatience any longer, they puffed their chests, stretched their throats, and crowed lustily, beckoning the sun to make intimate contact with their proud red combs.

The sun took a deep breath and began its morning chores. With a long-handled sunbeam, it dusted the veils of mist off the trees. Then it set about warming the paddy tops before knocking on the doors of the various coops. The air filled with a faint throb that grew in intensity as it came down the hill: Duk. Duk. Duk. The thumping of Majid's Royal Enfield Bullet as it wound its way down the dirt road to his house. Parrots raked the skies with their screeching, and doves gurgled from within the hollows in the walls of the well.

Shankar removed the wooden planks with which at night he turned his tea shop into a matchbox. As the planks went down, the sun darted in crumbling the mask of the night. Shankar liked to watch the sun frolic in the tea shop.

He took out the two wooden benches and positioned them at the entrance. He hung up the plantain bunches which the sun eyed lasciviously. He tuned the radio for the early morning news broadcast. Minutes later the samovar began to hiss. Shankar's Tea Club was open for business.

This extract is taken from *The Better Man*, published by Penguin Books India.

Shankar rinsed out the glasses and arranged them in sentinel rows. The sun, tired of caressing the plump, inert contours of the plantains, turned its attention to the glasses. Born coquettes, the glasses sparkled when the sun flirted with them. A fickle admirer, however, the sun disappeared when the first bus from town ground to a halt outside Shankar's tea shop. Shankar walked to the bus to pick up the bundle of newspapers that arrived in the bus every day, and plonked it on the counter from which he surveyed his domain.

Shankar's Tea Club stood at the crest of the hill. Opposite it were the few shops that catered to the needs of the village. A fish shop that sold various kinds of dried fish. An all-purpose store that stocked rice, sugar, tea, oil, bolts of cloth printed with gigantic flowers in oranges and mauves against lush green leaves, notebooks, batteries, and even condoms. A rice mill, the barbershop, and a little cubbyhole in which the lone tailor of the village cut and sewed. The last three shops were all housed in the building Hassan had built some years ago when he came back from Kuwait for good during the Gulf War. A hundred feet away, as if distancing itself from all such commercial activity, stood the post office.

Achuthan Nair had always believed himself to be a progressive soul. Long before the village had even heard of a new-fangled idea, he would have assimilated it into the fabric of their lives. When a post office was sanctioned for Kaikurussi, he took it upon himself to make everything possible to hasten its arrival in the village. He built a two-room house at the bottom of the garden and this, he decreed, would house the Kaikurussi post office. No one dared ask why not somewhere else more convenient to the whole village. And from that hub soon, one by one, the rest of the shops sprouted.

Many years later, when the people who ran the two buses that plied to and fro between Kaikurussi and the town came to inspect the route, they looked at the motley collection of shops and jeered, 'The city, ha!'

The name stuck. It rolled off the tongue easily. It was so much simpler to say, 'I'm off to the city for a tea and a beedi' than 'I'm going to the shop opposite Shankar's Tea Club for a beedi'. If Shankar resented losing his landmark status, he hid it well. After all, as people waited for the bus, they strolled in for a cup of tea and some gossip.

The house stood halfway up the hill, crouched on the land like an old man bent over. Aging by the minute, but seemingly indestructible by time. Mukundan looked at the house and tried to fathom what it was about it that disturbed him so. The cobwebs had been pulled down, the dust swept away, the floors mopped, and the woodwork made to gleam. And yet the house continued to wear the look of a chronic sufferer. Its gloom enhanced by the trees that crowded around it like commiserating aunts. A beard of unkempt grass almost thigh-high covered the terraced hillside that was broken only by gnarled old trunks of trees that neither bloomed nor bore fruit.

For a moment Mukundan thought the house raised its hooded eyelids and peered at him. Now that I have you in my clutches once again, there is no way you can escape, it seemed to say with diabolical pleasure. He shook his head in annoyance and told himself not to be silly. He decided to go down the hill. There was a certain pleasure in breaking off a dried old branch from a tree nearby and swinging it like a machete through the grass as he tried to trace a forgotten path.

'Why don't you use the road?' Krishnan Nair called out. Mukundan pretended not to hear him and walked on.

The grass scratched his calves as he stumbled over the stones. Suddenly the hill became steeper, ending abruptly in a high precipice of mud. Beyond it was a deep ditch. Alongside, the road ran on less dangerously. He wished for a moment that he had chosen the road.

The fields were everywhere. Endless shades of green that stretched into the horizon on one side and the foot of the Pulmooth mountain on the other. Speckled only with the bright blouses of the women as they stood ankle-deep in water-logged mud and pulled out the young paddy plants. When a breeze blew, the tops of the paddy rippled and turned the sheets of sedate jade into gleaming splashes of emerald. He knew that soon the sun would disappear behind thick grey clouds that would frown down unrelentingly. Then it would be time to seek the dry confines of the house. Until then he would stay here and look at the view he had banished from his memories for many years now.

Mukundan leaned against the trunk of an old tamarind tree. His left foot firmly planted in the mud, his right one sidling, in the manner of a furtive crab, on the dune-like indentations of the bark. For the past one week, he hadn't strayed from the boundary of the house. He had examined everything and everyone from a distance. It was as if he knew that if he were to let in a wave of warmth or a sense of bulk, then he would lose this dreamlike trance he had drifted into. In this hazy world, there was no room for cumbersome thoughts.

He turned the leaves over with his stick. When his eyes lit on a grey curve, he lazily pondered, Was it a twig or a dried leaf?

He looked around him thoughtfully. What is it about age that shears everything around of its grandeur? It was as if by simply growing old, he had dwarfed the universe and robbed it of its awe-inspiring qualities. Even the Pulmooth mountain was no longer that huge mountain that reached into the sky insurmountably.

There was a time when the wooded slopes and steep paths of the mountain were forbidden to him. 'Little boys are not allowed to climb the Pulmooth mountain. For once you have climbed it, then in the eyes of the village you are a man. Which means they will expect you to do manly things,' Krishnan Nair had told him each time he begged to be taken along on the eve of the harvest festival.

He had to wait till he was twelve before he was allowed to join the men when they trudged up the mountain on the day before Onam. The muscles in his calves had ached as he trekked up, but he had refused all offers of help. He had waited for this for a long time, dreaming of the day he would scale the Pulmooth mountain and see for himself the wonder of the mountaintop; he had heard the men describe it time and again. And then when they were on top of the mountain, he felt a sweep of disappointment cloud his vision. It was as flat as a football field.

'Do you see that?' Krishnan Nair pointed out to him a strip of water that slimed through the brown fields of the neighbouring village several miles away. 'That's the Kunti river.'

Mukundan didn't know what he had expected to find there. But in his imagination the top of the mountain had been a peak that spiked high into the sky beyond everyone's reach. A needle's point that only he would be able to scale. And he dreamed of the villagers describing his valiant efforts to his father. Of how Achuthan Nair would ruffle his hair affectionately and say to him, 'I'm proud of you, my boy. Who did I say I'm proud of?'

Mukundan along with the rest of the village knew that Achuthan

Nair ended every conversation with a question. The listener was meant to answer the question so that Achuthan Nair knew for certain that the gospel truth of his words had been understood by the inferior intelligence of the person standing before him. But this time Mukundan would have gushed happily, 'Of your son. Of me.'

The flat brown plain almost made him want to cry. He swallowed and retorted, 'It looks like a gutter to me.'

Krishnan Nair placed a hand on his head and swivelled him around to face him. 'It is all in your mind. If you want to look around you and see mountains, forests, and oceans, you will. Or else you will see little mounds of earth, sparse bushes, and piddling streams.' A peacock screamed and rose in the air.

Mukundan moved away from the rest of the men and went to sit on a cashew tree bough. And as he sat there, he watched the magnificence of the landscape grow. There was a world beyond the valley he lived in. A world he would someday escape to. Far away from his father. Far away from the village.

The next time he climbed Pulmooth mountain, Meenakshi went with him. They had sneaked out in the afternoon so that Meenakshi could see for herself this splendid world he had described to her. By the time they reached the top, sweat was running down their backs and they were panting with thirst. But they forgot all about parched throats and aching legs as they looked down on the rest of the world. In a voice hushed with awe, Meenakshi whispered, 'Someday, I'm going that far.' And she pointed to the horizon that shimmered in the heat.

'Me too,' he whispered back.

They sat in the shade of a cashew tree catching their breath. 'Do you think that life will be different elsewhere?' Meenakshi voiced the doubt that had niggled in his mind ever since he had glimpsed heaven from the top of Pulmooth mountain.

'I don't know,' he said thoughtfully. 'But it must be infinitely preferable to this.'

'I guess we will never know until we leave.' Meenakshi stood up. It was time to go back. If they were missed and someone found out what they had been up to, there would be endless recriminations and accusations.

They ran down the hill. A boy in a pair of khaki shorts that owed their existence to a pair of trousers long discarded; a girl in a skirt patterned with flower sprigs, a shabby pink blouse, and two long shiny plaits. At the bottom of the hill, they stopped for a drink of water from a well by the paddy fields. The water was cold and sweet. They gulped down mouthfuls, sluiced their faces, hands and legs and then by silent consent went back separately.

Other children had brothers and sisters, companions to share their giggles and nightmares with. The wonder of a peacock's feather, the triumph of bringing down a mango with one perfectly pitched stone, the agony of scraped knees and splinters under the skin. Mukundan had Meenakshi—his girl cousin once removed; companion and soul mate. They crawled together as babies. They paddled together in the pool and when they were a little older, they learned to swim together. Diving from the top of the stone wall, slicing through the water and surfacing at almost the same moment from different corners of the pool. When they were three years old, Ezuthachan, who ran the local primary school, was invited to conduct their vidyarambham ceremony. With a gold ring, he traced the sacred letter Hari Sri on their tongues and guided their forefingers through a plate of raw rice to form the letters that invoked the blessing of the gods. By word and deed, they were deemed fit and old enough to acquire learning. And so together they began studying the alphabet, sharing a book and a necklace of consonants and vowels. They recited the multiplication tables and long poems about steam engines in one breath. They knew each other's bodies and minds as well as they knew their own.

And then suddenly one day they were considered to be too old to spend so much time in each other's company. Mukundan was given a room to himself. He was asked to put aside his short pants and switch to a mundu. He was encouraged to bathe with the rest of the men and asked to stay away from the pool when the women bathed. As for Meenakshi, she was forbidden to go wandering around the fields and cashew groves as she once used to in Mukundan's company. 'Put aside your books and fancy talk. It is time you learned to cook,' her mother nagged. She frowned whenever she saw them huddled together and invented excuses to separate Meenakshi from Mukundan. When Mukundan came looking for her, she would whisper into Meenakshi's ear that it didn't matter whether the leaf fell on the thorn or the thorn fell on the leaf, it was the leaf that was hurt for life. So sprang a distance between them, which they furtively tried to bridge. And because their meetings were so infrequent, they began to function as two separate beings.

For the first time in their lives, they had secrets from each other. His dreams were no longer hers. Her plans no longer his. When they met, they never had enough time to say everything they wanted to. The first few precious moments were spent trying to regain the closeness that they once had. It was frustrating for the two of them, and they weren't old enough to understand it or even know how to handle it, and so once in a while they fought. Mukundan never won those fights. His need to be with her was more than hers. They fought in whispers but there were times when he couldn't control his anger. Then he would seize her arm and press his fingers into its softness, enjoying seeing the pain fill her eyes with salt. Sometimes she would let him draw his secret vicious pleasure from her pain. Sometimes she would raise her foot and expertly kick him in his balls. Painful enough so he would let her go and light enough to cause no real injury. But their differences, like their plans to escape, were a secret.

Stalinist and Indian:
E.M.S. Namboodiripad

Ramachandra Guha

The paradox of Indian Marxism is that its practice has always been more appealing than its theory. The Naxalite theoreticians dismiss swidden or shifting cultivation as a 'primitive economic practice', bound to disappear with modernity, yet their cadres organize tribals to protect their traditional forest rights, in most cases the right to cut swidden in land usurped by the government. The Communist Party of India (Marxist) swears by Soviet-style central planning, but in West Bengal they have taken the process of political and economic decentralization further than has any other party anywhere else in India.

Communists used to speak of 'socialist internationalism', that is, the right to take their orders from Moscow or Peking, yet they are now, and have been for some time, the most patriotic of Indians. Certainly it is only in the Communist Party of India and the CPI(M) that one finds politicians who have enjoyed power for long stretches but are not known to take bribes or maintain Swiss bank accounts.

E.M.S. Namboodiripad, who died in March 1998, was a fundamentally decent and public-spirited man whose mind was messed up by reading too much of J.V. Stalin and V.I. Lenin. In his tribute to EMS, published in *The Telegraph*, Ashok Mitra called him a 'great Marxist theoretician whose thoughts had a pure classical grandeur'.

With due respect, this is one party man talking about another. While Namboodiripad wrote many works of history and political theory, none rose above the second rate. Even if one allows the qualifier '*Marxist* theoretician', EMS does not begin to compare with men such

This extract is taken from *An Anthropologist Among the Marxists and Other Essays*, published by Permanent Black (2001).

as D.D. Kosambi and Ranajit Guha, who stretched Marxism to its limits, going beyond economic determinism through the incorporation of insights from archaeology, linguistics, numismatics and, above all, anthropology.

As a historian, Namboodiripad interpreted everything through the lens of class struggle and the inevitable victory of revolutionary communism. As an ideologue he followed a man greatly inferior to Karl Marx, and even Lenin, namely Stalin. I have before me a booklet called *On Organisation*, published by the undivided CPI in 1954, and based on a series of lectures delivered by its leading theoretician to the Central Party School in Delhi. Stalin has just died, but Nikita Khrushchev's famous speech repudiating him lies a safe two years in the future. EMS thus begins his talks with the obligatory salutation: 'As Comrade Stalin explained in his *Dialectical and Historical Materialism* . .' Some pages later we find a worshipful reference to Stalin's 'last work on the *Economic Problems of Socialism* in the USSR', followed again by a long quote. Deeper into the tract are excerpted some gems from Stalin's *Foundations of Leninism*, another book that quickly and deservedly fell into oblivion.

In his writings, Namboodiripad was a craven follower of a crude despot, but as a practising politician EMS was one of the finest in the land. He was, for most of his life, a leading light of the most progressive party in the most progressive state in India.

Much has been written about the Kerala miracle: the strides in health, education and land reform and the quality of governance that has made this possible. As a column of the left and twice chief minister of the state, EMS was a key player in all this. His work for his people was repaid by a deep and genuine affection. On one of his last birthdays, 10,000 Malayalis contributed voluntary labour to desilt a long stretch of an irrigation canal, the patriarch looking on. It was a remarkable tribute, when compared especially with how the birthdays of politicians in other parties are remembered by their followers.

The moral distance between men like EMS and those who now rule India was underlined some years ago by an incident little noticed at the time. In January 1992, P.V. Narasimha Rao's government decided to award the second highest national honour, the Padma Vibhushan, to EMS and to Atal Behari Vajpayee.

It was a noble gesture, recognizing contributions to national life by people other than Congressmen—one cannot see governments headed by Indira Gandhi, Rajiv Gandhi or Sonia Gandhi displaying such generosity of spirit. Now while Vajpayee accepted the award, EMS declined, for his personality would not allow attention to be drawn to his achievements. Some weeks later, his home in Kerala was robbed. The police caught the burglar, repossessing for the original owner the stolen goods amounting to one gold sovereign and Rs 800. This after fifty years in public life.

Mitra speaks of the 'purity' of EMS's thought, but we might speak with more justice of the purity of the lived life. In her novel, *The God of Small Things*, Arundhati Roy makes the unfortunate claim that EMS transformed his family home into a luxury hotel. As everyone in Kerala knows, this was another Namboodiripad with similar initials: the Communist EMS had in fact donated his property to the party, an early example of a lifelong and always unselfconscious asceticism.

When one considers what kind of man EMS was, one must also consider it a great pity that he mortgaged his mind to Stalinism. Namboodiripad, of course, did not regret this. He liked to write of how he left his landlord family to join the Congress, then helped start the Congress Socialist Party, then broke away altogether to become a communist, the last constituting, in his view, the decisive step towards the promised land. Both Mahatma Gandhi and Jawaharlal Nehru he criticized as 'bourgeois' leaders who could not transcend the ideology of their class.

There is a most revealing moment in his book, *The Mahatma and the Ism*, where he complains of the poverty of Gandhi's intellect. This man, he says, came as a student to London in 1889, when *Das Kapital* had just appeared in its first English edition, when the Fabian Society of the great Bernard Shaw and the greater Sidney Webb was taking its first bold steps. And yet, writes a non-comprehending EMS, Gandhi chose to join Henry Salt's Vegetarian Society.

The Marxist was bewildered, but bourgeois thinkers like myself see Mahatma Gandhi's vegetarianism as a prelude to his mature political philosophy. For his later attitude to compatriots and adversaries was steeped likewise in *ahimsa* and *karuna*, the ideas of non-violence and compassion. Namboodiripad could not understand this, which is why, in the late thirties, he left the Congress for the CPI.

In the next decade his new party committed a series of colossal errors: the support to the British during the war, the support to the Pakistan movement, the ridiculous Russian-inspired attempt to foment an armed revolution immediately after India gained independence. But what if EMS and other like-minded patriots had followed Gandhi instead of Stalin? And what if socialists like Acharya Kripalani and Jayaprakash Narayan had also chosen to stay within the Congress? Might not the party that came to power in 1947 have then had a first-rate set of organizers providing the support that Nehru so desperately lacked to challenge the bunch of conservatives and reactionaries he was instead left with?

This did not happen and EMS and his comrades went on to lead a double life of bankrupt ideology and meaningful practice. Totalitarian thinker and practising democrat, subservient Stalinist and proudly patriotic Indian: this was the tragedy as well as the achievement of E.M.S. Namboodiripad.

The bonsai tree

David Davidar

Vijai's father came home early from work that day. The boy watched him park the car and come up the driveway. It was still light though black shadows had started sliding up the low hills that surrounded the bungalow.

'Hello, son.' Vijai ignored the greeting. He sensed his father turn away and go into the house.

They had announced the party to him a week earlier with a slightly wary look, knowing the news would not be well-received. Always shy, their son seemed to have retreated even further into himself ever since he had gone away to boarding school. Although Vijai hadn't remonstrated with his parents on the day they brought up the party, he had stopped talking to them. This hadn't seemed to affect them in any manner he could see, and he felt foolish. But he was determined not to make up.

He loathed the parties his parents gave. He wasn't sure who he hated more: the guests or the people his parents became. His father, normally reserved and poised, turned hearty and laughed a lot. His mother, naturally fluttery, would talk incessantly with an accent he found irritating. And she liked Mr Bopanna. Vijai disliked the planter's broad face, broad moustache and broad country speech. A fortnight earlier at the club, after he'd become bored with a game he had been playing with some other children, Vijai had gone to find his parents. His father, engrossed in a game of poker, had waved him away. He found his mother in the club's deserted smoking room, sitting very close to Mr Bopanna. Their voices were low and his mother was talking fast, the way she did when she had had too much to drink. The atmosphere in the room had been curiously unpleasant. Mr Bopanna had noticed him and had called out. Getting up quickly his mother had hustled Vijai out of the room. She insisted to his father, that they go home immediately. Vijai had noticed that his mother and Mr Bopanna were holding hands. Mr Bopanna was coming to the party that evening.

He could hear his mother calling him to tea. He decided he wasn't going to have any. Nor would he have any dinner. Let them have their party, he thought. He was going to starve.

The first mists of the evening slipped over the hills. Vijai loved this time of the day in the high isolated Peermade tea country. It was so different from the brutal heat and dusty reality of the plains where he went to school. The aqueous light, the hills helmeted with tea bushes, the sibilance of rain, the mist—all these seemed to enclose him, hide him away in a private sanctuary that soothed and enchanted him. Especially at times like this. As he sat there, letting himself relax under the influence of the evening light, he remembered something from a few days ago. They had gone for a drive, as they sometimes did when his father came home early from work. About an hour from the house, it had begun to grow dark. Great columns of mist, grey and big as cathedrals, had gathered and begun to sweep down the hills on either side of the road. As he had strained to see through the milky whiteness that enveloped the car he had spotted a tiny tree perched almost at the top of a hill like the foresight of a rifle. Imprinted on a sheet of mist, it had looked as pretty as a Japanese bonsai. He thought about the tree now and wondered how it would look in the garden.

The door to the veranda opened, and his father came out. Vijai thought he was going to talk to him and hunched deeper into the wicker chair he sat on, but his father walked past him and headed down to the garden. Vijai could hear him whistling as he worked, pinching off the vast sagging heads of blown roses.

His mother came out of the house. Vijai drew his legs up onto the chair and looked at his frayed sneakers. 'Put your legs down, Vijai.' He didn't look at her. 'I said put your legs down. Right now.' Still not looking at her, he put his legs down.

'Mani,' his mother called.

'Yeah, what's up?' his father shouted from the bottom of the garden.

'Tell your son to stop sulking and go and have his tea. Why on earth can't he behave himself?'

His father came slowly up the lawn. He held a bunch of roses in his hand. 'Here, honey. These should do, I think.'

'Mani, you'd better talk to your son. This is getting ridiculous.' His mother went back inside.

His father sat down on the steps of the veranda. 'Why don't you go have some tea, son?' Vijai decided not to say anything.

'Are you boxing this year?' his father asked after a long silence.

'No.'

'Tennis?'

'Yes.'

'What's the matter?'

He didn't reply. His father got up and Vijai heard his knee joints crack. He studied his father covertly. Still slim, tall and erect, silvering hair worn slightly long at the back. Vijai wondered why he disliked his father. Was it because of his looks, his presence, his success? Why wasn't he the same way? Bastard, he said to himself, and liking the sound of the word repeated it.

'Vijai.'

Surprised, Vijai looked at him. His father never addressed him by name, always calling him 'son'. Coming from him it sounded formal and distancing.

'Is there anything I can do for you, son?' This time even the 'son' sounded different. Kinder, Vijai thought.

The moment passed and the boy grew hostile again. What did his father care? He was only being nice to him because of his stupid party. Bloody hypocrite. To hell with him and his mother. If she loved him, if they both loved him, they wouldn't have their party. After all, he was home for only a week more.

'Do you want to go for a drive? Look, it's beautiful outside. Maybe we could go see if we can get some jungle-fowl. Would you like that? Come on, you've always liked to go shooting.'

'No. I don't want to go shooting.'

'Then what do you want to do?'

'Nothing.'

His father shrugged. Most of the yellow had left the sky and mist swirled on the hills. Vijai suddenly remembered the beautiful tree he had seen. 'I want the bonsai, Dad,' he said.

*

By the time they reached the spot, it was getting dark. As they parked the car, Vijai panicked for a moment thinking he wouldn't be able to find the tree. Then he saw it, a faint feathery shadow on grey. His father took a shovel and pruning knife from the trunk; Vijai took the knife. As they started up the hill. Vijai said: 'Dad, it's OK, isn't it? Ma won't mind.' His father said: 'No, son. She'll understand. Don't worry about it.'

They were nearly at the top of the hill now and Vijai started panicking again, for there was no sign of the tree. Ahead of them, the broad back of another hill stretched under a wind-whipped bank of mist, and beyond it, another hill rose indistinctly. To Vijai's dismay, the tree was on that hill. And it had seemed so close from the road! His father had spotted the tree too. The boy's mind rushed back to the quarrel his parents had had just before his father and he had set out.

'Don't spoil him, Mani,' his mother said when his father told her what he was planning to do. 'Why should it always be like this? I slave to bring the child up properly and you go and ruin it all.'

'It's OK, let me handle this.'

'Fine, you handle it. And you stay at home and handle his tantrums, you pack his trunk when he goes to school, you make him study.'

'Listen, Kiri.' His father had put his hands on his mother's shoulders but she had shrugged them off angrily. Vijai had cringed. Now he would be held responsible for everything, for ruining the party, for making his parents fight. If he knew his mother, she wouldn't talk to his father for a week. Absurdly, he wondered who would pack the trunk he took to school. His mother always got his things ready. Then a petulant anger had reasserted itself and he had been glad when she had run up the lawn and into the house, slamming the door behind her. When his father had come slowly up to him Vijai's anger had quickly faded to be replaced by an almost unbearable anxiety. How was his father going to deal with the situation? His father had smiled at him wearily. 'Come on, son, let's go get your tree.'

They trudged up the next hill slowly; Vijai's legs began hurting and he was cold, frustrated and angry. Finally, as his breathing grew laboured, they reached the top of the hill. Vijai looked at the third hill and realized with a dull fatalism that they wouldn't go through with it. His father was looking into the distance, not particularly focusing on the tree clinging black and minute to the top of the hill before them. When he spoke, his voice was calm and reasonable. 'Listen, son, I don't think we can get the tree today. It's already very late. Why don't you bring the mali and get it tomorrow?'

Vijai didn't look at him. Fine, go back, he thought, go back but I'm not going back with you. Go back to your car, go back to your party, go back, and do you know that last year I was knocked out in the school boxing championships because it was a grudge match and though I'm a lousy boxer, I took on the school's best boxer because he called you a fancy dressed up sissy, and all you care about is your goddamned party. I hate you, you bastard, go back to your goddamn party, you don't care for me, you care only for your friends and you love only Ma. But do you know that Ma was holding hands with Mr Bopanna at the club and I never told you because I love you Dad and all you can think about is your goddamn party, go on leave me here, you bastard, I'm never going to come back with you.

As he succumbed to the fear and the fury coursing through him, the boy started screaming his thoughts out, tears sliding down his face. He stopped abruptly, wondering what he'd said, how much he'd said aloud. 'I'm sorry, Dad,' he sobbed. His father had not moved. He stood looking at Vijai thoughtfully. The boy's body heaved as he gulped in air between great choking sobs. He looked down at his sneakers; he was gripping the pruning knife fiercely, the wooden handle painfully hard in his hand. Slowly he released his grip. The wind and mist on his drying tears felt cold.

*

When they reached the tree, Vijai was surprised by its size. It was nearly as tall as him, though it stood bent almost parallel to the ground, its trunk twisted and contorted into grudging submission by the wind and rain. Moss furred the silver oak's dwarfed, misshapen branches and trunk. The leaves stood out in dull flashes of grey-green.

'It's beautiful, son, just like a real bonsai.'

Vijai said, 'I told you, didn't I?'

He made a slashing movement with the knife he carried and his father said, 'Careful.' It was quite dark now and the wind had dropped. His father gave the tree an experimental shake. It did not move. He picked up the shovel from where he had dropped it and began loosening the earth around the tree. The ground was hard and unyielding, and the tree was firmly rooted. His father removed the jacket he wore and Vijai could see the sweat popping up on his bare forearms.

Vijai watched his father uncover the tap root, which was almost as thick as the trunk. The digging seemed to go on forever, and Vijai grew anxious again. He wondered what his mother would say, and he remembered with fear and shame the incident on the previous hill. What had possessed him? How could he have dared abuse his father? For a dirty, ugly old tree? He was suddenly angry and swung his knife at the tree. It glanced off one of the branches; white gleamed where the knife had struck. He kicked the tree. 'Easy, son,' his father said.

'No Dad, let's go home. This horrible tree . . .' He was close to crying.

'Stop it now. Behave yourself.' There was an edge to his father's voice. He straightened and put the shovel down. He didn't look at Vijai, and when he spoke, his voice was quiet. 'I hope you realize you can't lose your temper every time things don't go exactly the way you want them to. You won't be a boy much longer, Vijai, and it is my dearest hope that you will grow up to be strong, determined, successful . . . But the only way that is going to happen is if you learn how to deal with adversity and situations that test you. They will make a man of you, but only if you stand up to them. Look at this tree. It started with nothing—poor soil, blasted every day by the wind and the weather, but just look at it, it will survive till the end of time, whereas its fellows, well-watered and nourished and living the good life will go down in the first storm . . .' His voice trailed away. He seemed very tired. Vijai wanted to go to him, touch him. Instead, he stood quietly where he was. A moment, two, then his father bent to work again.

Eventually they took the root off, as far down as they could. As the tree began to topple over, his father wrestled it to the ground. 'Christ, it's heavy,' he said. 'Can you get the shovel, son? I'm going to need both hands for this one.' Vijai picked up the shovel and stuck the knife into his belt. His father hefted the tree on to his shoulder and set off down the hill. As he followed, Vijai looked at the tree, its branches with their plumed tufts of leaves swaying with his father's stride. The tree would look good in the garden. He looked back to where it had been. Mist slid silently over the spot; he couldn't even see the gashed earth where they had dug so recently.

*

When they got home, they rousted the mali from the servant's quarters and installed the bonsai tree in an old kerosene drum. Then Vijai and his father scurried into the house to change for the party. Like children anticipating adult ire for some small offence, they crept down the silent passage to their bedrooms, shutting the doors behind them ever so softly.

The party was a disaster; Vijai's mother was even more fluttery than usual and spoke to his father only when it was necessary. She ignored her son altogether but he didn't mind too much, preoccupied as he was by everything that had preceded the party.

Later that night, before dropping off to sleep, Vijai ran the evening's adventure through his mind once more. It remained as clear and precious as when it had taken place, and he had a vague idea that he would be able to call it up whenever he had need of it. He spent the next day painting the drum with a can of silver paint that he had found in the garage. As a final flourish, he painted a broad red band round the middle. They installed the tree at the entrance to the driveway.

A few days later, he left for school. His mother, who had broken her silence only the day before his departure, packed his trunk as usual.

When he came home the next year, Vijai was glad to find the bonsai tree still in place in the driveway. The silver paint on the drum had dulled and the red stripe had faded, but there were more leaves on its tiny branches. Vijai spent a few mornings watering the tree and admiring its tortured beauty. Then the monsoon rains came, and he spent most of his time indoors studying for his exams.

A fortnight after the monsoons broke, it was time to leave for school. They set off early as their progress would be slow on the ghat road made treacherous by the unending downpour. As the car turned out of the driveway, its headlights picked out the bonsai tree briefly, the deformed branches ghostly in grey rain.

Mundu, meesha, kumbha, koda: The sartorial splendour of the Malayali male

Geeta Doctor

It must be the lush tropical climate.

After a season of rains, the moist red earth teems with a cacophony of green. Heart-shaped leaves of caladium spotted with white, pink and red vie for attention with slender tapioca plants hiding their swollen tubers under the ground. Spongy ferns fill the crevices that have not yet been occupied by the violently coloured creatures that chirp and crawl, and climbing vines creep along tree trunks, buttonholing the passer-by with tiny bursts of orange and white flowers. Under the surface of the water that has flooded through the canals and backwaters, the karimeen flips over on its side and in a fatal display of vanity, allows itself to glitter against a sudden beam of sunlight, only to be caught.

Is it a wonder then that the male of the species, the Malayali Male or MM as we shall call him, should be just as filled with a keen devotion to the spectacle he presents to the world around him? When he steps out into the world he is flamboyantly arrayed in a fine white mundu, a rectangular length of cloth wound round the waist and tied correctly, if he is a Hindu, to the right side. The Muslims, or moplahs, show their preference by knotting their mundu to the left. The MM's meesha, or moustache, has been trimmed and polished to regimental perfection. His waistline, kumbha, protrudes ever so lightly over the bulge of the tucked-in end of his mundu, where he keeps his money purse, to indicate to the world that he is a man of substance. He has had his breakfast of puttu and crab curry that morning. To complete the picture, no self-respecting MM would ever step out without his koda, his black umbrella, furled as tightly as a morning glory bud that has yet to burst out in the sunlight.

At this time of the early morning, bathed and fresh, the MM is a sight to behold. He is as full of pride and a splendid sense of exaltation as a green tree-frog sitting on the uppermost branch of a tree and distending its neck in a booming croak that alerts his mates that an important individual has just arrived. The MM stops when he meets a fellow citizen, delicately flicks up the end of the mundu and enquires politely, with that portmanteau word, 'Pinhe?' It could be translated to 'What gives, old cat?' or 'So then?' or even 'Top of the morning to you!'

Outside of his home state, the MM is a timid creature, somewhat ordinary, even obsequious in his ways. At the Dubai airport for instance, where fortune and a blood relative have placed him behind a glass counter full of Seiko watches, he smiles a trifle too readily, betraying the typical Kerala male's weakness for a mouth a little too full of teeth. It could be that he is ill at ease in his readymade terylene suit and white shirt two sizes too large for him that he has just borrowed from his cousin-brother, and smiles broadly to distract attention from these constraints. He might even make a gesture that involves cupping a hand in front of his mouth to hide his smile, somewhat in the manner of a refined Geisha entertaining a client and holding her fan politely in front of her face, to indicate merriment.

In his case of course, the grin and the gesture are a sign of embarrassment. He comes from an environment that in theory is so fertile, that no MM is ever expected to coarsen his hands with work. That's why he holds up a delicate hand. If he has started to earn a living, it's only for a couple of years, until he can get back to his native soil and let the women of the household take the responsibility for allowing him to enjoy the privileged life of a male born in a tropical climate. In an ideal world, the MM reclines in the comfort of a veranda, on an easy chair, wearing a fine white mundu and shaking his legs at the knee joints as though he were playing an imaginary accordion with his thighs. It is for such moments of bliss that the MM is willing to struggle under strange skies to make his packet of money and return home. He is a dreamer with a built-in accordion player between his legs.

The rich Gulf-returned king-makers who return periodically to recruit young nephews and delinquent cousin-brothers for the job market in whichever country is open to them, are the nerves and sinews of the Kerala brotherhood of bachelor boys who seem to be everywhere. They are forced to leave home to make their fortunes in whichever part of the world affords them a bed and a shared lungi. The lungi is the badge of the de-racinated MM. The first time he affects a lungi might be as a comrade-in-arms as a newly liberated student learning to give up bourgeois values of ownership and identify himself as a prole, willing to live in a sloppy lungi, worn by a common student collectorship. The next time round it could be while sharing a common chumri, or hostel room or dormitory, with others who are on the ladder of opportunity offered by the system of capitalist enterprise. The lungi is their badge of freedom, the only moment when they can revert to being the carefree laid-back lads that they used to be in their ancestral homes.

The lungi is to be worn in the real world or at night. It's a mere tubular piece of checked or striped woven cloth, nowadays even a cloth printed in post-modernistic batik designs of virulent colours that is treated with the contempt that it deserves. It's actually borrowed from the Tamils next door and as everyone knows, the innumerable uses to which the Tamil subjects his lungi, from towel to turban to bed sheet at night, is not worth contemplating. Why, even when he decides to take his life, he twists his lungi into a rope and hangs himself from the nearest branch and when a kindly neighbour cuts him down, the same bit of cloth is used to drape the corpse.

The mundu, on the other hand, is a sacred piece of white cloth to be worn on returning to the family hearth. The more exalted the person, or the occasion, the finer the cloth. The marriage mundu for instance is of such a fine quality, so diaphanous, that even when it is worn in the form of a double mundu, that is a longer version of the single mundu, folded to a double thickness, it is possible to catch glimpses of the brand and style of underwear affected by the bridegroom. Who knows, maybe like the famous advertisements for a particular style of bras that used to portray the wearer in all kinds of improbable situations wearing her 'maidenform' bra, the Malayali bridegroom might also be saying to himself, 'I dreamt I was getting married in my Y-front Rhinoceros brand underwear!'

For the fact is that traditionally, the MM likes to appear with the least amount of clothes possible. Again, it's the climate. In such a warm, humid atmosphere, the male body, lightly glazed with a residual film of coconut oil, actually looks quite delectable with just a mere wisp of clothing.

'The natives cannot understand why Europeans clothe themselves to such an extent in India,' writes an early visitor to Kerala. He goes on to add, using his own spelling for a member of the Namboodiri community, 'A Namboorie visiting the house of an European gentleman, after meditating for some little time, suddenly pointed to a wine bottle which had a worked cover, and exclaimed, "Well, you are a curious race of people, not only do you clothe yourself from your head to your feet, but put clothes upon your wooden table and petticoats on your bottles!"'

What is equally interesting is the impression made by the Zamorin of Kozhikode, at that time one of the most powerful rulers on the Malabar coast, when he received the Portuguese adventurer Vasco da Gama at his palace.

'He was a very dark man,' says the account rendered by Da Gama's entourage. 'Half-naked and clothed with white cloths from the middle to the knees; one of these clothes ended in a long point on which were threaded several gold rings with large rubies which made a great show.' The description then lists with a growing sense of amazement, the quantity and variety of jewels that the Zamorin wore about his person. He had a diamond 'the thickness of a thumb' that hung pendant from the arm bracelet on his left arm, while around his neck, falling to the level of his waist, he wore a double strand of pearls the size of hazelnuts, we are informed. This was quite apart from the rubies, the emeralds, the pearls and gold earrings that he wore around his neck, in his hair, and pierced ear lobes. In short, the Zamorin might have been naked, but he carried his treasury about his person.

The Portuguese upstart, on the other hand, was dressed from head to toe in the manner of his country in lavish silk gown, cape, leather boots, and a feather waving on his hat. It's not surprising that this encounter led to a certain misunderstanding. 'The Zamorin,' we are told, after watching Da Gama and friends drink the water that had been given to them to wash their hands, 'then sent for figs and fruit for them to eat, and laughing most immoderately at them whilst so engaged, Da Gama became nettled and declined to enter into any conference, unless conducted to a more private room.'

More to the point, however, is that Kozhikode was at that moment in time, the trading post for the finest cloth produced in the Coromandel. The calicos and muslins were as delicate as the morning dew lying upon the grass, as sheer as the wings of the dragonflies alighting upon the surface of the water-lilies thrusting their heads out of the bathing ponds. This was the favoured garment of the royalty and if today the MM affects the same delicately woven fabrics, it's only on special occasions, weddings for instance, or ritual appearances at the temple.

The kasavu mundu, or gold-bordered cloth that is worn by MMs on festive occasions, as they troop into the temples, bare bodied from the waist upwards, with perhaps just an upper body cloth (angavastram) loosely draped about the shoulders, a gold chain around the neck, is quite a spectacle. Accompanied by the blowing of conches, gorgeously lit brass lamps, the swaying ambulatory movement of the temple elephant, whose skin contrasts just as effectively with lavish gold ornaments as it is led around the outer passage of the temple, the mundu-clad procession takes on an epic quality.

'The moment I get back to Kerala I automatically slip into my mundu. It's only then that I feel that I am a true Malayali,' explains a trim, elegantly dressed hotelier, who could not be more distant from such primitive spectacles in his daily life. 'I think the first time I wore my mundu was when I was around six. It's a rite of passage. I had to get into one for some wedding that we were attending in my grandfather's house because all my cousins were wearing mundus. I had to wear a belt to hold it up, but not anymore. When I look back at all the more important occasions of my life, I have worn a mundu, so it's very much a part of who I am.'

The MM is never content to just let his mundu hang; he uses it to convey a whole range of signals. There is for instance, the simple half-hitch signal. The wearer stands at ease, legs slightly apart, with his mundu hanging down, then he gives a casual back leg flick and in the same instant grabs the fabric from the lower edge and knots it loosely in the front. As performed by the famous actor Mamooty, whose sartorial language conveys more than any script that a writer could invent, this is the MM at his most confident. 'Why don't you come and see me sometime, babe?' he seems to be saying.

On the other hand, a forward kick of the mundu, causing it to fly up, like a subdued Bruce Lee kickboxing blow, is inclined to be a warning gesture. The knot is much more briskly tied; the mundu now becomes a tight shield of self-defense around the wearer's waist. 'Don't mess with me, brother,' he seems to be saying. Or if he has girded his mundu taut in front of a comely maiden who happens to be passing by, the message is much more explicit. It's a prelude to all those heavy breathing Malayalam flicks that go under the title of 'Her Nights'.

For, unlike his male counterparts in the rest of the country, the MM is fully aware of his tenuous position in the richly pulsating landscape of continually proliferating life that surrounds him. The endless stories of husbands who returned home to their temporarily linked partners, only to find, Freud be praised, another MM's spear, sword, or pair of slippers outside the door, are just an indication of the insecurity that the MM has to face. He has to shape up or face up to the fact that someone else will take his place. It's not so much a question of infidelity as availability, an excess of males in a closely guarded society of family members who cross-pollinated, until very recently, only within a carefully observed hierarchy of available females, controlled by an implacable matriarchy.

It's the mothers, aunts and grandmothers who control the destiny of the pampered males in the typical Malayali family. They see to it that he has his daily Malabar banana, his egg fried and sunny-side up—'Moneh, have you had your mutta?'—with his breakfast delicacies, the steamed and boiled quota of starch, and that last thing at night he retires to bed with: a warm and milky, malt-flavoured drink.

'My son will not go for his bath unless I lay out his clothes. Now I hope his new wife will do that for him,' says a proud mother. One twitch of his mundu and he will be back at her side.

Much as the Victorians raised or doffed their hats to members of the opposite sex, or to those who were socially superior, or older and more influential in subtle ways only explicable to the doffer of hats, the MM raises and lowers his mundu in similar fluctuations. 'Sometimes, to save myself the bother, I just wrap one end of my mundu around my finger,' explains a young MM. 'It makes it easier for me to walk. At the same time, I am showing respect for any of my elders that I might meet along the way.' For some of the famous Malayali actors, showing off their well-rounded calves between the folds of their tied up mundu is the equivalent of a heroine displaying her cleavage.

If the continual lowering and raising of the mundu in social situations reflects the sensitive feminine side of the MM, the bristling moustache, the prominence given to a display of the fine upper body, the kumbha or belly included, and the somewhat aggressive posturing with the koda, or black umbrella, reflect his instinctive understanding of the need to show off the masculine element. It's the outward man.

'A Malayali man without a meesha is like a boiled egg without salt,' explained a fond mother. That being the case, it's quite extraordinary how frequently the style for moustaches has changed. In the era of David Niven, when the heartthrob of the Malayali screen was Prem Nazir, the fashion was for a pencil moustache, known as a 'podi meesha'. A little earlier, the trend had been for the bottlebrush variety, the most famous exponent—besides a certain vile German dictator—being Charlie Chaplin. From those minimalist times, the fashion has changed to include the massive congee strainer moustache affected by Mamooty. Or, in the style known as 'Komban meesha', one that sweeps and curls along the edge of the upper lip, like the horn of a bull.

In the era of black and white films, the trend was also to plaster the surface of the face with a layer of Cuticura powder, and the soap of choice amongst a certain class of MMs was always 'Pears' which was pronounced as 'Peers'. No doubt they felt that they would be elevated to Peers of the ruling British class if they persisted in using British goods. Their moustaches were blackened to Salvadore Dali standards and in every MM's personal vanity case, there would be a tiny pair of scissors with pointed ends, made only in England, that would be wielded with all the skill and fetish of a Samurai learning to trim the eyelashes of an enemy, using just his broadsword.

That perhaps is where the answer lies. In his original state, the

MM was very much an aficionado of the martial arts; he could leap about the air with amazing skills. His every joint and muscle was oiled and exercised to such a pitch that even today in certain parts of North Malabar, songs are sung and stories told about the extraordinary feats of valour by a hero such as Tacholi Othenan. The Japanese tradition of warrior or Samurai is but another term for the old Zamorin traditions of Kozhikode. He was also known as the Samuri, or Samuthiri, and he was surrounded by a shining army of bare-bodied warriors who could fight with a sword 'as bright as a drop of water', a shield 'of cow's hide as large as a portion of a cloud'.

In his heart, the Malayali Male is a warrior, a homegrown Samurai. When he steps out into the world, freshly oiled and bathed, encased in a starched white mundu, holding aloft his shield and sword, for one bright instant he becomes that Samurai, and the past becomes the present. He is a wonder to behold!

Siddharth Das

The town they come from

C.P. Surendran

The day was a high vault of gray steel. He should have got hold of an umbrella. But if he did, he wouldn't have felt free. Should he walk, or should he catch a three-wheeler to Geetha's place? By a rick he'd be at her place in less than ten minutes. Too short a time to brace for the occasion. A walk across the paddy fields, and over the narrow bridge leading to the main road and her house, would calm him down.

Ramu glanced at his watch. It showed ten past three. She must be sleeping, he said to the fields flying in the moist monsoon wind. He picked his way over the narrow ridge separating large squares of paddy fields, and set his foot on the bridge just as the sky gave in, each drop a whale's spout. He thought of running for cover, but the nearest tree was in the dream he'd had the night before. There was nothing to do but surrender to the pouring rain. He stood and took it, grinning at the cold, his shirt bleeding blue, his hair plastered, his love burning him up from inside through the cold, lightning couched in cloud, his fear drying him up, his heart racing ahead of him like a ripple before the wave, his desire slowing him down like a stone, a state of suspension where everything was at once possible and then again not; he was a whole meteorology of excitement.

Ramu leaned over the railings of the bridge. Below, the level of the river was rising in the rain, and in a few minutes he would be able to touch its muddy waters. Maybe a fish or two would then cross the bridge, having come to it. He stood there till the river rose to the level of the bridge and the muddy water lapped over and across his feet. Then he made his way forward, an exodus of one. The sea parted, and he trod the bed wet and soft and wrinkled, towards the Promised Land.

At Geetha's place, it was quiet. Were they all sleeping, Jew and gentile, in the holy city of Jerusalem? He trapezed the polar distance in his head between pressing the bell and knocking on the door, and settled on knuckles. Perhaps he could knock with such ardour, only she would hear him. Be my love's lone bat. She would know it was he, come to claim her, her hero-lover lost in the mists of time and found again, emerging from a veil of rain centuries later, knocking at her door with tremulous hands, love-lorn fingers seducing music from dead wood, a tattoo of sounds of longing and desire and terror, a high symphony of the spirit only she could hear. Ramu knocked, paused to sum up a sad smile of ripe hurt to wring from her heart the warm blood of pity. He forgot to fix it in place as the top green square of the four-part door opened, and an old bald head furrowed like sand framed itself in the vellum of space, the sanatorium pallor of the face stark against the shuttered dark of the hall.

'Yes?' said Geetha's grandfather.

Sonovabitch, Ramu thought. He wants me to tell him who I am all over again, for the sixth time in as many weeks.

'Yes,' the old man asked again. He had developed, on the instant, stilettos for vocal chords.

'It's me, Ramu,' said Ramu. He was astonished at the claim he was making. Was he Ramu? What did being Ramu entail? Wasn't trying to be Ramu a risk to his life?

'Ah, yes,' the old man said.

'Well?'

'Yes?'

'Is Geetha home?'

'She could be.'

'I thought I'd drop in and meet her...'

'Just like that, eh?'

'Well...'

'What do you want to see her about?'

'It's about a candle.'

'A candle?'

'Yes, a candle. It burns between my thighs.'

The old man frowned. 'Are you trying to be smart?'

'I guess.'

'Been plenty smart myself in my days.'

'Imagine.' This was futile, Ramu thought. He should put a stop to this nonsense, irony and all, salvage the wreck of the evening from the choppy waters of this dialogue. He felt ashamed at losing his cool so fast, for accelerating into rudeness so quickly. He looked up at the old man with plaintive eyes. But he saw age was turning ugly with anger, and so said, helplessly, 'Old men must act their age.'

'You stand there, flooding my porch and teaching me manners?'

Ramu looked down at his feet, and saw from his trousers dripping onto the floor the map of Africa. Was he responsible for this artwork? What was he doing here on this rainy day, looking for a love that, in the final count, was as ephemeral as these raindrops, picking up an argument with an old man who like him might drop dead even as he turned towards his armchair? The idea of death, that termination was possible at this very moment, rendered all enterprise absurd. Human life was accidental. That was only part of the problem. The more painful part to confront and survive was that it would end, and that it would end anytime. Surely, then, no relationship could warrant the respect of design? Surely, then, no single experience could be considered central to one's evolution?

'I'm sorry,' Ramu said, and turned towards the gate. Oh, I feel sad, the kind of sadness that sits immovable at the heart of a stone. Ramu walked down the lane running with water. Ah, ever to walk this lane with such sadness, he exclaimed to the ten hard-working little men down below. He wiggled his toes. I'm the king of all my woes.

He turned right at the corner of Warriam lane and walked slowly up the deserted Library Road towards the Town Hall. He sat on the wide steps leading to the Public Library on the ground floor. The sky was low, like a black canopy ripped loose from its moorings. A heavy wind blew the leaves back, and the trees reared back to their last bone. Why is there nothing between the sky and the trees? A large castle in flight would do the occasional sheltering trick, wouldn't it?

'Ramu.'

He turned. It was Geetha.

'*Mon sembable, mon frere*,' Ramu said.

'Don't tell me what it means.'

'Oh, it just means I love you.'

'I'm sure not.'

'Does it matter? It's a line from one of my cousins, and the wonderful thing about it is that it can mean anything, just like all good lines.'

'When did you get back from Kozhikode?'

'Last night. Really, this love that I bear for you...'

'Yes?'

'It's very beautiful.'

'I am sure. How is your new teaching job?' She smiled, pink, pliant lips opening to reveal pearls in the purse of her mouth.

Do not cast them before a swine, Ramu screamed in his throat, but said in a difficult whisper, 'A grief ago I was at your place.'

'Oh, Ramu, poetry is wasted on me.'

'Oh, it's not mine, really.'

'Whatever.'

'I'm afraid I was rude to your grandfather.'

'My grandfather. What did you do to him that you wouldn't want to be done to you?'

'I had words with him.'

'Regarding me, of course?' Geetha sighed.

'Regarding you. I asked to see you. He was not interested in true love.'

'Was he an impediment to its course?'

'Yes.'

'Never mind. And here we are, anyway.'

'I love this rain.'

'It's a beautiful rain, though we have no hand in it.'

'You believe in Tansen singing his art out and the rain arriving on call?'

'The power of music and all that?'

'Something very like that. You know, hope? Will? That things can happen for no other reason than a wish.'

'Why do you wish to have me?'

'Isn't love independent of all wishes? A state of affairs, a situation, over which you have no power?'

'I think you're mad.'

'I think this is, after all, a lovely day, despite your grandfather.'

'Be nice to him. He's my favourite grandfather.'

'Yours maybe, but not mine.'

Geetha glanced at him, and smiled. And he thought, I love her. A love hard as a diamond, the genuine final product of his spurious feelings. Something he could reach out and touch even, and reaching out and touching it and not reaching out and touching it, both hurt him. But, unlike everything else, except perhaps for the shock of his birth, he knew it was there. No question. It was knowledge. And its completeness was so exhilarating, even death could be laughed at.

'Care for a stroll?' It seemed to him a simple enough question. He could put it in words, and not be misunderstood.

'In this rain?'

'Well, I'm wet to my teeth anyway. And you have a nice little umbrella, I see.'

'Well, all right, maybe a short walk home then, because I really have to rush.'

'All right,' he said, and got up from the wide steps of the library. A gust of wind made his bellbottoms flap against his shin like the ears of an elephant. Ah, this wind blows me into mahout land.

'Why are you walking as if you are sitting on a horse or something?' Geetha asked.

'An elephant, not a horse.'

'Well, I don't like the idea of you riding an elephant while I humbly walk by your majesty's side.'

'Majesty? Mahout is more like it.'

'You are embarrassing me.'

'All right, then,' Ramu said, and straightened his legs.

'Thank you.'

They walked past the stadium where children were playing football in the rain and cut through its back entrance towards Geetha's house. She seemed remarkably dry under the umbrella except for her feet and ankles and they looked flower-fresh under the running water. Witch. Which is why.

'You want to come in under the umbrella?'

'No,' Ramu said, watching a crow, heavy with the black rain, alighting on Geetha's umbrella. It was a Japanese umbrella of red silk, igniting at irregular intervals in clusters of white roses. The crow sat right on top of the umbrella, and just gazed all around. It was a crow of magisterial regard. Some dead judge, no doubt. His friend George's father? Geetha looked exotic, like a portable landscape. No warmth in her invitation, Ramu thought.

'There's a judgmental crow riding on your umbrella,' Ramu said, as they approached Geetha's house.

'I know,' Geetha said.

'Oh, you did?'

'Yes, I thought, let it ride.'

'Is poetry the mystery of a thing, or its common truth?'

'What are you talking about?'

'Oh, nothing.'

They were at the gate of her house. As she opened the gate, the crow took off.

'Your grandfather doesn't like crows either?'

'You want to come in?' Geetha said, one hand on the gate.

'No,' Ramu said, wishing he were a crow. Life might be simpler.

'When are you off to Kozhikode again?'

'Monday, I guess.'

'So long then.'

'Right,' Ramu said. I wish I hadn't met you, you beautiful polite bitch. 'I'll be along, then,' he said, without looking at her. Geetha gazed at him through the grillwork of the window. There was so much rain between him and her. She stayed at the window till he turned the corner, and then drew the curtains.

*

Ramu walked towards the bus stop. He wished the rain would stop for a moment, so he could take off his shirt and wring it. A cup of tea to collect my thoughts? he asked the darkening air. He made his way to Banana Krishnan's.

Krishnan's shop was a tiny affair raised on six short bamboo poles, planted into the low paddy field on the side of the road. The shop was crammed with yellow, red and green bananas hanging from their stalks from hooks and rope-loops. Krishnan stayed mysteriously behind the banana screen, and once in a while added his face to the wonders of the world by rudely forcing the bananas apart with his strong hands. It was a famous face. Big, dark, luminous eyes parted by a bulbous nose; the rest of the gleaming face was lost in the pitch-dark forestry of his beard. Krishnan's thick, red, paan-soaked lips constantly moved, as if in flight from the persecution of their own debauched habits.

'Hello,' Ramu said from this side of the hanging wall of bananas. 'Anybody home?'

'No,' Banana Krishnan said. 'Who's it?'

'It's me, Ramu.'

Krishnan stuck his face out. 'What're you doing out in this rain? Running after that girl with your distended dick?'

'You got a cup of tea for me?'

'We got better. Come on in,' Krishnan said, opening the flimsy excuse of a door on one side.

'Here,' said Krishnan dragging a stool from a corner of the shop for Ramu to sit. 'In a minute,' he said, lighting a lantern and hanging it on a hook. It swung for a minute in the wind, and then steadied. 'I got the right thing for you here,' he said. He got up from the small blue trunk on which he was sitting, opened it and brought out a bottle of arrack. 'Good stuff. Like Smirnoff.' Krishnan twisted the cap open and handed the bottle of hooch to Ramu. 'Here, just smell.'

Ramu brought it up to his nose. 'Ahhh! Just like Smirnoff.'

'You need to change into something dry, kid,' Krishnan said. 'Or you will come down with a cold.' He ferreted about inside the trunk again, and this time produced a lungi, a pink synthetic silk on which white boats sailed under a full moon.

Ramu peeled the dripping clothes off his body. He wrapped the lungi around him, lifted a slithering corner of it and used it like a towel to dry his hair. 'Are you a much travelled man, Krishnan?'

Krishnan sat down on the floor. He poured the arrack into two glasses, and handed one to Ramu. 'Here, drink it up.'

Ramu held the glass in one hand against the lantern. Deep inside, in its liquid heart, a flame shone. He tossed it down. 'This is strong stuff.'

'Yeah, sort of lights your torch.'

It was cosy inside the shop. Raindrops fell on the tin-roof and were muffled by the tarpaulin stretched over it. It was like sitting inside a drum while a percussionist played on it without conviction. 'It's like sitting in a drum,' Ramu said.

'We are all sitting inside one drum or another,' Krishnan said. 'And no, I'm not a much travelled man.'

'I want to travel a lot.'

'I guess you can't afford to fall in love, then,' Krishnan said, pouring out another glass of arrack for Ramu.

'Why's that?'

'You want to travel a lot, you've got to be light in your mind and luggage. Love's a burden.'

'Have you been in love, Krishnan?'

'Twice.'

'What happened?'

'Oh, you don't want to know, really.' Krishnan put his glass aside, conjured up two eggs from the inexhaustible blue trunk and put them to boil on a kerosene stove. 'You've fallen for that Geetha girl, haven't you?' he said, pumping the flame to a hissing blue jet.

'Yes.' And I'm drunk, Ramu thought. He no longer felt the cold. A warm flush of elation, that he was part of the freedom of life in general, put him out of his mind. The physicality of his being jolted him like a friendly thump on his back. He no longer worried. Everything would shape up. What was he worried about, anyway? To hell with Geetha. To hell with every one. 'This is better than Smirnoff,' he said, shaking what was left in his glass against the light from the lantern. The glass threw a long shadow across the floor. 'Yes, I love her,' he said. 'The trouble is, I don't know if she loves me.'

'I don't think she does.' Krishnan shook his head.

'What makes you think so?'

'I saw you two walking up the road. If she loved you, you would have been sharing her umbrella.'

'She asked. I said no because I was wet and dripping anyway.'

'That's not the point.'

'Maybe you're right.'

'Or maybe she's still in two minds about you.'

'What do I do?'

'Help make up her mind.' Krishnan poured the dregs of the bottle evenly into both glasses, and offered Ramu his. He put the stove off, took a spoon and transferred the eggs into a mug of cold water. 'You know, sort of influence her decision.'

'How do I do that?'

'I'm not sure.' Krishnan shelled the eggs. Then he took a knife, dipped it in a pot of pepper and salt, and carefully cut each egg vertically into four pieces, so each piece had its share of the frills. 'Have an egg,' he said.

'I love her like crazy.'

'Abduct her.'

'Are you mad? And?'

'Make love to her.'

'And?'

'Make her your woman, man.'

'This is Smirnoff talking.'

'You've no balls.'

'If I carry out your idea, I might land in jail.'

'Well, that's not such a bad thing, if you're hoping to become a writer.'

'On the other hand, she might fall in love with me.' Hell, on the other hand, I'm drunk, Ramu thought. Very drunk, and very wanting Geetha. Ramu want, want. He looked at Krishnan and saw that Krishnan was in many places. Maya in the marketplace? On the other hand, Krishnan, you're a bloody god. The other hand was the one you had to look out for. That was the tricky hand.

'That other hand's a good hand,' Krishnan said.

'Will you help me abduct her?'

'Maybe I will. We've got to be careful, kid.'

'What the hell, we'll be careful. You bet we'll be careful.'

'Very careful.'

'Very, very careful,' Ramu agreed.

'Strike while the iron is hot.'

'Discretion is the better part of valour.'

'Cowards die a thousand deaths.'

'To sleep, perchance to dream,' Ramu said, and crumbled to the floor.

Krishnan had his egg. He sat there, on the floor, staring at Ramu for some time. Still staring at him, Krishnan ate the leftovers from Ramu's plate. Then his hands dived into the depths of the blue trunk again, and came up with a shirt. He shoved Ramu's hands into its oversized sleeves, buttoned the shirt up. He opened the door of the shop and put his palm out. The rain had stopped. And the road was deserted.

He sat Ramu on the carrier of his old military-green Hercules cycle, and pushed him forward so his head rested on the saddle. With one hand round Ramu's back, Krishnan rolled the cycle up the road towards Ramu's home. It took him a good forty minutes. Once there, he got off the cycle, flexed his heavy muscles under the one star which had made a shy appearance right in the middle of the low-hung roiling dark sky, and lifted Ramu off the cycle onto his shoulder. The house was in the dark. Krishnan gently leaned Ramu against the door, and pressed the bell twice. Then he turned around and walked, and heard Ramu hit the floor in a heap just as he reached his cycle. Krishnan cycled fast towards his shop. He hoped the bananas wouldn't rot in the rain. He looked up. The star was missing. It was a good night to abduct. A season to sin.

The swamp

Kamala Das

in malabar during the rains after one singularly dark week and one hot
morning our backyard was a swamp my feet cracked the grey crust and
i sank with a wail my lover ageing without grace says why do you want
my child i am your child yes yes yes then again and again this tragic
sport that has made of us its addicts he undressing my soul effortlessly
blindly reaching the locus of anguish but still i shake my head i leave
unsatisfied for what does he bare for me on the bed in his study except
his well tanned body

the bhagavatis oracle took two steps forward to swing back again the
chosen one with the long hair the waistlet of bells and the scimitar
he spoke to my great grandmother in a warble not his own i shall
protect
your descendants from illness and untimely death is this not
enough and the old one her hands folded her eyes closed said yes it
is enough i cannot ask for more

virtue is the richest jewel said my great grandmother she wore
invisible jewels that respected one while the family sold every bit
of gold to retrieve lost land the maids turned anaemic
i was born fair but within months like the rolled gold bangles on my
ayahs arms my skin grew tarnished i was the first dark girl in the
family there was something tainted in me of this i was aware but my
mother told my bridegroom be gentle she is the most innocent being
you will ever meet

when i was ill my three year old son was brought to me amma he

This poem is taken from *Only the Soul Knows How to Sing: Selections from Kamala Das*, published by DC Books.

said leave this hospital come home with me even if i had died that
week i would have walked as a ghost to my home

and him so much of me was taken out and sent in jam jars to the
pathological lab but what the lab did not need lay under white
sheets in room number five sixty five and thought longingly of that
little boy

my beloved is armed with cunning and violent hate and mistrust but
he comes to my arms unarmed and when the last of strengths in
drops is shed i call him my baby i hold him to my breast but often
after taking leave i open his door and see him at his desk signing
letters with the glasses on with the stern look with the do you want
something the change is so complete that i am silent and in silence
must move away

i am the tainted bush the poisonous snakes retreat at three a m while
the others sleep i have no name of my own and my past is a desolate
terrain where memory like tall trees grow to my malabar home years
ago on hot noons the devil dancers came walking past the bright rice
fields behind them the pariahs reed wailed a long wail rising from
the heat like a ribbon of pain

he is the richest the strongest the deadliest i lit one thousand and
one lamps at our snakeshrine praying for a mate such as he he said
power and money two and two make not four but twenty two he is
simple politics and a little bit of love each day he did not read
books or walk on marine drive or swim i am the puppet on his
string virtue is the richest jewel said my great grandmother yes yes i
know but he is the jewel i prefer to wear he rubs oil on me he puts
me in his bathtub i cower before his incurious stare the warm water
grazing my harbours his eyelids droop he is about to fall asleep like
frankensteins brutal toy i shall rise one day i shall stalk out of his
bed i shall walk along the marine drive he will then become just
another man just another season and the summer then will burn to
ashes in his garden

Notes on contributors

Balachandran Chullikkad, one of Kerala's best-known and loved poets, has published six collections of poetry and a book of memoirs.

Alexander Frater is a travel writer based in the UK. He has contributed to many publications, including *Punch* and the *New Yorker*, and is the author of the best-selling *Beyond the Blue Horizon*.

Shashi Tharoor is the author of *The Great Indian Novel*, *Show Business*, *India: From Midnight to the Millennium* and *Riot*. He is based in New York.

C.V. Raman Pillai (1858–1922) graduated from the University of Madras in 1881, was the founder–editor of *Malayali* and contributed to other Malayalam and English dailies. *Marthanda Varma*, published in 1891, was his first attempt at fiction, and was the first book of a trilogy of historical romances written by him.

B.K. Menon (1907–1952) was educated in Ernakulam and Madras. He gave up his job as the Secretary of Nedungadi Bank in his early thirties to concentrate on his writing. He wrote poetry in Malayalam and articles and short stories in English. *Marthanda Varma* was his only major work of translation.

V.K. Madhavan Kutty is a senior journalist and writer based in New Delhi. He is the author of *The Southern Discomfort*, a book that explores the North-South divide in India.

Thakazhi Sivasankara Pillai (1912–1999) is the author of more than twenty-five novels. *The Scavenger's Son* (1947) was the first work to win him acclaim. *Chemmeen*, *Two Measures of Rice* and *Kayar* are some of his well-known novels. He was awarded the Padma Bhushan in 1985.

V.K. Narayana Menon was one of the first Ph.Ds in English in India. In the course of a long and distinguished career, he served as the Director General of All India Radio and the Chairman of the Sangeet Natak Academy.

Jeet Thayil's third collection of poems, *English*, co-published by Rattapallax Press in New York and Penguin Books India in New Delhi, will appear in Spring 2003. He lives in New York City where he writes for a newspaper and teaches poetry.

William Dalrymple's first book *In Xanadu* was shortlisted for the John Llewellyn Rhys Memorial Prize. Other books include *City of Djinns*, *From the Holy Mountain*, *The Age of Kali* and *White Mughals: Love and Betrayal in Eighteenth-century India*.

Vaikkom Muhammad Basheer (1908–1994), one of Kerala's finest writers, has written several books in Malayalam, of which the best-known is *Me Grandad 'Ad An Elephant*. He revolutionized the art of story-telling in Malayalam using lively, colloquial idiom to describe everyday matters. He was awarded the Padma Shri in 1982.

V. Abdulla retired as Divisional Director of Orient Longman. He has translated the works of Vaikkom Muhammad Basheer, M.T. Vasudevan Nair and S.K. Pottekkat among others.

Ammu Joseph is a writer and media-watcher based in Bangalore. Among her publications are two books: *Whose News? The Media and Women's Issues*, co-authored/edited with Kalpana Sharma (Sage, 1994) and *Women in Journalism: Making News* (The Media Foundation/Konark, 2000).

Abu Abraham is a well-known columnist. His books include *Abu on Bangladesh*, *Emergency*, *Private Views* and *Arrival and Departure*. He has also edited the *Penguin Book of Indian Cartoons*. He lives in Thiruvananthapuram.

O.V. Vijayan broke new ground in Malaylam literature with his novel *The Legends of Khasak*. Since then, he has published several novels, short stories and essays. He is also an accomplished political cartoonist.

Pankaj Mishra is the author of a travel book, *Butter Chicken in Ludhiana*, and a novel, *The Romantics*.

Jayanth Kodkani, a senior journalist with *The Times of India*, resides in Bangalore.

M.T. Vasudevan Nair has won the Jnanpith as well as the State and Central Sahitya Akademi awards for his contribution to Malayalam literature. He is the editor of the leading Malayalam daily *Mathrubhumi* and is also a successful screenplay writer with several award-winning films to his credit.

Gita Krishnankutty has translated several Malayalam novels and short stories into English, including the work of M.T. Vasudevan Nair, Paul Zacharia, Lalithambika Antherjanam and Kamala Das.

Suresh Menon, one of India's youngest newspaper editors, is currently writing a book. His son shows no serious aftereffects of having had his father sing Yesudas lullabies to him.

Ayyappa Panikker is an academician, poet and critic based in Thiruvananthapuram.

Salman Rushdie is the author of *Midnight's Children* (the 'Booker of Bookers'), *Grimus, Shame, Haroon and the Sea of Stories, The Moor's Last Sigh, The Ground Beneath Their Feet* and *Fury*.

Lalithambika Antherjanam (1909–1987) is the author of many collections of short stories and one novel, *Agnisakshi*, which won the Sahitya Akademi Award. Most of her stories reveal the little-known world inhabited by the Namboodiri women of her time and the agonizing experiences they endured because of the severe social restrictions they had to live with.

Paul Zacharia is one of Kerala's best-selling writers. Three collections of his stories exist in English translation: *Bhaskara Pattelar and Other Stories*, *Reflections of a Hen in Her Last Hour* and *Praise the Lord: What News, Pilate?*

A.J. Thomas is the Assistant Editor of *Indian Literature*, the journal of the Sahitya Akademi. He has translated the work of Paul Zacharia among others.

Ravi Menon is a senior sports journalist who lives and works in Kozhikode, Kerala.

M. Mukundan was born in Mahe (Mayyazhi), a former French enclave in Kerala. He is the author of twenty-seven books in Malayalam including a selection of essays and a play. He won the Sahitya Akademi Award in 1993 and his novel *On the Banks of the Mayyazhi* won the Crossword Award for Indian language fiction in English translation (1998). The second Mayyazhi novel, *God's Mischief*, has just been published by Penguin Books India.

Bill Aitken is Scottish by birth and a naturalized Indian by choice. He has written on travel and tourism for newspapers and magazines in India and is also the author of several books including *The Nanda Devi Affair*, *Seven Sacred Rivers* and *Riding the Ranges: Travels on My Motorcycle*.

Arundhati Roy is the author of *The God of Small Things*, which won the Booker Prize in 1997, and *The Algebra of Infinite Justice*, a collection of essays. She lives in New Delhi.

Shashi Warrier is the author of three thrillers—*Night of the Krait*, *The Orphan* and *Sniper*—as well as two books for children—*The Hidden Continent* and *Suzy's Gift*.

Shreekumar Varma is a poet and playwright, and has written a novel *Lament of Mohini* (Penguin) and a book for children, *The Royal Rebel*. He has completed a second novel, *Maria's Room*, and is working on a biography of Chennai city.

Jaishree Mishra is the author of *Ancient Promises* and *Accidents Like Love and Marriage*. She lives in London and is currently working on her third novel.

Vijay Nambisan is a poet and journalist, whose published works include *Bihar Is in the Eye of the Beholder* and *Gemini*, a two-poet volume which features a selection of his poems.

Ramachandra Guha is based in Bangalore. He is the editor of *The Picador Book of Cricket* and the author of *A Corner of a Foreign Field: The Indian History of a British Sport*.

David Davidar is the author of *The House of Blue Mangoes*.

Geeta Doctor is a Chennai-based journalist and writer who writes on art and literature. Never having lived in Kerala, she does not believe in ancestral home worship but nonetheless finds Keralites an endless source of amusement.

C.P. Surendran was born in Ottapalam, Kerala. He started his career as a lecturer in English, before he took up journalism. He is a Senior Assistant Editor with *The Times of India*, Mumbai. His poetry collections are *Gemini II*, *Posthumous Poems* and *Canaries On the Moon*. He has stopped writing poetry and is currently working on a novel, an extract from which has been carried in this volume.

Kamala Das (Suraiya) is an award-winning poet, fiction writer and essayist who writes with equal felicity in Malayalam and English. She is based in Kochi.

Copyright acknowledgements

The editor and the publishers gratefully acknowledge the following for permission to reprint copyright material:

The Random House Group Limited for the extract from *The Moor's Last Sigh* by Salman Rushdie, published by Jonathan Cape;
IndiaInk for the extract from *The Village Before Time*;
East West Books for 'The Garden of the Antlions' by Paul Zacharia and the extract from *On the Banks of the Mayyazhi* by M. Mukundan;
Permanent Black for the extract from *An Anthropologist Among the Marxists and Other Essays* by Ramachandra Guha;
Prema Jayakumar and the Sahitya Akademi for the extract from *Marthanda Varma* by C.V. Raman Pillai;
Stree for the extract from *Cast Me Out if You Will: Stories and Memoirs* by Lalithambika Antherjanam; original Malayalam text © Saritha Varma, this English translation © Gita Krishnankutty;
Kerala Sahitya Akademi for 'The Blue Light' by Vaikom Muhammad Basheer;
Jaico Publishing House for the extract from *Chemmeen* by Thakazhi Sivasankara Pillai;
Penguin Books India for extracts from *India: From Midnight to the Millennium* by Shashi Tharoor, *Chasing the Monsoon* by Alexander Frater, *Butter Chicken in Ludhiana* by Pankaj Mishra, *The God of Small Things* by Arundhati Roy, *Karkitakam* by M.T. Vasudevan Nair, *The Legends of Khasak* by O.V. Vijayan, *Hangman's Journal* by Shashi Warrier, *Ancient Promises* by Jaishree Misra and *The Better Man* by Anita Nair.